Multicultural Issues in
DEAFNESS

Multicultural Issues in
DEAFNESS

—————— Edited by ——————

Kathee M. Christensen
San Diego State University

Gilbert L. Delgado
New Mexico School for the Deaf

Longman

Multicultural Issues in Deafness

Longman, 10 Bank Street, White Plains, N.Y. 10606

Associated companies:
Longman Group Ltd., London
Longman Cheshire Pty., Melbourne
Longman Paul Pty., Auckland
Copp Clark Pitman, Toronto

Acquisitions editor: Kenneth J. Clinton
Sponsoring editor: Naomi Silverman
Development editor: Susan Alkana
Production editor: Linda Witzling
Cover design: Susan J. Moore
Production supervisor: Anne Armeny

Library of Congress Cataloging-in-Publication Data

Multicultural issues in deafness / edited by Kathee M. Christensen and
    Gilbert L. Delgado.
        p.   cm.
    Includes bibliographical references and index.
    ISBN 0-8013-0752-X
    1. Children, Deaf—Education—United States.   2. Children of
minorities—Education—United States.   I. Christensen, Kathee M.
(Kathee Mangan)   II. Delgado, Gilbert L., 1928-
HV2440.M85   1993
362.4′2′089—dc20   92-8258
                                                          CIP

1 2 3 4 5 6 7 8 9 10-MA-9695949392

Dedicated to
Robert R. Davila
with appreciation

Contents

Preface

It is no longer necessary to travel great distances in order to learn about cultural diversity. As one looks around an average contemporary classroom, the presence of children from a variety of racial and ethnic backgrounds is apparent. Classrooms for Deaf children also reflect this racial and ethnic diversity, along with an important added dimension—the recognition of Deaf culture and signed communication.

Deaf children represent a population whose major need is one of communication development in at least two languages, the visual-spatial, natural language of American Sign Language (ASL) and the auditory-oral-written language of English. Deaf children from families who use a language other than English or ASL as the primary mode of communication present a unique trilingual challenge. This population is growing, particularly in the states that border Mexico and the Pacific and Atlantic oceans. The focus of this book is on four special populations of Deaf children. Deaf children from African American, American Indian, Hispanic, and Asian/Pacific Island families will be considered from both educational and cultural perspectives.

The premise of this book is that all Deaf persons are members of a larger Deaf culture. In the lives of some Deaf individuals, however, two or more cultures are combined to create a human experience that differs from each singular cultural experience. The experience of a Deaf Hispanic individual, for example, differs in many important aspects from the experience of a Deaf Anglo-American or a hearing Hispanic person.

The Office of Demographic Studies (1989–1990) at Gallaudet University in Washington, D.C., reported the following national ethnic profile of Deaf children in their 1989–1990 census:

Ethnicity	*Percentage*
White (Anglo-American)	63
Black (African American)	17
Hispanic	13
Native American	.7
Asian/Pacific Island	3.3
Other (including multiethnic)	3

On the other hand, approximately 94 percent of all teachers of the Deaf describe their ethnicity as white (Corbett & Jensema, 1981). In a study of 487 Deaf teachers of the deaf, Mobley (1991) reported the following:

Ethnicity	*Number*
White (European American)	470
Hispanic	6
Black (African American)	5
Asian/Pacific Island	3
American Indian	2
Other	1

There is a critical need for teachers, both Deaf and hearing, to learn more about the cultures of the children whom they teach. It is estimated that by the year 2000, one-third of school-age children in the general population will be from African American, Hispanic, American Indian, or Asian/Pacific Island families. In fact, in large metropolitan areas, approximately 42 percent of the general school-age population will be children from these ethnic groups (American Council on Education, 1988). The demographics of the school-age Deaf population will change in much the same manner. The purpose of this book is to help teachers of Deaf children understand some fundamental concepts with regard to multicultural issues in the education of Deaf children. With an increase in awareness of the strengths and needs of Deaf children from the four groups on which we focus, teachers may be better able to help these children reach their academic potential.

HOW THIS BOOK IS ORGANIZED

The text is divided into three main sections. Section I presents the issues. In Chapter 1, Tom Humphries, a leading author in Deaf culture, presents an overview of that area and introduces the concept of multicultural Deaf identity. Kathee M. Christensen expands on this overview in Chapter 2 and considers the impact of bicultural and multicultural identity on the cognitive development of Deaf learners. Cynthia A. Grace concludes Section I with a description of a program to enhance understanding among multicultural families, teachers, and other school staff.

Section II considers the populations of Deaf learners who constitute the focus groups of this text. In Chapter 4, Oscar P. Cohen discusses the needs of African American and Hispanic Deaf students from both academic and cultural viewpoints. Chapters 5 and 6 are centered on the situation of Hispanic Deaf children in the United States and Mexico. Barbara Gerner de Garcia presents her perspective as both a trained English as a Second Language (ESL) teacher and also a certified teacher of Deaf children. In Chapter 6, Donna Jackson-Maldonado shares research that she has conducted with Deaf children in Mexico and the United States and presents current information on nonbiased communication assessment. The overall cultural situation of Asian and Pacific Island children is described in Chapter 7 by Li-Rong Lilly Cheng. C. Tane Akamatsu continues the discussion in Chapter 8 with a specific focus on Asian/Pacific Islander Deaf children. Section II concludes with a look at the situation of American Indian Deaf children and youth by two professionals, Sue Anne Hammond and Linda Hagar Meiners, who have worked extensively with Deaf students from the Arizona reservations.

Section III completes the text with two chapters that envision the future of education of ethnic and racially diverse Deaf populations. In Chapter 10, Joseph E. Fischgrund and C. Tane Akamatsu challenge us to rethink our priorities and stretch the boundaries of education as we have known it. In the final chapter, Kathee M. Christensen directs our attention to a strong multicultural commitment as we enter the twenty-first century.

The field of education of Deaf children has a long history of controversy, debate, and discord. This text calls for a child-centered curriculum based on a fundamental acceptance of differences in communication and interpretation. The development of self-esteem and independent decision making in learners can occur only when the professionals who work with them are open-minded, observant, and able to view communication from a variety of perspectives.

This text does not strive to provide simple answers to complex educational questions. Instead, it provides information from which professionals can gain insights to apply in their work. Multicultural teaching and learning is presented as an ongoing, dynamic process. Diversity is celebrated as a positive force through which teachers can motivate all learners, seek the individual, natural strengths of each learner, and use these strengths to facilitate growth and the acquisition of new abilities.

It is our profound hope that the chapters in this book will foster greater understanding of Deaf children who are from African American, Hispanic, American Indian, or Asian/ Pacific Island families. Through them, all of us can gain insights about ourselves as members of a multicultural society.

ACKNOWLEDGMENTS

The authors would like to thank Susan Alkana, Naomi Silverman, and Linda Witzling of Longman Publishing Group for their meticulous editing and constructive comments. We appreciate the prepublication reviews and helpful comments made by David F. Conway (University of Nebraska at Omaha), Robert D. Moulton (Lamar University, Beaumont, Texas), and Bruce F. Godsave (State University of New York at Geneseo). In addition, the editorial assistance of Amy Hina and Karen Stein was of great value. A special thank-you is given to Dr. Kenneth R. Mangan for reviewing the entire manuscript with professional care and wisdom. Finally, all of the contributors to this book are friends as well as colleagues. We would like to thank one another for the many years of dialogue, mutual support, and heated debate that have resulted in the successful completion of this project!

REFERENCES

American Council on Education. (1988). *One-third of a nation: A report of the commission on minority participation in education and American life*. Washington, DC: Author.

Corbett, E., & Jensema, C. (1981). *Teachers of the Deaf: Descriptive profiles*. Washington, DC: Gallaudet University.

Mobley, R. (1991, February). *Deaf teachers of the deaf*. A paper presented at the conference of the Association of College Educators in Hearing Impairment, Jekyl Island, GA.

Office of Demographic Studies. (1989–1990). *Annual census of deaf children and youth*. Washington, DC: Gallaudet University.

Contributors

C. Tane Akamatsu
Michigan State University
East Lansing, Michigan

Li-Rong Lilly Cheng
San Diego State University
San Diego, California

Kathee M. Christensen
San Diego State University
San Diego, California

Oscar P. Cohen
Lexington School for the Deaf
Jackson Heights, New York

Gilbert L. Delgado
New Mexico School for the Deaf
Santa Fe, New Mexico

Joseph E. Fischgrund
Pennsylvania School for the Deaf
Philadelphia, Pennsylvania

Barbara Gerner de Garcia
Horace Mann School for the Deaf
Boston, Massachusetts

Cynthia A. Grace
Lexington School for the Deaf
Jackson Heights, New York

Sue Anne Hammond
Community Outreach Program for the Deaf
Flagstaff, Arizona

Tom Humphries
San Diego Community College District
San Diego, California

Donna Jackson-Maldonado
University of California–San Diego
San Diego, California

Linda Hagar Meiners
Arizona State Schools for the Deaf
    and the Blind
Tucson, Arizona

CRITICAL THE

ISSUES

SECTION I

The Issues

Foreign language study in the United States has long been part of the
secondary school curriculum, but rarely has it been emphasized as
it is in other countries. Only a small percentage of English-speaking
Americans are fluent in a second language, and even fewer are "fluent" in
another culture. Learning to speak and understand a second language and to
understand a foreign culture are tasks often perceived as time-consuming and
difficult.

As we move toward a more global society, more and more Americans are
beginning to see the need to operate in a multicultural context. For one
American population, however—Deaf people—the need to operate
multiculturally has always existed. For most Deaf children in the United
States, who learn first to communicate in some form of signed language,
English is a second language. Imagine, then, the communications implications
for a Deaf child who is born not into the dominant culture, but rather into a
culture significantly different from the population at large. A Deaf child from
a non-English-speaking background may well have to operate within a Deaf
culture and language, a dominant English culture and language, and a third
culture and language in which he or she is immersed at home. Such a child
must become, for all intents and purposes, tricultural and perhaps trilingual.

Section I examines the communications issues facing this multicultural
Deaf population in the United States.

CHAPTER 1

Deaf Culture and Cultures

Tom Humphries

Deaf people must live almost entirely within the world of others. This peculiar social condition leads to a longing of their own, a longing to live lives designed by themselves rather than those imposed by others.

Padden and Humphries

To begin to talk about the cultural history of people who are deaf, it is essential to be aware that deaf people in countries all over the world who are signed language users consider themselves to be separate cultural groups from the societies of hearing, spoken language users among whom they inevitably live. Therefore, in the United States, for example, to be deaf and an American Sign Language (ASL) user, and also interact and use English well in the hearing society, is to be bicultural and bilingual. This is just for starters. To be a deaf signed language user *and* African American, Hispanic, Asian/Pacific Islander, or American Indian in the United States is to be multicultural. This chapter discusses the bicultural and multicultural nature of deaf peoples and some issues central to their lives and education.

EMERGING DEAF CULTURES

In the 1970s there arose a strong groundswell of research and political change that brought, at long last, a great public awareness of the existence of ASL and the culture of Deaf people from which this language evolved over hundreds of years (Baker & Battison, 1980; Klima, et al., 1979; Padden & Markowicz, 1976; Siple, 1978; Stokoe, 1960, 1975; Supalla, 1978; Wilbur, 1979). Suddenly, by the end of the 1970s, Deaf people in the United States began to use a new vocabulary in describing themselves. American Sign Language, previously denied the status of a "real" language, suddenly was a language. Deaf people who were less than fluent in English and considered "language delayed" were acknowledged to have a first language, ASL; therefore, English was their second language. A very different proposition, indeed (Charrow & Fletcher, 1974; Goldberg & Bordman, 1975; Humphries, Coye, & Martin, 1978; Kannapell, 1978).

Concurrently in other countries of the world, particularly in Europe, there emerged a strong body of research first in the signed languages of each of these countries and, later, descriptions of the ethnicity of communities of signed language users (Kyle & Woll, 1983). From being thought of as "deficit," "handicapped," and sometimes "languageless" individuals, in the space of a decade, Deaf signed language users became central groups with first and second languages. "Deaf culture" became the label of choice for describing Deaf people and the ways that they design their lives.

This change in how Deaf people were perceived led to early discussions of the need for new models of human development and education that account for the bicultural and bilingual nature and needs of Deaf people, and, in particular, the needs of Deaf children (Cokeley, 1978; Erting, 1978; Goldberg & Bordman, 1975; Humphries, 1978; Humphries, Coye, & Martin, 1978; Kannapell, 1978; Lane & Grosjean, 1980; Stokoe, 1975; Woodward, 1980). Complicated issues of biculturality and, indeed, multiculturality, needed to be considered. Although this discussion continues today, one thing seems clear: The idea of the Deaf person as a fully integrated and well-developed cultural person by means of ASL and a community of Deaf people is now the point from which to begin, as well as the base from which the Deaf person can achieve biculturality and even multiculturality.* What does it mean to start from this base? What must it be like for a Deaf signed language user in the United States today, and how must these new models address him or her? Consider the hypothetical story of Jay, a deaf person who grew up in the United States.

Jay's Story

Jay is twenty-six years old. He has graduated from high school, but it was tough going since English is his second language and his ability to speak, read, and write it is not very good. He is aware that other people find him to be very different. He knows that others think he is incapable of a lot of things that he really can do very well. He knows that they don't understand him and have a lot of stereotypes about him and his people. He finds that people discriminate against him in many ways, most of the time unintentionally. By now he is accustomed to living in a world full of people who use a different language and seem to have a different way of looking at things. To improve himself he has been going to a continuing education program to try to learn to read and write better English.

Jay finds that he often needs a translator at work and to gain access to many social services, and even to buy a car. Sometimes he is able to arrange for an interpreter with public assistance, but most of the time he is on his own and must handle the language

---

*A common convention, the capitalized term *Deaf* is used throughout this text to refer to a condition of being part of a culture that uses a signed language, as distinguished from a condition of not hearing, or *deafness*. Whenever relevant, a nationality or community identification is also used to specify a culture or language, as in "Deaf people in the United States," "Deaf people of Mexico," or "black southern Deaf signers."

problem himself. He sees this as a normal part of his life, however, and doesn't give it much thought. Apart from what he considers a normal and usual amount of conflict and mutual misunderstandings with English speakers, he thinks his life is fairly normal.

He has a wife and two small children. Although he and his wife do not use English much in the home, their children do seem to be learning English pretty normally. Both Jay and his wife make an effort to expose the children to English via the playground and school, and the children seem to be learning everything to which they are exposed. The children spend time with relatives, some of whom are native English speakers and others who are very fluent. They also play with the neighbors' children, from whom they learn much.

For the most part Jay and his family interact socially with people of their own group who share their language and culture. This community of people is a vibrant one with networks that support its members in many ways. Jay is most comfortable and happy when he is with his family and the other members of his community. He works hard to preserve the culture and language of his people, of which he is very proud. He has no desire to give up his language or to become more like "them." He wants to remain the way he is, one of his own people and not have to become one of "them."

DEAF PEOPLE IN THE UNITED STATES

Perhaps Jay's story sounds similar to that of a family recently arrived in the United States from another country where the language and culture are different. His experiences seem much like those of millions of people who are making the transition from another culture to living in the mainstream of American culture. In fact, the experience of feeling discriminated against is probably more than a feeling. It is probably a fact of life for people like Jay who are not yet fluent in English and who strive to remain a part of the culture of their family and their community.

But Jay is not foreign born. Nor is he a second generation American, the child of foreign born parents. He is not from Mexico, the Philippines, or Poland. He does not speak Spanish, Tagalog, or Polish. He is a Deaf man born in the United States. His first language, American Sign Language (ASL), is what he uses with his family and friends who are also Deaf. He is one of several hundred thousand Deaf people born and raised in the United States who use ASL and belong to a Deaf cultural group.

However, not all people who do not hear are native users of ASL and are part of a community of Deaf people. We know that culture is learned through interaction with the people of a given cultural group. Many people are born without hearing, and many later in life find themselves without hearing. Unless they have access to the language and culture of Deaf people in the United States, they will not be a part of this linguistic community.

Ultimately then, even though it is an important element, hearing or not hearing does not determine the cultural and linguistic heritage of people like Jay (Markowicz & Woodward, 1975; Padden, 1980; Padden & Humphries, 1988; Padden & Markowicz, 1975). It is not uncommon to find third-generation Deaf children (of Deaf parents and grandparents) able to hear well enough to use the telephone, for example, and speak English clearly. Nor is it uncommon to find people without much hearing or ability to speak English who know no ASL and have never met anyone from a Deaf cultural group.

COMPETING VIEWS OF DEAF PEOPLE

Perhaps it still seems strange to many to be discussing Deaf people as a cultural group. There is a strong belief in American society, and in most of the rest of the world, that anyone who does not hear is a person with an affliction, not a person with a culture different from the mainstream culture of people who hear. But the people of this cultural group, these Deaf people, these ASL users, do not see themselves as having an affliction (Padden & Humphries, 1988). Jay will say that his real problem is that he must function in a world where he is viewed as having an affliction while trying to maintain his identity as a whole person, a person whose language and cultural development are intact, in the form of ASL and the culture of Deaf people in the United States.

Thus, in this chapter we are not talking about "medical" definitions of *deafness*. In such a definition, people who do not hear are described in terms of a pathological condition or a dysfunction that requires certain "interventions." We are talking, instead, about people who do not hear but who learn the language and culture of the Deaf people among whom they live.

We are not talking about Deaf people as special or unique, as marvels of adaptation, or as having adjusted to a special circumstance of finding themselves without a human sense. Such terminology evokes the image of adjustment from a disability. We are talking about normal human development in which the language and culture to which one is exposed is learned spontaneously and naturally. And this language and culture derives not from a clinically defined condition, but from the historical transmission of ways of being, of knowledge and ideologies, and, of course, language from one generation of Deaf people to the next (Padden & Humphries, 1988).

Under these circumstances, there is no room within the culture of Deaf people for an ideology that all Deaf people are deficient. It simply does not compute. There is no "handicap" to "overcome" or to which one must "adjust" or "adapt." These two theories of who and what Deaf people are (handicapped or linguistically and culturally intact) often compete with each other and sometimes lead to tension between those who assume the respective views of these theories.

Since the history of the way of being that Deaf people maintain does not incorporate the ideology of themselves as disabled, Jay has no desire to give up what he is to become one of "them": a person who is "hearing." He does know the difficulty of interacting with hearing people whose language, English, he does not hear and has some difficulty learning. But Jay has attained some level of biculturality. He grew up in the United States and knows a great deal about general American culture and a great deal of specifics. He has spent all of his life interacting with people of this culture and has learned much.

Although Jay is more comfortable and chooses to interact mostly with other Deaf people and his primary language in the home is ASL, he still, like most Deaf people, is functional in his daily life as an American. He holds many of the same beliefs and perceptions as people who hear. He does many things in the same ways. The content of his education has been the same as for any other hearing person in the United States. He is more of an expert in interacting with hearing people than they are in interacting with him, because he has done it every day throughout his entire life. Most hearing people, on the other hand, may never spend more than a few hours with a Deaf person. Jay's experience may differ from that of those who hear, but he is not ignorant of American life.

There are issues in Jay's life that are important to him: issues such as how to gain equal access and equal opportunity in a society that is basically designed for people who hear and which uses a spoken language. There are issues of how best to educate Deaf children (and Deaf adults, for that matter) to prepare them for their lives as Deaf people in the United States. There are issues of others' denial of Deaf language and culture and of efforts to assimilate people who do not hear by forbidding or refusing the use of any signed language in schools. Even today, many schools in the United States neither officially accept ASL nor acknowledge a culture of Deaf people. Most of the hearing public is still skeptical of ASL as a language, relegating it to the level of a prosthesis that Deaf people use because they cannot speak or hear. These are basic issues that concern many cultural minorities in the United States, namely, educating their children, maintaining the integrity of their native language, and standing up to outside pressure to reduce cultural diversity.

DEAF CULTURES AND SIGNED LANGUAGES OUTSIDE OF THE UNITED STATES

If Jay, who was born in and grew up in the United States, finds himself in a situation demanding biculturality, what must it be like for Deaf people of other signed languages and Deaf cultures who find themselves in the United States? Indeed, there are many other signed languages and Deaf cultural groups—perhaps as many signed languages as there are spoken languages. American Sign Language and presumably most other signed languages are not derived from the spoken languages of the hearing societies among which the Deaf people live. British Sign Language (BSL) and ASL, for example, are very different languages even though the spoken languages of the American and British hearing societies are very similar. American Sign Language, in fact, is related to French Sign Language (Langue Signe Française) historically, but today the two are very different. Knowing ASL will not prepare one to understand LSF.

Although ASL is used in most of Canada, Deaf people in some parts of Canada, notably in Quebec, use another signed language, Langue Signe Quebec (LSQ). Deaf people in Mexico also use varieties of different signed languages. And so on, throughout the world. Each of these signed languages is a product of the Deaf community from which it evolved, and each Deaf community testifies to the diversity of the human condition.

DEAF PEOPLE IMMIGRATING TO THE UNITED STATES

Deaf people from other signed language communities who immigrate to the United States have before them a task, therefore, of learning two cultures and two languages (ASL and English). First, they need to learn to be Deaf people in the United States. Much of the access to American educational, social, and economic achievement is through systems developed to allow access through ASL, and translators (interpreters) are unlikely to know any other signed language. Educational opportunities are accessible only through ASL and English. The use of ASL is also important in order to interact effectively and satisfyingly with most Deaf Americans. Deaf Americans have available to them a body of knowledge about how to live a life as a Deaf person in the United States. They use available resources that other Deaf people have been making use of or have developed over many generations. To use these resources requires a great deal of learning and assimilating by Deaf people new to the United States.

Second, Deaf people who come to this country need to learn English and the culture of hearing English speakers. There is great economic and social pressure to do so. These pressures are considerable, since they involve daily communication with employers, service persons, shopkeepers, educators, and the many other interactions that English speakers take for granted.

Some will argue that it is more important to learn English and function among hearing Americans (Gustason, Pfetzing, & Zawolkow, 1972) than to learn ASL and function among Deaf Americans. It hardly seems to be a matter of priorities. The need to be able to function among both linguistic communities is so great that to be unable to do either or both would undoubtedly mean extreme hardship for the individual. It can be argued persuasively that the better one functions in ASL and among Deaf Americans, the more likely one will be able to use the considerable resources of that community to improve interactions with English users. An example of this, on a concrete level, is that many Deaf people find jobs through contacts provided by friends and relatives, presumably many of them other Deaf people (Schein, 1968). On a less tangible level, but equally important, are the knowledge and perceptions that American Deaf people have regarding how to maintain oneself as a linguistically and culturally intact Deaf person in the face of the larger society's attempts to describe Deaf people as afflicted and lacking in some way (Padden & Humphries, 1988).

ASSIMILATION: DEAF PEOPLE'S VIEW

There is pressure on Deaf Americans to be assimilated as completely as possible into mainstream hearing society. Perhaps unintentionally, many of the educational and social designs for deaf children are for this very purpose. Forbidding the use of signed language in some educational programs for deaf children, for example, is presumably based on the reasoning that they should be spoken English users only. Significant segments of the public, including doctors, educators, parents, and the media, have been fascinated with medical interventions such as the recent experimentation with surgically implanting electronic devices into the cochleas of young deaf children in hope of improving the quality of their lives. The trend toward "mainstreaming" or educating Deaf children in public schools rather than in large local, regional, or state programs for Deaf children is another design to maximize assimilation.

The premise in all of these designs proposed for Deaf people is that the more one looks, talks, and behaves like a hearing person, the more one is a hearing person. Not an unusual concept as far as ethnic Americans, in general, are concerned. There is African American pride, Hispanic pride, and even Deaf pride, of course, but the fact remains that the definition of successful assimilation is more narrow than broad. The view that one can remain fully integrated into the culture of one's heritage *and* be integrated into American life, switching as needed, is not a driving force in the American scheme of things. But for Deaf people, it is an especially necessary view.

There is one difference between efforts to assimilate Deaf people and efforts to assimilate other hearing ethnic groups: Those who advocate English only for Spanish-speaking children, for example, are generally aware that they are advocating cultural and linguistic assimilation. However, those who advocate that Deaf children become as much as possible like hearing children are often unaware that there is a Deaf culture or that ASL has the validity and value of a language such as English. Thus, in their view they are not proposing one culture and language at the expense of another. Most hearing people involved with Deaf people probably don't see it as an issue of linguistic or cultural assimilation. But in Deaf people's view, it is.

Deaf people have strong and realistic views about the need to remain Deaf while functioning well in the English-speaking world. Their concept of integration, however, is different in significant ways. They see ASL as one of the most important ways to access the American social service and educational systems. Through use of interpreters or translators and through steady growth in the number of people in this country who are able to use ASL to some extent, Deaf people see their participation and acceptance increasing. In this sense, ASL is as important as English to the integration process. This differs from the traditional view that signed language will not help a Deaf person when he or she must interact with the hearing world. Deaf people perceive, quite correctly, that the quality of their lives as integrated Americans is ensured by the presence of and access to a large Deaf community which provides a rich cultural and social life. Their history is replete with symbolic stories of isolation among hearing people and the constant search for and seeking out of others like themselves (Padden & Humphries, 1988).

Deaf people are conscious, too, of the danger in the mythology that the rest of society has about them. This mythology has two opposing forms. On one hand, there is the notion of the deaf person as unable to function in few ways that others find "normal." In this notion, the absence of hearing is limiting. On the other hand, there is the myth of the deaf person who has overcome these limitations and speaks, lipreads, and uses prostheses to hear. Deaf people's view of integration includes neither the idea of accepting a limited role nor the idea of devoting one's life to being what they consider to be the impossible: the deaf person who isn't. The historical view of the folly of devoting one's life to trying to be like a hearing person is illustrated in this translation from ASL of a story told by Robert McGregor in *The Irishman and the Flea*, part of a series made by the National Association of the Deaf in 1913 to preserve signed language on film:

Ladies and gentlemen . . . always when I hear about the "restored to society deaf," it reminds me of the story of the Irishman and the flea. The Irishman had this flea that would pester him here, there, and everywhere on his body until finally he could no longer stand it. He stripped off his clothing to get at it and managed to catch it but as soon as he caught it in his hand, opened his hand to look at it, it would jump back on his body. He'd have to look for it again, catch it but as soon as he caught it, opened his hand to look at it, it would jump back on his body and so on. He could never catch it. This is exactly how it is when often one hears about some deaf man out in Boston: clever, sophisticated, speaks like the hearing, lipreads faultlessly. We'd say, "Really?" and get on the first train out, arrive and ask "Where is he?" "Oh, must be some mistake, he's out in New York!" "Really?" and then we'd hightail it to New York on a horse, "Well, where is this man? Clever, sophisticated, speaks like the hearing?" "Oh, he's in Chicago!" "Drat!" and we'd get back on the train for Chicago but of course, we'd never find him. Always (like the flea), he'd be here, there, or everywhere. Now, I ask you, will we ever find someone who is just as they say: clever, sophisticated, speaks like the hearing, mingles effortlessly with people? Never! (Padden & Humphries, 1988, p. 112)

Assimilation and integration for Deaf people, therefore, is acceptable in a context in which Deaf people retain their language and their community. Then, and only then, are they able to center themselves and approach functioning in the world of others (Padden & Humphries, 1988).

DIVERSITY AMONG AMERICAN-BORN DEAF PEOPLE

Of course, Deaf people in the United States are people of different ethnic heritages. The community of Deaf people in the United States is as diverse in this way as the general hearing population. This does not mean that they are not part of a general Deaf culture any more than it means hearing people of Hispanic or Asian heritage are not Americans. There is variation among communities of Deaf people just as there is variation among communities of hearing people. There is regional, ethnic, and linguistic variation.

The variations, or dialects, of ASL usually don't interfere greatly with communication among Deaf signers. There is variation in the vocabulary and the diction of white southern signers and black southern signers, for example (Woodward, 1976). There is variation between white southern and white northern signing. Unfortunately, most of the research into the lives and language of Deaf people has tended to be unspecific in reference to particular communities or classes of Deaf people, leaving us to assume that most descriptions of Deaf culture and ASL in the United States are based on studies of white, middle class Americans of indeterminate local community. It is also clear that inquiry in general, including inquiry into how best to educate Deaf people, has not focused very well on issues of ethnicity among American Deaf people—although that is a growing trend, as evidenced by the chapters in this book.

Variation in racial and ethnic background of Deaf people in the United States means that a large and significant number of Deaf people are among the most multicultural people of this country. It also means that many of these Deaf people face all of the social and political implications of being of a racial or ethnic minority in the United States. These are the Deaf ASL users who are of African American, or Hispanic, or Asian/Pacific, or American Indian heritage. Of course, the pattern of language use and fluency, as well as the degree of assimilation into each of these various cultures, will vary by individual, but there is no denying the unique experiences of these individuals in their specific communities. The individuals are the products of these experiences, and their identities and social orientation are determined by these experiences.

MULTICULTURAL ISSUES FOR NATIVE-BORN DEAF AMERICANS

With this backdrop of issues related to the biculturality of Deaf people, multicultural issues can be divided into two categories: those that concern native-born Deaf Americans and those that concern naturalized Deaf Americans. This section discusses Deaf people born and raised in the United States. The next section discusses issues for those who have immigrated to the United States.

As has been pointed out, every native-born Deaf person who is part of a community of Deaf ASL users is, regardless of ethnicity, in a bilingual situation in the United States. The two languages involved are English and ASL, and the cultures of the two language communities are different. White, native-born Deaf Americans interact with two languages and two cultures. An issue for them as well as for ethnic Deaf Americans born in the United States is the recognition of the bilingual, bicultural nature of their lives and the implications it has for education. Should educational problems for Deaf people be bilingual programs? Should English be taught as a second language, rather than as *the* language? Is there a place in the curriculum for the cultural heritage of Deaf ASL users? Discussions of *multicultural* Deaf people, then, must be placed within the context of a society that is not even totally prepared to think about *bicultural* Deaf people.

From Deaf people's point of view the most central issue in education of Deaf people in the United States has been and remains: How can deaf children grow up to be Deaf adults and yet function within a larger social and economic structure of others? This issue emerges in various forms, such as in the insistence that Deaf children must have "role" models in the form of Deaf adults. Or it may be manifested in the struggle Deaf people have kept up to maintain the presence of a signed language of their community in the education and daily lives of Deaf children. Most recently, it has been evident in the questioning of Public Law 94-142 and its interpretations, which have resulted in the isolation of large numbers of deaf children in mainstream educational programs where they may have no access to a community of Deaf people and where they may be limited to seeing a form of signing unacceptable to the Deaf community or to any informed user of a signed language. It may be seen, quite clearly, in the "self-determination" movements, the most famous of which was the students' closing of Gallaudet University in a successful attempt to have a Deaf person appointed as university president in 1988.

At the bottom of these issues is the belief that a Deaf person must be rooted in the language and community of Deaf people. From this community the Deaf person will learn how to function among hearing people and develop a strong identity and social stability. People outside of the community have always believed that they must teach Deaf people how to function in non-Deaf society. The realization will come hard to outsiders that Deaf people prepare one another for the outside world. Deaf people have rarely felt that they have had sufficient presence in the lives and education of young deaf children.

The number of Deaf people working as teachers in U.S. educational systems to educate other Deaf people is small, and the proportion of these Deaf people who are African American, Hispanic, Asian/Pacific Islander, or American Indian is minuscule (Woodward, Allen, & Schildroth, 1987). The ethnocentric attitudes in this country, working against the development of cadres of educators of various ethnic heritages, have combined with practices and attitudes that limit the participation of Deaf people in society and create a situation in which the administrator, the teacher, and the counselor who have the most impact on the ethnic Deaf person's life are white, hearing persons. Deaf African American children, for example, are unlikely to have either hearing African American adult consultants or Deaf African American adult consultants in their school environment, although they need both if they are to function as Deaf African American adults.

Aside from the issue of the ethnic diversity of those who staff our educational systems for Deaf children, what educational practices will we use to educate Deaf children in schools or programs in which there is a concentration of two or more ethnic groups? Since most of what we know and do in education for Deaf people is grounded in what applies and what may work for white, middle-class Deaf persons, this issue takes on particular relevance to Deaf people of other racial and ethnic backgrounds. It is no more appropriate to apply expectations of white Deaf Americans to African American Deaf Americans or Hispanic Deaf Americans than it is to apply the expectations of white hearing Americans to hearing Americans of other racial and ethnic heritages. There are class and cultural differences in how people of different ethnic groups view the role of school and how they interact with school and text (Heath, 1983).

Traditionally, we have adopted one set of practices or methods and used it uniformly with all students regardless of ethnic background or language used in the home. Only in recent years have we at the program level begun to recognize the need for diversity of methodology as well as of staff. Some diversity of methodology is presented in this book, and it is certainly a step forward. But it is clear that the greater number of Deaf students in the United States are not in an educational system that has significantly considered either their cultural orientation or their multilanguage needs. Research that has attempted to suggest ways to teach in hearing multicultural classrooms has proliferated in recent years, but very little of it has trickled into the classrooms of Deaf children. At issue is when and whether Deaf children will share in the benefits of the well-designed, multicultural educational practices that are becoming more feasible in the American educational system. Underlying this issue is the question, Will we continue to view these children as without hearing and, in our zeal to deal with that, overlook ethnic and language differences?

MULTICULTURAL ISSUES FOR NATURALIZED DEAF AMERICANS

Often Deaf adults and their families set out quite deliberately to immigrate to the United States seeking a better life for themselves. These Deaf adults may be skilled and knowledgeable in a profession, trade, or craft. Or they may be young, school-age children coming from good educational systems where they may even have learned some English or ASL. They come seeking to further their education, or to gain employment, or to escape from political strife. Whatever their reasons, these Deaf people know what they want and have the resources within themselves and their families to get it. Their needs vary, but they must find other Deaf people and a community of signed language users in order to learn the systems of access in this country. In order to become multilingual and multicultural, as they most certainly now must do, they must learn to be Deaf people in the United States.

The situation is much more difficult for Deaf people and their families who immigrate to the United States from countries that historically have had negative views of deaf people, their education, and their place in the community. These Deaf people may have quite different expectations regarding education and employment, family relationships, religion, medical practices, and sex roles, which do not agree at all with American views on the same subjects. Many of us who work with people such as these know the problems of outreach to Deaf people within families from other cultural orientations. Many of us have learned the hard way about contact with families who have different systems of politeness. Many of us have experienced firsthand the challenge of communicating without a common language, sometimes relying on gesture or intermediaries who are only slightly more skilled in translation than we are.

We have also seen deaf people of all ages who have had little or no previous education or training for employment other than menial or domestic tasks. These people often have learned neither the spoken nor signed language of their former country well. Whether they are six years old entering a school for deaf children or twenty years old entering a continuing education or vocational education program, their needs are extensive. They may have little family, community, or personal resources to function well in this new country.

Access to programs established to meet the needs of new arrivals to this country is severely limited for the Deaf person. Access to elementary and secondary school programs for Deaf children from families who have moved to the United States is also problematic. By default, these people end up in special classes, programs, or schools designed to meet the needs of Deaf people but not necessarily of Deaf people from other cultural backgrounds. If, as is the case in my own community college district, the effort is made to adapt for their needs, then the method and materials used are still very likely to be instinctively put together from experience rather than grounded in research. Much of our effort as a profession in this direction has been ad hoc at best. The major issue of our profession is that there is little guidance for organizing programs or resources to teach students who are Deaf and from another country and culture. Indeed, there may not be recognition that there is a need to do so.

The needs of these students can be extremely complicated. For example, many young deaf children are in hearing families that do not use a signed language at all and are in the process of learning to speak English themselves. In school, the child may be learning ASL and English. The child may go home at the end of the school day to a family that is not learning ASL and which has no expectation that the Deaf child will leave the family and become independent. The family may have chosen to maintain its spoken first language in the home, but the Deaf child might not have mastered it. It is unlikely that the school will teach the child how to speak or read and write the first language of the family: English and possibly ASL, yes, but Spanish or Vietnamese, probably not.

Deaf adults in this situation have the added pressure of needing to be independent immediately. They often cannot afford the time it takes to learn English and ASL and become integrated into a Deaf community before they have to support themselves or contribute to the family support. For this reason, an integrated system of educational programs and social service agencies, both privately funded and government sponsored, is absolutely necessary. There must be a strong educational program designed to work with Deaf adults as second language learners; there must be an advocacy and counseling program in the community that helps with community integration; and there must be a program, such as vocational rehabilitation, which counsels, assesses to determine employment potential, and supports the student financially. Although most educational programs and social service agencies acknowledge that there are many Deaf people who need this kind of systematic approach to service, there is still little effort to organize such systems. At issue is whether this country and our profession are prepared to make the effort.

We must consider the important issue that the Deaf person, child or adult, who comes to this country may find it difficult to reconcile the new culture with the old. Expectations are likely to be different. Role definitions are also likely to be different. For example, a Deaf person from a hearing family that values an extended family support system may experience the pull of a Deaf community of people not of his or her old culture. This is because of the support that the Deaf community can give, which includes greater ease of communication in ASL and access to a social world not available for the deaf person within the hearing family. There is an ongoing uncertainty about what is best for the Deaf person in this situation. What can we do to assist a person faced with conflict over this issue? At the least it will take a commitment to preserving the right and privilege of such Deaf persons to make choices that maintain their multiculturality, and providing educational and community resources to help them live by their choices.

CONCLUSION

Deaf people have a vision of integration that is different from what hearing people envision for them. Deaf people see a grounding in the culture and signed language of the Deaf community in which they live as the most important factor in their lives. Integration comes more easily and more effectively from these roots. In short, Deaf people teach one another not only how to be Deaf people in the United States, but also how to function in the world of others. How can the vision of Deaf people be incorporated into the educational processes for Deaf children in this country? How can we increase the presence of Deaf people in the lives and education of Deaf children? How can we increase the presence of *ethnic* Deaf people in the lives and education of Deaf children?

It may be more difficult for African American, Hispanic, American Indian, and Asian/Pacific Island Deaf people to achieve a sense of community in the United States because of several factors: The social forces that isolate people of different races and ethnicity may isolate Deaf people of ethnic backgrounds from white Deaf communities as well. The forces that isolate Deaf children from Deaf adults may be even more effective among ethnic groups. There are few ''models'' of white Deaf people in the lives of Deaf children, and there are even fewer African American, Hispanic, American Indian, and Asian/Pacific Island Deaf role models in the lives of Deaf children.

We know that there are very important questions to be answered about how children of different cultures and class approach learning to read and write. Family practices that foster the development of children vary from culture to culture. They vary among families of Deaf children of differing ethnic backgrounds as well. How can we move from applying what we do with white, middle-class Deaf children to new strategies and configurations for effectively educating ethnic Deaf children? Perhaps the chapters that follow will help to answer these questions and others that pertain to how we will educate and serve an increasingly diverse Deaf community in the United States.

BIBLIOGRAPHY

Baker, C., & Battison, R. (1980). *Sign language of the deaf community*. Silver Spring, MD: National Association of the Deaf.

Charrow, V., & Fletcher, J. (1974). English as the second language of deaf children. *Developmental Psychology, 10,* 463–470.

Cokeley, D. (1978). Program considerations in a bilingual ASL English approach to education. *Proceedings of the Second National Symposium on Sign Language Research and Teaching*. Silver Spring, MD: National Association of the Deaf.

Erting, C. (1978). Language policy and deaf ethnicity in the United States. *Sign Language Studies, 19,* 139–152.

Goldberg, P., & Bordman, M. (1975). The ESL approach to teaching English to hearing impaired students. *American Annals of the Deaf, 120,* 22–27.

Gustason, G., Pfetzing, D., & Zawolkow, E. (1972). *Signing exact English*. Rossmoor, CA: Modern Signs Press.

Heath, S. (1983). *Ways with words*. New York: Cambridge University Press.

Humphries, T. (1978). A rationale for a comprehensive, culturally sensitive language program objective. *Teaching English to the Deaf, 5*(1), 4–5.

Humphries, T., Coye, T., & Martin, B. (1978). A bilingual, bicultural approach to teaching English. *Proceedings of the Second National Symposium on Sign Language Research and Teaching*. Silver Spring, MD: National Association of the Deaf.

Kannapell, B. (1978). Linguistic and sociolinguistic perspectives on sign systems for educating deaf children: Toward a true bilingual approach. *Proceedings of the Second National Symposium on Sign Language Research and Teaching*. Silver Spring, MD: National Association of the Deaf.

Klima, E., & Bellugi, U., with Battison, R., Boyes-Braem, P., Fischer S., Frishburg, N., Lane, H., Lentz, E., Newkirk, D., Newport, E., Pederson, C., & Siple, P. (1979). *The signs of language*. Cambridge, MA: Harvard University.

Kyle, J., & Woll, B. (Eds.). (1983). *Language in sign: An international perspective on sign language*. London: Croom Helm.

Lane, H., & Grosjean, F. (Eds.). (1980). *Recent perspectives on ASL*. Hillsdale, NJ: Erlbaum.

Markowicz, H., & Woodward, J. (1975). *Language and the maintenance of ethnic boundaries in the deaf community*. Paper presented at the Conference on Culture and Communication, Temple University, Philadelphia.

Padden, C. (1980). The deaf community and the culture of deaf people. In C. Baker & R. Battison (Eds.), *Sign language and the deaf community*. Silver Spring, MD: National Association of the Deaf.

Padden, C., & Humphries, T. (1988). *Deaf in America: Voices from a culture*. Cambridge, MA: Harvard University.

Padden, C., & Markowicz, H. (1975). *Crossing cultural group boundaries into the deaf community*. Paper presented at the Conference on Culture and Communication, Temple University, Philadelphia.

Padden, C., & Markowicz, H. (1976). Cultural conflicts between hearing and deaf communities. *Proceedings of the Seventh World Congress of the World Federation of the Deaf*. Silver Spring, MD: National Association of the Deaf.

Schein, J. (1968). *The deaf community: Studies in the social psychology of deafness*. Washington, DC: Gallaudet College.

Siple, P. (1978). *Understanding language through sign language research*. New York: Academic.

Stokoe, W. C. (1960). Sign language structures: An outline of the visual communication systems of the American deaf. *Studies in Linguistics, Occasional Papers, 8.*

Stokoe, W. C. (1975). The use of sign language in teaching English. *American Annals of the Deaf, 120,* 417–421.

Supalla, T. (1978). Morphology of verbs of motion and location in American Sign Language. *Proceedings of the Second National Symposium on Sign Language Research and Teaching*. Silver Spring, MD: National Association of the Deaf.

Wilbur, R. (1979). *American Sign Language and sign systems*. Baltimore: University Park.

Woodward, J. (1976). Black southern signing. *Language in Society, 5,* 303–311.

Woodward, J. (1980). Some sociolinguistic problems in the implementation of bilingual education for deaf students. *Proceedings of the Second National Symposium on Sign Language Research and Teaching*. Silver Spring, MD: National Association of the Deaf.

Woodward, J., Allen, T., & Schildroth, A. (1987). English teachers of the deaf: Background and communication preferences. *Teaching English to Deaf and Second-Language Students, 5*(2), 4–13.

CHAPTER **2**

A Multicultural Approach to Education of Children Who Are Deaf

Kathee M. Christensen

Considerable research data suggest that for groups who experience disproportionate levels of academic failure, the extent to which students' language and culture are incorporated into the school program constitutes a significant predictor of academic success.

J. Cummins

Profoundly, congenitally Deaf children, in most cases, encounter two languages during their formative years. Adults with normal hearing typically communicate with these children using spoken English or a form of signed English. Deaf adults and older Deaf children may provide American Sign Language (ASL) models. This chapter discusses the notion of bilingualism as applied to the Deaf ASL and English user. Trilingual and multicultural educational issues, which arise when the parents of a Deaf child are members of diverse ethnic and racial backgrounds, are considered. This chapter is founded on the assumption that Deaf individuals have unique personal and collective experiences that differ significantly from those of hearing persons. In all cases, the term *multicultural* refers to issues of both culture and communication.

Multicultural groups have been described as groups whose collective and personal experiences differ significantly from the mainstream. More specifically, the term *culture* ''denotes an historically transmitted pattern of meanings embodied in symbols . . . by

17

means of which men communicate, perpetuate, and develop their knowledge about and attitudes toward life'' (Geertz, 1973, p. 89). The U. S. government uses the term *linguistic minority* to refer to individuals who are not functional in English. Professional educators in the United States have been slow to reach a consensus regarding the educational needs of multicultural linguistic groups, in general, and they have barely started to address the needs of multicultural Deaf children. In fact, educators are still debating in some circles whether or not Deafness represents a separate cultural group. It is the premise of this text that Deaf culture is a vibrant, living dimension of human experience.

Deaf students with normal intellectual abilities are seldom provided with early access to natural (primarily visual) communication. Early natural language deprivation may explain the reason why these children often do not reach their potential in English language usage and, therefore, are penalized educationally in the predominantly ''English focused'' American public school system. Communication develops through cultural necessity. When the cultural experience of an individual is devoid of sound, natural communication grows out of a predominantly visual environment.

A profoundly, congenitally Deaf child is a member of a ''language different'' culture. Frequently the natural, visual cultural behavior of the Deaf child is disregarded by ethnocentric hearing individuals, and the child becomes a marginal member of the culture of his or her hearing, speaking family. To superimpose on a Deaf child an unnatural cultural experience, one based on the ability to hear, is to overlook an opportunity to understand the Deaf child socially and psychologically. In other words, one must seek to understand all components of a visually oriented Deaf child's natural behavior in order to achieve an unbiased understanding of the child's communicative strengths and potentials. The foundation for an educational program for Deaf children must be centered on the ''three Cs'': cognition, communication, and culture.

The majority of profoundly, congenitally Deaf children are born into an environment that requires of them early bicultural awareness. Approximately 90 percent of all Deaf children are born to parents with normal hearing ability. These children do not have easy, natural access to the communications system used by members of their family or, indeed, in the cultural environment at large. Cultural information that is transmitted through primarily oral communication is not completely accessible without visual modification. By necessity, Deaf children seek alternative means for understanding others and making themselves understood. They learn to observe carefully and make connections through observations.

A Deaf child of hearing parents is a member of a unique language community without access to early, natural, and comprehensible linguistic input at home. Visually salient information becomes critical to the developing Deaf child as he or she begins to take risks in order to gain knowledge. Educators can learn much about this process by interviewing Deaf adults and reading autobiographies of successful Deaf individuals. Bragg, in his highly readable autobiography entitled *Lessons in Laughter* (Bragg & Bergman, 1989), recalled his own strategies as a four-year-old Deaf child involved in the task of interpreting his world visually. At an early age, this son of Deaf parents designed creative ways to cope with obstacles.

> One afternoon I saw a group of children hitting a ball with a broomstick. I tried to join them, but they kept moving their mouths at me and finally waved me away. This was the first time my deafness became a barrier to me, although at the time I still did not realize

what that meant. . . . I do not remember how, but I conceived the idea of going back outside with a crate containing all my toys. I dumped them on the pavement and, one by one, the kids abandoned their game, trotted over, and began to play with my toys while I supervised them to make sure they would handle the toys properly and not appropriate them. (p. 4)

COGNITIVE DEVELOPMENT

Much of the early learning of hearing children is a result of information gained through observation of daily routines. These routines provide a conceptual framework for the development of cognition and language. Children about the age of two frequently invent their own cause-and-effect relationships based on observation of commonly occurring events. Often these cause-and-effect equations are totally incorrect. In Piagetian terms, such original interpretations are labeled *transductive reasoning*. In transductive reasoning, the young child observes natural, daily occurrences and interprets cause-and-effect relationships on the basis of his or her child logic. Transductive reasoning is one of the early, culturally bound cognitive roadblocks for deaf children.

For example, perhaps Daddy normally comes home every day at 6:00 P.M. Soon after his arrival, dinner is served. When Daddy decides to take the afternoon off and comes home at 1:30 P.M., the transductive child assumes that it is dinner time. The phenomenon of transductive reasoning is a normal step in the cognitive developmental process of all children and therefore occurs in the Deaf child's development, also. The hearing child, however, is able to test his or her hypotheses through oral attempts and to receive immediate, salient feedback from more mature speakers who perceive and monitor the early cognitive misinterpretations. The parent of the two-year-old hearing child in the example situation could explain easily the reasons why, in fact, it was not time for dinner.

What does the Deaf child do in order to test original interpretations of the environment? Unless the child is able to ask a logical question and receive a salient answer, the explanation for a disruption in the normal daily routine will remain a mystery. This dilemma requires the Deaf child to make adjustments early in life in order to achieve what Piaget termed *intellectual equilibrium*. The process of early adjustment through a visually salient environment lays the cultural foundation for adjustment throughout all stages of intellectual and psychosocial development across the life span. It is critical for primary caretakers, parents, and others to understand and support the bicultural situation of Deaf infants in order to facilitate the ability of these children to function successfully both in a natural visual culture and in a less accessible cultural environment based on fundamental knowledge acquired through the ability to hear and to speak.

An example of transductive reasoning occurred recently in our clinical program at San Diego State University. One of our graduate clinicians, who was working with a three-year-old profoundly Deaf girl, frequently gave stickers as a reward for good work during the clinic session. Typically, the stickers were awarded when it was time to go home; however, during one session, the stickers came out early. The little girl made her choice, said good-bye, and got up to find her mother. The clinician was able to explain, using American Sign Language (ASL), that it was not time to go home and that the sticker was given early because they were going across the hall to join another activity for the rest of the session. The three-year-old understood the explanation and was able to store that experience in her "logic bank." Instead of feeling confusion or frustration, the child learned that clinic sessions had an element of flexibility and that stickers did not necessarily signal time to go home. She may have begun, at this point, to understand the multidimensionality of her world.

Relatively little research has addressed the intriguing question of how very young deaf children come to a point of knowledge and develop increasingly complex cognitive schema as they attempt to make sense out of a world that for them is dominated by visual stimuli. It has been suggested that spontaneous gestural communication of congenitally deaf infants and young children may provide insights into the ways in which these children interpret the environment (Christensen, 1988; Goldin-Meadow, 1985). This early communicative behavior may be viewed within a Piagetian framework. Piagetian theory is founded on close observation of the activity of infants prior to the development of word usage. Stage I, Sensorimotor Development, comprises a sequence of six substages that lead to the eventual acquisition of the first referential word, typically about the age of one year for children with normal hearing. Passage through each substage is critical to the eventual acquisition of expressive communication.

In the young deaf child, the acquisition of the first word (signed or spoken) may be delayed significantly because of limited comprehensible input during the early stages of physical development. Nonverbal communication acts, however, do occur and can serve as the basis for verbal (signed or spoken) communication. Close observation of the nonverbal communication of young deaf children with limited expressive language has revealed cognitive behaviors at Piagetian stages II (Preoperational) and III (Concrete Operations). However, these phenomena have not been documented to the fullest extent.

Research has not, for example, probed the effect of profound, congenital hearing loss on the assimilation and accommodation processes of the child with regard to cognitive stimuli. It would be interesting to study ways in which Piagetian Stage III reversibility behaviors might vary when perceived and demonstrated through predominantly visual cues. How might reversibility behavior be influenced by early access to a complete, natural visual language? This and other significant questions must be addressed by persons who nurture the intellectual development of Deaf children.

Future research in the area of Deaf culture and cognitive development must consider ways in which an experience is perceived and understood when perception is solely visual rather than visual and auditory. Investigation of the cultural experience of profoundly, congenitally deaf infants and young children will lead parents and educators toward an understanding of how complete experiences can be communicated in a mutually comprehensible mode between Deaf and hearing individuals. Knowledge and acceptance of a basic ASL/English bilingual or dual language environment with cultural and cognitive underpinnings is primary to this research.

Figure 2.1, based on the dual iceberg theory of Cummins (1984), presents a model for parallel acquisition of ASL and English. When common visual features of both languages are introduced and used consistently among young Deaf children and their family members and teachers, the possibility for natural acquisition of both languages is enhanced. The most logical and easily adapted common features include eye contact, facial expressions, and basic hand shapes. Teachers who are fluent in both languages can assist young children in the use of a natural visual language to acquire competence in a primarily auditory spoken language, thus producing basic bilingual ability.

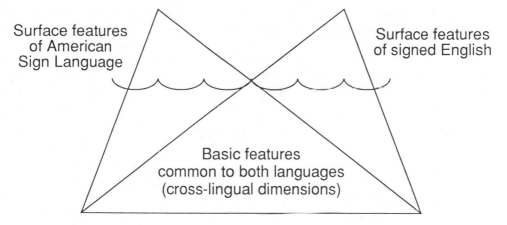

FIGURE 2.1.   Bilingual ASL/English acquisition

SOURCE: J. Cummins (1984). *Bilingualism and special education: Issues in assessment and pedagogy.* Multilingual Matters, Ltd., Bank House, 8A Hill Road, Clevedon, Avon BS21-7HH, England. Adapted with permission.

Deaf children from diverse ethnic and racial backgrounds represent an additional dimension of the Deaf experience. The environment of Deaf individuals from African American, Hispanic, American Indian, and Asian/Pacific Islander families must be viewed from a trilingual and tricultural perspective. This view includes the home language and culture, the school language and culture, and the natural, visual language and culture of the Deaf community. A fundamental assumption is that multicultural Deaf children have normal cognitive potential, which will develop and flourish when educators apply a trilingual and tricultural perspective when working with them and their families. Public Law 99-457 requires the inclusion of families in early intervention decisions for deaf children. The interpretation of this law must extend to include the language of the family, as well as the academic languages of ASL and English and the cultures represented by Deaf and hearing family members.

In her book, *The Foundations of Dual Language Instruction*, Lessow-Hurley (1990) pointed out that dual language instruction has been available since ancient times when conquered groups were forced to learn the language of their conquerors. Although school programs in those societies typically emphasized the language of the dominant culture, there is no evidence of an interest in systematically destroying local languages. In modern times, a country such as the Republic of China reveals much about its history and immigration patterns through the parallel use of several living languages, among which are an aborigine language, Japanese, Taiwanese, and Mandarin. The academic language is Mandarin; however, children grow up at least bilingual, and more often multilingual, as they encounter the languages of their families, their neighborhood, and the educational and political arenas. There is ample evidence of the ability of these children to learn to communicate effectively in more than one language and to adjust comfortably to unfamiliar cultural environments (Bhatia & Ritchie, 1989).

These languages will, however, influence one another. As Grosjean (1982) pointed out, "Language borrowing is the legacy of those who live with two languages" (p. 341).

Language borrowing is not necessarily a negative phenomenon. Early research, which held that dual language environments were detrimental for hearing infants and young children, has been challenged in recent times. McLaughlin (1984) asserted that so-called language interference could be reduced if the domains were clearly defined and if the two languages were maintained in balance. A primary challenge in the education of Deaf children is to provide a bilingual environment where English and ASL are clearly defined and balanced.

BILINGUAL AND TRILINGUAL EDUCATION

For many people, bilingualism is a way of contemporary life, and multicultural sensitivity is a positive social force. It is possible to apply this concept to acquisition of one or more visual-spatial languages in combination with one or more auditory-oral-written languages. It seems logical to assume that visual-spatial/auditory-oral-written bilingualism is a positive answer to a modern educational dilemma—the dilemma of bridging the natural visual communication mode of the Deaf child and the less comprehensible mode of spoken English. A critical component in a successful bilingual and bicultural educational program is the availability of teachers who are bilingual and bicultural. University teacher preparation programs that require bilingual/bicultural competencies are rare, but two examples can be found in the California State University system. Both San Diego State University and California State University at Northridge have given priority to the addition of bilingual and multicultural coursework and practicums in their graduate curricula.

When a third language is used by a Deaf child's family, the communication environment should include opportunities for all members to achieve comprehensible communication. Research in the area of trilingual education has supported the use of signed language as a bridge between two different spoken languages. In one study, Spanish-speaking parents were able to acquire the rudiments of ASL when signed communication was presented along with spoken Spanish. Parents reported an increase in communication with their Deaf child and a greater understanding of the condition of deafness (Christensen, 1985).

At the international Deaf Way in Washington, D.C., in summer 1989, I watched with fascination as Deaf people from all over the world met in the lobby of the Omni Shoreham Hotel and negotiated highly abstract conversations through nonverbal and verbal visual-spatial means. The motivation to communicate and to exchange ideas was stronger than the need to establish a preferred language. Conversations evolved using bits and pieces of formal signed languages combined with gesture, mime, and other nonverbal, visual-spatial communication techniques. The result was a demonstration of multilingual and multicultural communication with the common, unifying link being deafness. Anyone who was a witness to this scene would admit to the obvious existence of a unifying Deaf culture among these individuals from all parts of the world. The next cultural level, of course, would include the country in which an individual was raised, for example, American Deaf or French Deaf culture.

ETHNOGRAPHY

A bicultural or multicultural approach to education of children who are deaf must involve an ethnographic (qualitative and observational) perspective toward assessment. Communication is defined by the larger context of any exchange of information, rather than by the more narrow definition of information exchanged through a specific language (English) or even more narrowly through a specific language modality (speech). In an ethnographic approach to assessment and instruction, any attempt to explore or to communicate is counted. Nonverbal as well as verbal acts are accepted. Formally signed or spoken acts are viewed equally from a linguistic point of view. Attempts at home language communication, signed or spoken, are valued as highly as attempts at school language communication. In other words, communication assumptions or biases on the part of the observer are put aside in order to view objectively the natural communication strengths of the Deaf child.

The varied abilities of individuals from different language environments are observed in a context where meaning is negotiated through any and all modes available to the participants. The burden in such an approach is placed on the teacher or investigator to evaluate the existing communication rather than to describe ways in which the communication is deficient according to prescribed standards. The teacher is challenged to find the communicative strengths of each Deaf child instead of creating myths on the basis of what should or could take place if the child had natural access to comprehensible standard English. Educators are obligated to present information in a predominantly visual mode, so that Deaf learners can assimilate and accommodate all aspects of academic input naturally.

One can observe the communicative behavior of Deaf children as they respond to visually salient cues. Vision is the natural "voice" of the profoundly, congenitally Deaf child. By encouraging Deaf children to seek and use their natural, cultural "voices," educators can learn much about these children and about ourselves in relation to them.

CULTURAL COMPLEXITY

Profoundly, congenitally Deaf children from African American, American Indian, Hispanic, and Asian/Pacific Island families have unique cultural and linguistic challenges. They may be faced with the acquisition and maintenance of a delicate personal balance among a home culture, the dominant culture of the United States, and the culture of the Deaf community. This is further complicated by the finding of a 1981 study that only 13.6 percent of teachers of deaf children reported having a hearing loss themselves, and the "population of teachers of the hearing impaired is overwhelmingly dominated by those who classify their ethnic background as 'white' " (Corbett & Jensema, 1981, p. 12). These figures have not altered drastically in the past decade. Mobley's study (1991) informed us that, of the 476 students enrolled in teacher preparation programs throughout the United States during 1990–1991, only 17 were from underrepresented ethnic groups. On the positive side, however, the Conference of Educational Administrators Serving the Deaf (CEASD) awards an annual scholarship of $1,000 to a Deaf or hearing member of an underrepresented ethnic group enrolled in a university or college program in preparation to become a teacher of Deaf children. Wide-scale recruitment efforts and scholarship support are needed if diversity is to be represented equally among Deaf students and their teachers.

Trueba, Jacobs, and Kirton (1990) described the cultural conflict found in American public education. The insensitivity of educators resulted in "school created disabilities" for students from different cultures. This situation, the authors suggested, must be countered with the development of "culturally congruent instructional models which are effective and nondamaging" to students (p. 104). Educators must assign high priority to the acceptance of cultural values other than those of the mainstream American culture and integrate these values into the overall curriculum. Teacher training programs, textbooks, educational media, and computer programs typically ignore in-depth treatment of diversity issues and emphasize, instead, the culture and values of middle-class white citizens of the United States. The recent English-only movement in California is an example of this ethnocentricity. These factors add to the at-risk status of Deaf children from the four ethnic groups discussed in this text.

CURRICULUM DEVELOPMENT

A Piagetian approach to the education of Deaf children promotes the active participation of the learner in the process of cognitive and linguistic growth (Christensen, 1990). Language learning is a complex, "multifaced problem-solving activity" (Lessow-Hurley, 1990). Classroom activities that include diverse cultural experiences are likely to stimulate the interest and participation of children who can relate to a particular experience and share the perspective of a native of that culture. Cognitive development, particularly the ability to perceive positive relationships among differing entities, will be enhanced when teachers and children respect and value diversity from a social perspective. With regard to the development of communication, a child is likely to be open to the consideration of linguistic variation and expansion if he or she understands at an early age that there are multiple solutions to cognitive problems and many ways in which these solutions may be expressed. Rather than fearing to attempt "incorrect" communication, that child might become involved in creative self-expression through written, signed, or spoken variations of his or her home and school languages.

Successful two-way educational programs for hearing children that combine monolingual English-speaking children and monolingual Spanish-speaking children were first implemented in San Diego in 1975. This approach, based on an additive bilingual and bicultural model, is being replicated in several places across the United States (Lessow-Hurley, 1990). At least two center schools for the deaf—one in Indianapolis and another in Fremont, California—have plans to implement bilingual and bicultural ASL/English educational programs. A study of successful bilingual, bicultural programs for hearing children and for Deaf children might result in a model for bilingual, multicultural education of Deaf children. A bilingual, multicultural approach would encompass ASL, English, Deaf culture, and the cultures represented by the families of the student population in a specific school. Foreign language interpreters would be as common as signed language interpreters. Texts and other classroom materials would reflect the cultural experiences of African American, European American, American Indian, Hispanic, and Asian/Pacific Islander groups in the United States and in their land of origin.

Although the acculturation of teachers may be more difficult than the acculturation of children, resources exist to facilitate this process. The Teachers of English to Speakers of Other Languages (TESOL) international organization recently formed a section for educators of Deaf students. This active subgroup is an ideal place for the integration of cultural and linguistic information from the parent organization with the growing body of information on ASL/English bilingual biculturalism. The annual convention of TESOL provides a forum for research in ASL/English educational practices within programs for Deaf learners.

The Council on Education of the Deaf (CED) endorsed a new standard in December 1990 that requires the inclusion of multicultural coursework in university programs which prepare teachers of the deaf. The national Conference of Educational Administrators Serving the Deaf (CEASD) regularly sponsors a symposium on multicultural issues in deafness and has an active committee on ethnic and multicultural concerns. And the Convention of American Instructors of the Deaf (CAID) has a special interest group on multicultural issues in education of the deaf. All of these groups have been formed within the past decade. The oldest one, the CAID-Ethnic Multicultural Special Interest Group (SIG), was founded at the CAID convention in 1983. Cooperative ethnic and multicultural projects and programs that involve CEASD, CAID, TESOL, and the Association of College Educators in Hearing Impairment (ACE-HI) are being planned for the future.

PARENTS

A sociolinguistic model of language acquisition relies heavily on the comprehensibility of linguistic input from parent to child. Language competence is acquired through dynamic social interactions involving the child and family members (Owens, 1988). Studies of Deaf parents who use ASL with their Deaf infants revealed that these children acquired natural, salient, two-way communication in a manner parallel to that of hearing infants' acquisition of spoken language (Vernon & Andrews, 1990). African American and Hispanic children are less likely than white children to have a signed language used at home (Jordan & Karchmer, 1986). This may be the result of lack of access to signed language classes, lack of accurate information regarding signed language, or, for Hispanic parents, lack of ASL classes taught in Spanish. The disproportionate representation of African American and Hispanic Deaf children in classes for children with so-called additional learning disabilities may be a result of limited early comprehensible communication at home.

Few attempts have been made to provide signed language classes for families who speak a language other than English. An experimental trilingual education project that presented televised signed language instruction for Spanish-speaking parents of Deaf children found that these parents were successful in the acquisition and use of a rudimentary signed language when instruction was provided in Spanish (Christensen, 1986). Videotaped copies of the trilingual programs are in use in several schools and programs for Deaf children around the United States. Although the trilingual project represented a beginning attempt at bridging the communication gap between home and school languages—in this case Spanish and Conceptual Sign—additional programs are required to meet the communications needs of other ethnic groups. The videotaped format has proved successful and could be replicated for use with other cultures and languages.

CONCLUSION

The demands of life in a multicultural society can and should be met by individuals and institutions. For a Deaf individual, the "three C's "—cognition, communication, and culture—develop from a visual center and interrelate as each individual encounters unique life experiences. Whether or not the academic potential of a deaf learner is realized during the years that he or she spends in school depends primarily on the visual salience of the school environment, the linguistic consistency of school personnel, the opportunities for creative self-expression, and the positive interaction between school and home settings.

Many Deaf individuals achieve academic and professional success "in spite of" their educational experiences. Many more could achieve success if adults at school and home valued the visual culture of people who are Deaf and if home and school settings were designed to maximize growth in communication and cognition by tapping the visual strengths of Deaf learners. Through ethnographic (observational) methods, teachers and others can learn to participate in the visual culture of Deaf children. Although, this may mean shedding some preconceived ideas of what should happen in school with regard to language, the rewards in the form of motivated learners should more than compensate for the cultural struggle of the hearing teacher toward the goal of visual literacy.

If one is to take a multicultural approach to the education of Deaf children seriously, then there must be closer communication between the school and the social and vocational levels of the community. Multicultural sensitivity, by definition, cannot thrive in a vacuum. It requires exposure to the cultures under consideration; that is, the Deaf cultures, which may include the African American cultures, the Hispanic cultures, the Asian/Pacific Island cultures, and the American Indian cultures.

Including members of these cultures in the academic program of Deaf children can be done in a variety of ways. When possible, it is important to hire teachers and other educational support personnel who are themselves Deaf. Equity in hiring has yet to be achieved in educational programs for Deaf children. Although, at present, multicultural equity in hiring is not seen as a high priority in most school districts, it is encouraging to see professional organizations such as CEASD begin to sponsor national symposiums that address the needs of Deaf children from diverse ethnic, racial, and linguistic backgrounds. It would be a positive step to see individual school districts follow this lead by providing inservice education for teachers and support staff at the local level. Another step toward cultural integrity in the schools would be the inclusion of multicultural information across the curriculum. Issues related to the Deaf community, in general, as well as issues related to specific ethnic groups within the Deaf community will better prepare all children to meet the challenges of life in a multicultural society.

BIBLIOGRAPHY

Bhatia, T., & Ritchie, W. (Eds.). (1989). *World Englishes: Special issue on code-mixing*. New York: Pergamon.

Bragg, B., & Bergman, E. (1989). *Lessons in laughter*. Washington, DC: Gallaudet University.

Christensen, K. (1986). Sign language acquisition by Spanish-speaking parents of deaf children. *American Annals of the Deaf, 131*, 285–287.

Christensen, K. (1988). I see what you mean: Nonverbal communication strategies of young deaf children. *American Annals of the Deaf, 133*, 270–275.

Christensen, K. (1990). Thinking about thinking: A discussion of the development of cognition and language in deaf children. *American Annals of the Deaf, 135*, 222–226.

Corbett, E., & Jensema, C. (1981). *Teachers of the deaf: Descriptive profiles*. Washington, DC: Gallaudet University.

Cummins, J. (1984). *Bilingualism and special education: Issues in assessment and pedagogy*. San Diego: College-Hill.

Cummins, J. (1988). From multicultural to anti-racist education: An analysis of programmes and policies in Ontario. In T. Skutnabb-Kangas & J. Cummins (Eds.), *Minority education: From shame to struggle*. Philadelphia: Multilingual Matters.

Geertz, C. (1973). *The interpretation of cultures*. New York: Basic Books.

Goldin-Meadow, S. (1985). Language development under atypical learning conditions. In K. Nelson (Ed.), *Children's language, Vol 5*. Hillsdale, NJ: Erlbaum.

Grosjean, F. (1982). *Life with two languages: An introduction to bilingualism*. Cambridge, MA: Harvard University.

Jordan, I. K., & Karchmer, M. (1986). Patterns of sign use among hearing impaired students. In A. Schildroth & M. Karchmer (Eds.), *Deaf children in America* (pp. 125–138). San Diego: College-Hill.

Lessow-Hurley, J. (1990). *The foundations of dual language instruction*. New York: Longman.

McLaughlin, B. (1984). *Second language acquisition in childhood. Vol. 1: Preschool children*. Hillsdale, NJ: Erlbaum.

Mobley, R. (1991). *Teachers of the Deaf*. Paper presented at the conference of the Association of College Educators in Hearing Impairment, Jekyll Island, GA.

Owens, R. (1988). *Language development: An introduction*. Columbus, OH: Merrill.

Trueba, H., Jacobs, L., & Kirton, E. (1990. *Cultural conflict and adaptation: The case of Hmong children in American society*. New York: Falmer.

Vernon, M., & Andrews, J. (1990). *The psychology of deafness: Understanding deaf and hard-of-hearing people*. New York: Longman.

CHAPTER 3

A Model Program for Home–School Communication and Staff Development

Cynthia A. Grace

> *We have our own built in prejudices about the way certain kids can learn, or how they talk and how they walk or dress. . . . I don't see a lot of efforts to counter that.*
> *Mary Hatwood Futrell*

This chapter describes a staff training program designed to enhance home–school communication by increasing educators' sensitivity to the needs of African American Deaf children and their families. Although the training program focuses on the African American Deaf child, it can be used as a model to increase educators' knowledge and awareness of the needs of Deaf members of other stigmatized racial or ethnic groups. It underscores the need to mobilize more vigilance, more commitment, and more resources in addressing the needs of those who are doubly stigmatized.

The demographics of American schools are shifting rapidly. It is projected that by the turn of the century, more than 40 percent of the nation's public school students will be African American,* Hispanic, Asian, or of another non-European ethnic group. In many large city school systems, over 80 percent of the students are children of color (Feistrizer, 1985). There will be deaf children in this growing pool, thereby creating an overwhelming

---

*The term *African American* is used throughout this chapter to refer to persons of African descent. This would include, but is not limited to, persons born in the Caribbean, South America, Africa, and the United States. The term is used in this manner for better readability; however, it is extremely important to keep in mind that while there are cultural themes that unify persons of African descent, there are many significant differences that distinguish each of the subgroups.

need for educators who are familiar with the unique concerns of the children of color who are deaf. Many educators are unaware that some of the problems that many of these children experience in school are linked to their participation in a culture that is very different from the one that serves as a basis for the design of this country's school systems.

Educators typically have very little awareness of the sociocultural realities of children from families with little economic or political power. When the children are racially or culturally different, educators' knowledge of the children's experiences is sometimes even more limited. The deaf child who is excluded from the mainstream because of racial or cultural differences seems to be functioning in a culture submerged within a culture.

McCay Vernon, in the foreword of Hairston and Smith's (1983) *Black and Deaf in America*, stated:

> When the conditions of blackness and deafness are combined in one person, the individual effects of prejudice, discrimination, and negative self-image are compounded exponentially. For example, a disproportionate percent of Black deaf youth are educated in urban schools where the programs are often unbelievably bad. In many of these schools, the Black child is mainstreamed or else he is placed in classes with retarded children or those having other disabilities totally unrelated to his own. The results are devastating. (p. i)

The experiences of many African American Deaf children, particularly when they are from economically distressed families, mirror those of other Deaf children who are members of more than one stigmatized group. The isolation of many African American Deaf youngsters from the mainstream is further compounded by the effects of poverty. African American Deaf children are more likely to come from poor homes than are white Deaf children. Their family members are less likely to know a signed language and are less likely to be aware of services for Deaf children and themselves. Consequently, the African American Deaf child may be more dependent on persons outside the family for information, support, and guidance. Without special training, the average educator is unprepared to assist African American Deaf children and their families in combatting isolation and obtaining needed services.

THE ROLE OF STAFF TRAINING

We are now undergoing a rapid and important cultural evolution as the nation becomes more and more culturally diverse, and as disabled and other stigmatized members of our society recognize their worth and potential and adjust their expectations accordingly. Some welcome this evolution. Others, in a variety of ways, resist it. This conflict impedes productive and timely adaptation to change, thereby creating a need for creative, thoughtful solutions to the problems that result.

Recently there has been a renewed interest in human relations training as a possible solution to some of these problems. Human relations training has allowed for the exploration of an array of issues, including gender roles, work relationships, and cultural identity. Although its importance has been recognized for decades, it is during significant periods of social and cultural transition that *the role and potential usefulness of sensitivity and group relations training* is most obvious.

The Cultural Sensitivity and Skills Training Program was developed at the Lexington School for the Deaf to increase staff awareness of the needs of African American deaf children and their families. The program evolved out of the recognition that African American children scored far below their white peers on measures of cognitive ability, communications skills, and other measures of educational achievement (Wilson, 1986). The interactive effect of being both African American and Deaf resulted in a relatively lower level of academic achievement on the part of African American deaf youngsters when compared with white deaf students and their hearing peers, both African American and European American.

Differences in socioeconomic status account for some of the differential in performance between white and African American children. There is growing awareness, however, that some of what we are seeing has less to do with poverty or low socioeconomic status than is typically thought. There is growing support in the literature that a major contributing factor is a failure on the part of educational institutions to provide African American deaf children with the kinds of experiences that would foster academic success (Stewart & Benson, 1988). These experiences would include *activities that provide knowledge of their heritage* and pride in themselves as black deaf people.

Preconceived notions about the capabilities of African American deaf people have been a major stumbling block in the personal and professional advancement of these individuals (Anderson & Bowe, 1972). School personnel, for the most part, have not had available to them educational experiences that foster appreciation and respect for cultural diversity. Many are unprepared to utilize cultural differences to enhance the curriculum process. Instead, there is frequently the tendency to ignore or minimize unique cultural differences, as exemplified by the frequent insistence on the part of some educators that deafness precludes minority group status. It is erroneously assumed that because the children are deaf, they do not think about being Asian, African American, or Italian. A lack of understanding of the values, motives, behavioral codes, and language of African American deaf children and their families frequently results in low expectations and unwarranted generalizations about the children's educational potential.

School is a major transmitter of culture and makes a significant contribution to the developing identities of students. It is a major source of internalizations of aspects of personal and occupational identities. For African American children, and African American deaf children in particular, the internalization of positive role models is rendered difficult, not only because they are not available, but also because educators often do not recognize their significance. Teachers, administrators, and other school personnel typically do not receive the training and experience necessary to ensure that they are knowledgeable about the cultures of the children and families with whom they interact. Therefore, they miss the opportunity to utilize this knowledge in a manner that promotes learning and effective cross-cultural exchange. Too often the learning that does occur is not consistent with the development of positive group identity.

Frequently on the institutional level, and more subtly on the interpersonal level, African American children and their parents find that educational environments offer reminders of black people's devalued status. On the institutional level they see that lower status employees are frequently nonwhite, and that higher status employees are usually white.

PARENT–TEACHER EXPECTATIONS

Because the school is a vital subsystem of the community and shares the responsibility for the socialization of children, the relationship between the school and the home is of paramount importance. A mutually hostile and uncooperative relationship between school and parents can seriously threaten a child's willingness and ability to make a commitment to learning. Training provides an opportunity to examine how educator and parent expectations, co-cultural dynamics, and particular attitudes contribute to both productive and dysfunctional communication patterns. Participants in the training are guided in exploring how they can help to create a learning environment that is both part of and supportive of the child's community.

Most educators believe that parent participation in school activities is a necessary and good thing. However, even this very basic belief is culturally determined. Many parents, depending on cultural orientation and socioeconomic status, may define educators' and parents' roles much more rigidly than the average educator would. In addition, parents and teachers may differ in their opinions concerning what is acceptable behavior in relating to authority figures. Some inner city parents may feel intimidated, because there is likely to be a socioeconomic status difference that favors educators. This may cause parents to believe that they have little to offer where school matters are concerned.

In many cultures, teachers are highly respected. To challenge, question, or behave as an equal with them would be considered impolite and, in some cases, in bad judgment. A parent with this view might be confused about the need for parent–teacher conferences to develop learning goals. During such a conference, what may appear to be cooperation and agreement is probably merely an attempt not to appear disrespectful. Often following a seemingly congenial and productive meeting, educators are perplexed by parent resistance to agreed-on goals.

When parents have been socialized to believe that the teacher is solely responsible for the education of children, attempts on the part of a teacher to obtain parental cooperation in the educational process may be met with resistance. For example, requesting that a parent correct his or her child's homework may be viewed by the parent as an impingement or even laziness on the part of the teacher. Such misunderstandings between parents and teachers occur because, in making requests that parents join in the educational process, teachers often are unaware of conflicting expectations or factors that might limit a parent's ability to participate. In the face of demands that seem excessive or unrealistic, some parents become angry and defensive.

The backgrounds and expectations of educators may also contribute to a widening gap between the school and the community. Many American educators are products of an educational experience that created and perpetuated the illusion of dominant culture superiority. Consequently, many have acquired negative attitudes and erroneous information and have internalized destructive myths about black families. This typically reduces educators' comfort in interacting with the parents of the children whom they teach.

In addition to having cultural roots, the values and behaviors of traditionally disenfranchised members of society tend to be related to their lower socioeconomic status. Furthermore, these values and behaviors are connected to conflicts with people who control or are perceived as controlling access to the things needed and wanted. Educators need to know how to communicate with parents who are of lower socioeconomic status, and less well educated, without humiliating them or making them conscious of their lower status. By avoiding excessive use of jargon, actively encouraging parental input, and making use of culturally appropriate ways to enter and leave situations, the potential for good communication is enhanced. The communication process unfolds more smoothly because there is less anxiety for either party and, consequently, more room for focusing on the tasks at hand. An atmosphere of mutual respect and appreciation is thus created. Trainees are sensitized to the need to mobilize these and other behaviors that facilitate the communication process.

Frequently, the issue of historical mistrust (Lockart, 1981) or cultural paranoia (Grier & Cobbs, 1968) is examined during training. This refers to a tendency on the part of disenfranchised members of society not to trust members of the dominant culture. It is often manifested by reluctance on the part of historically disenfranchised persons to self-disclose or verbalize feelings to members of the dominant culture. Participants in training are encouraged to understand and accept this view and the behaviors that accompany it.

Training provides an opportunity for participants to share and explore some of the myths about African American parents, the most popular being that African American parents do not care about their children's education. Usually, at some point during the training, some participants come to understand that African American parents have the same goals as the majority of parents. Often what is interpreted as lack of caring is really lack of familiarity with methods, procedures, and services.

Another prominent issue discussed during training is that of racial and ethnic differences in communication style. These differences have been identified as significantly contributing to the quality and process of cross-cultural exchanges for both deaf and hearing persons. The historical roots and significance of these differences are examined to bring participants closer to viewing the differences as differences and not necessarily deficits. The use of nonstereotypic verbal and nonverbal communication is encouraged. Usually, participants provide numerous opportunities to experience both stereotypic and more appropriate language during the training. These opportunities become learning opportunities with the help of participants and a skilled trainer.

The current training program differs from others that rely primarily on contact among culturally different individuals who have conscious awareness of their attitudes and beliefs. It was once naively assumed that simply mixing people of different races would lead to the development of positive attitudes. Studies of *desegregated* schools showed that often the result was greater intergroup hostility and conflict as children quickly learned who was valued and who was not (Davidson, 1976).

Experience has shown that prejudice is extremely difficult to eliminate. This has become increasingly the case, and the prevailing norm now appears to be an intellectual disavowal of prejudice and racism without much change in behavior. Moreover, many who do not consider themselves to be racist justify their racist attitudes and behavior with what they believe to be rational, unbiased explanations (Goleman, 1987). People are less likely to admit prejudice, but the tendency to behave in a bigoted manner, in some situations, is not lessening. Consequently, more direct access to prejudiced attitudes, for the purpose of altering those attitudes, is much harder to obtain.

The overall objective of the training program to increase staff awareness of the needs of African American students and their families is to enable educators to become aware of how racism affects students' lives overall, and to help them change their attitudes and behaviors toward African American children and adults. To accomplish these objectives, trainers devote considerable effort toward guiding participants in examining the unconscious manifestations of bias that are present during training.

STEPS IN IMPLEMENTING THE CULTURAL SENSITIVITY AND SKILLS TRAINING PROGRAM

An initial organizational structure was established consisting of a project director; an advisory board of experts in the fields of rehabilitation, education of the deaf, psychology, and anthropology; a full-time assistant; and a secretary. A subsequent step was to conduct a needs assessment. This included a thorough review of the literature, conferences, and correspondence with a variety of professionals in fields related to the goals of the project and meetings with students, parents, supervisors, teachers, teaching assistants, and other staff about their perceptions of the needs and experiences of African American deaf students and their families. Focus groups that were conducted to gather information provided the following recurring themes:

A Model Program

African American Students
Believe that teachers don't encourage African American students to achieve

Believe that teachers make assumptions about African American students, especially African American males: "Teachers are quick to think that black males are on drugs [when they misbehave]"

Expressed a need for more support from teachers and parents

Expressed a need for more role models: more African American teachers and administrators with whom to identify

Believe that the school environment is more supportive of white middle class culture than of other cultures

Tended to disparage African American students for lack of motivation and leadership skills

African American Parents
Need more information about their children's development, disability, and available services

Not clear about their children's educational and occupational potential

Believe that school personnel don't treat them with the same respect afforded white parents

Lack comfort, at times, in dealing with school personnel

Do not trust that teachers' and administrators' judgments reflect the best interests of their students

Staff
Expressed concern over lack of African American parental participation in school matters

Expressed a need to understand better the values, needs, and motives of African American students and their parents

The results of this needs assessment guided the development of the training model, whose target populations are teachers, teaching assistants, administrators, and support staff. A triphasic, eighteen-hour program was developed to promote the acquisition of knowledge, skills, and attitude change. As Table 3.1 suggests, Phase I of the training concentrates on helping participants to acquire an understanding of institutional and cultural racism and their impact on the experiences of African American deaf individuals. Phase II encourages participants to explore the culturally relevant values, beliefs, and behaviors that they bring to interactions with those who are culturally different. Throughout, emphasis is placed on the significance of deaf culture. Phase III addresses action strategies; its goal is to enable participants to acquire skill in eliminating or reducing the impact of racism and discrimination in the educational setting.

TABLE 3.1 Three Phases of Training

Learning	Attitude Change	Skills
Phase I		
Identify key elements of racism and discrimination	More positive attitudes toward deaf students and their families	Capacity to assess objectively strengths of African American people
Identify how racism functions in society	Decreased tolerance for racial and cultural bias and discrimination against disabled	Ability to challenge the myths and negative stereotypes pertaining to African American students, African American families, and deafness
Knowledge of deaf culture Knowledge of the interactive processes of being African American and deaf	Appreciate the significance of culture for the experiences of African American students and their families	
Phase II		
Self-knowledge as it pertains to cultural values, beliefs, and biases	More positive attitudes toward those who are different in culture, social class, and occupational status	Ability to articulate one's own cultural values, beliefs, and biases and their possible impact on behavior in work role
Identify factors that block effective communication	More positive attitudes in interactions with those who are different	Ability to communicate with someone who is different
		Ability to interact more effectively with African American students and their families
Phase III		
Identify necessity for action and appropriate steps	Decreased tolerance for institutional barriers to effective learning and intergroup exchange	Ability to implement action strategies appropriate to work role

PROCEDURE FOR IMPLEMENTING TRAINING

The success of the Cultural Sensitivity and Skills Training Program depends on the careful implementation of five steps:

    I. Contact/Needs Assessment
    II. Training
   III. Evaluation
    IV. Feedback
    V. Follow-up

When an institution has expressed interest in the training program and a commitment to implement the training, a training coordinator schedules a consultation with that institution's designated contact person. The goals of the training program, the time requirements, and the resource requirements are fully explained. An assessment of the institution's training needs is then conducted. The procedure for conducting the needs assessment includes an interview with the institution's contact person, information gathering sessions with small groups of staff and students, and a tour of the school. The basic training program may be altered to suit the particular training needs of each school. Training activities are

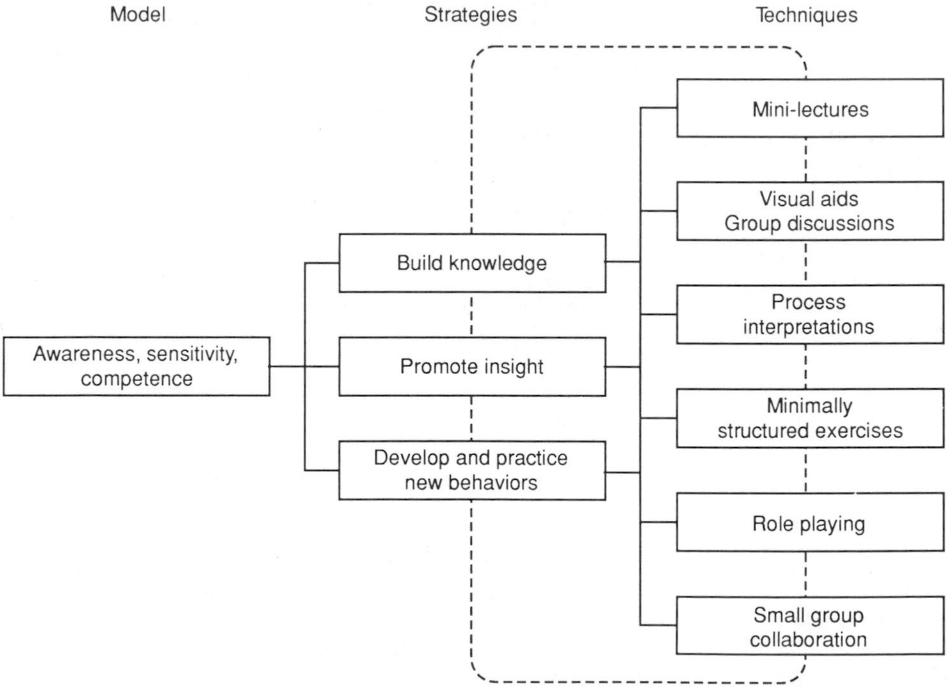

FIGURE 3.1   A model program: Cultural sensitivity and skills training

selected by the training coordinator, and the choice of training activities is guided by the outcome of the needs assessment.

Evaluation is one of the most important aspects of program implementation. The trainees' responses to each of the training activities and their overall evaluation of the training program serves as a foundation for the step that follows. It is extremely important that time be allotted after each session, and at the close of the training program, for participants to offer feedback.

The training coordinator arranges a feedback consultation, which should take place within one week of the final session of the training program. At that time, the evaluation of the training program is presented and recommendations for follow-up activities are made. Recommendations may include additional training, support in making institutional changes, or continued evaluation of the project.

The training program is not built around a series of loosely connected cultural awareness exercises. It utilizes a well-established group relations paradigm that recognizes the importance of unconscious beliefs, feelings, and motives as primary determinants of individual and group behavior. The basic premise is that a group will function optimally when it is relatively clear about its primary task and is relatively free of anxiety and counterproductive assumptions and motives. Group experiences foster a progression toward greater awareness of individual contributions to group attitudes and behavior. An awareness of larger systems dynamics that promote or impede positive group relations is also developed. With the help of consultants, participants examine ways of relating to others through observing and attempting to understand individual and group behavior. Emphasis is on how issues of difference affect the group's ability to reach its goals and fulfill its tasks. Groups vary in size, composition, and purpose (see Figure 3.1).

Several assumptions underlie the design of this model:

1. Experiential learning leads to greater transfer of knowledge and skills;
2. learning is an active process—therefore, passive acceptance of information is not learning;
3. if experimenting with new skills leads to success, then attitude change will occur; and
4. improved cross-cultural exchange will result from increased comfort brought about by greater understanding and increased respect for cultural diversity.

Dissemination of Training

The training program should be thought of as a first step in an ongoing process. Program participants, therefore, should not view themselves as having "graduated" from a training program, but rather as having been engaged in a process of change just at its beginning. It is hoped that participants will develop an understanding of the structural dynamics of racism and discrimination and, consequently, some commitment to working for change at that level. A consultant for periodic follow-up consultation, and postevaluation feedback sessions should be available to provide ongoing assistance.

To promote the continuity of training, when feasible, professional members of the school staff should be trained as consultants. This orientation requires a relatively sophisticated level of training and clinical sensitivity. Selection and proper training of candidates to serve as trainers is of paramount importance. The best trainers are well informed about the dynamics of racism, systems, and groups. They have wrestled with issues of racism and discrimination on a personal level and have emerged with a well-developed sense of their own relevant attitudes and beliefs. Trainers should be able to make available to the group not only manifest meanings of participants' communications, but also unconscious ones. In addition, they should be able to resist the tendency to emphasize similarities in people while dismissing or ignoring important differences.

Most important, trainers should be sensitive to defensiveness and other signs of vulnerability in participants. They should create a comfortable atmosphere in which defensiveness can be replaced easily by curiosity and a desire for self-knowledge.

Although training often contributes greatly to the development of intergroup relations that facilitate the tasks of schools, training alone cannot eradicate bias. It is but one among many balancing and counterbalancing forces. It is imperative that larger systems issues be addressed and that administrative support for the goals and objectives of the training be clearly expressed. Without such support, meaningful change is not likely to occur.

FADE-OUT AND ADMINISTRATIVE SUPPORT

No matter how powerful the effects of training are on individuals, their impact may fade out very quickly once the participants are back into the school routine. If participants feel that new behaviors acquired as a result of training will not be accepted and rewarded by others, particularly those in power, then they will not use these behaviors. The newly acquired behaviors are likely to be stored away and retrieved at a time when they are more acceptable. If the participants are continuously coached after training, then their chances of losing the gains afforded by training are significantly reduced.

Efforts by the school administration to support the goals of training are crucial. Administrators should openly support and participate in activities that promote cultural awareness and sensitivity. After training, the school's superintendent or principal might thank participants publicly for being a part of the training.

Training should not be the only intervention, and it should not be applied to only a few people. One strategy for institutionalizing the goals of training is to develop and dissemi-nate a policy statement that presents the institution's position on the cultural diversity issue. If a written policy does not exist, then the formulation of one could be an instructive and very valuable posttraining activity. Periodically, the school should evaluate its policy regarding cultural diversity for suitability and the extent to which it is consistent with current institutional practices. In addition, a plan could be developed to increase the pool of school staff being trained, especially when it may not be feasible to train more than a small number of staff at any given time.

The administration must make a commitment to identify and eliminate institutional bias by examining school policies and procedures for consistency with the school's stated position and goals. School policy should also be monitored periodically and its impact evaluated.

Participants should receive formal recognition from their supervisors and other key administrators in their schools. Special roles might even be created for participants that are consistent with their skills and interests. For example, an individual or team might be employed as a resource for curriculum ideas that address cultural issues.

Participants could also serve as group leaders or facilitators of subsequent staff development activities about culture and racism, or establish a newsletter to disseminate information to the staff who did not participate in the session. Attendance at conferences about cultural diversity should be strongly encouraged, and, when possible, financial support and other incentives should be offered.

The policies of many institutions serving economically deprived children and families reflect the "poverty centered approach." This approach de-emphasizes the significance of cultural diversity, race, and racism for understanding the needs and concerns of people. Instead, it focuses on economic deprivation, which the policies do little or nothing to eliminate. This often leads to a failure to tap the strengths that might be mobilized to empower people to make constructive changes in their lives. In schools for the Deaf, there may be a tendency for some staff to focus on deafness and what a child cannot do instead of focusing on strengths and abilities.

Perhaps the most common and the most difficult challenge for trainers is to help trainees overcome their resistance to acknowledging that racism is still a major national problem and is prevalent in the deaf community. Reconceptualizing the nature of intergroup relations in the United States challenges a valued component of the nation's self-concept. The view of America as a melting pot has for many decades been a source of national pride and a defense against the feelings engendered by recognizing the struggles and pain of ethnic groups that have attempted to join the mainstream and met resistance.

Americans have not quite come to terms with their nation as a conglomerate of unmelted ethnics. To do so would mean acknowledging and taking greater responsibility for the nation's failure to protect the rights and comfort of some of its citizens. This view of America as a melting pot is vehemently protected. Therefore, program trainers often encounter opposition to the idea that it is important to affirm cultural differences. The source of the resistance will be those individuals who have not succeeded at critically examining the dynamics of American ethnic groups, and who may have formed negative associations to some of the racial and cultural characteristics of those who are different.

There will be educators who will fail, out of ignorance, to affirm the cultural identities of the children they are attempting to educate. The challenge for the trainer, with respect to this group, is to increase awareness of the significance of culture as a vehicle for enhancing the intellectual curiosity, motivation, and self-esteem of all children. This is accomplished by both telling and showing that culture makes a difference.

Training should challenge participants to think about what it means to be white in America, and what it means to be hearing. In particular, issues of power and entitlement should emerge for exploration and understanding. Because these are sensitive issues for many people, it is imperative that the trainer understand, tolerate, and work with manifestations of "flight and fight." At times, participants will flee the issues. They may resist talking about racial bias, bias against the disabled, and cultural insensitivity. They may focus on other issues such as sexism and class—topics that, at the moment, appear safer. Attempts to refocus the group might be met with anger, some of which will not be obvious. The tasks here are to assist the group in managing the anger and to demonstrate that anger is not to be feared or avoided. Rather, anger can be a valuable source of information and often signals progress.

Above all, the trainer needs to be aware of his or her own sensitivities and gaps in knowledge with regard to race, culture, and bias. It is essential that facilitators have knowledge of the realities of racism and personal security. They must have the capacity to see people as individuals. They must possess respect for and appreciation of diversity. They must have the willingness to learn.

CONCLUSION

Cultural awareness and multicultural skills training for educators has promise as a partial solution to the failure of educational institutions to provide black, Hispanic, Native American, and Asian/Pacific Deaf children with the kinds of experiences that would foster academic success. The overall objectives of such training are to enable educators to become aware of how racism affects their lives and—in particular, how it impacts the educational experiences of their Deaf students—and to help them change their attitudes and behaviors toward black children and adults. To accomplish this objective, both the conscious and unconscious manifestations of racism and bias must be addressed.

In addition to having skill in managing group process, the trainer must also possess self-awareness and knowledge of the social, cultural, and political realities of people of color and of the disabled. The trainer must also take into account the limitations of training and work toward maintaining any positive gains that result from the program. If the training is successful, then culture becomes institutionalized as a key aspect of the learning process, and, over time, the home and school come to have compatible expectations and begin to speak a language that is understood by both.

BIBLIOGRAPHY

Anderson, G. B., & Bowe, F. G. (1972). Racism within the deaf community. *American Annals of the Deaf, 117,* 617–619.

Billingsley, A. (1968). *Black families among Negroes.* Englewood Cliffs, NJ: Prentice-Hall.

Cole, M. (1971). *The cultural context of thinking and learning.* New York: Basic Books.

Comer, J. (1988). Educating poor minority children. *Scientific American, 259,* 42–48.

Comer, J. (1989). Racism and the education of young children. *Teachers College Record, 90,* 352–361.

Comer, J., & Poussant, A. (1975). *Black child care.* New York: Simon & Schuster.

Davidson, D. (1976). Sociology of oppressed cultures: An analysis of the socio-cultural dynamics of colonialism. *Journal of Black Political Economy, 6,* 420–437.

Dubrin, A. (1982). *Contemporary applied management.* Plano, TX: Business Publications.

Feistrizer, C. (1985, July 16). A new baby boomlet hits the schools. *The Washington Post.*

Franklin, A., & Fulani, L. (1979). Cultural content of materials and ethnic group performance in categorical recall. In A. W. Boykin, A. J. Franklin, & J. S. Yates (Eds.), *Research directions of black psychologists* (pp. 449–473). New York: Russell Sage Foundation.

Futrell, M. H. (1986). *The Black teacher as leader.* Paper presented at the annual meeting of the National Alliance of Black School Educators. New York.

Goleman, D. (1987, May 12). ''Useful'' modes of thinking contribute to the power of prejudice. *The New York Times,* pp. C1, C10.

Grant, W. (1981, January). Racial attitudes of hearing impaired adolescents. *Journal of Black Studies, 12*, 39–52.

Grier, W., & Cobbs, P. (1968). *Black rage.* New York: Basic Books.

Hairston, E., & Smith, L. (1983). *Black and deaf in America.* Silver Spring, MD: T. J. Publishers.

Hale, J. (1980). The socialization of black children. *Dimensions, 9,* 43–48.

Hale, J. (1981, January). Black children: Their roots, culture, and learning styles. *Young Children, 36,* 37–50.

Hale-Benson, J. (1986). *Black children: Their roots, culture and learning styles.* Baltimore: Johns Hopkins University.

Hare, N. (1976, March). What black intellectuals misunderstand about the black family. *Black World, 25,* 4–15.

Lockhart, B. (1981). Historic distrust and the counseling of American Indians and Alaska Natives. *White Cloud Journal, 2*(3), 31–34.

Nobles, W. W. (1981). African-American family life: An instrument of culture. In H. P. McAdoo (Ed.), *Black families.* Beverly Hills: Sage.

Ogbu, J. V. (1978). *Minority education and caste.* New York: Academic Press.

Pascoe, E. (1985). *Racial prejudice.* New York: Franklin Watts.

Peters, M. F. (1981). Parenting in black families with young children: An historical perspective. In H. P. McAdoo (Ed.), *Black families.* Beverly Hills: Sage.

Sharma, M. P. (1985). How cross-cultural social participation affects the international attitudes of U. S. students. *International Journal of Intercultural Relations, 9,* 377–388.

Stack, C. (1974). *All our kin: Strategies for survival in a black community.* New York: Harper & Row.

Stewart, D. A., & Benson, G. (1988, July). Dual cultural negligence: The education of black deaf children. *Journal of Multicultural Counseling and Development, 16.*

Thomas, M., & Hughes, M. (1986, December). The continuing significance of race: A study of race, class and quality of life in America, 1972–1985. *American Sociological Review, 51,* 830–842.

Wilson, J. (1986). Race, culture and education: Some conceptual problems. *Oxford Review of Education, 12,* 3–16.

SUGGESTED READINGS

Acevedo, J., & Anderson, G. (1980). Bias and stereotypes in American sign language. *Bulletin, 11*(1), 3–9.

Boyd-Franklin, N. (1989). *Black families in therapy: A multisystems approach.* New York: Guilford.

Fantini, M. C., & Cardenas, R. (1980). *Parenting in a multicultural society.* New York: Longman.

Nixon, J. (1985). *A teacher's guide to multicultural education.* Oxford: Basil Blackwell.

Ramirez, B. A. (1988), Summer). Culturally and linguistically diverse children. *Teaching Exceptional Children,* pp. 45–51.

SECTION II

The Populations

All evidence suggests that the population of the United States is changing, and that before we are very far into the twenty-first century, ''minority'' populations will outnumber the ''majority.'' The linguistic and ethnic diversity represented by American students includes a proportionate number of Deaf students. Meeting the particular needs and fostering the linguistic and cultural growth of this multicultural group depends on an understanding of their cultural, linguistic, and cognitive development.

Section II offers insight into the Deaf populations from four ethnic and racial backgrounds: African American, Hispanic, Asian/Pacific Island, and Native American. The following chapters examine the demographic, historical, and linguistic aspects of these cultures in combination with their underlying social values. Our belief here, as throughout this text, is that educators can incorporate all languages and cultures represented by their Deaf students into the learning environment through respect and understanding.

Educational Needs of African American and Hispanic Deaf Children and Youth

Oscar P. Cohen

Our educational goals are not limited to instructional objectives but include the enculturation or socialization of children to values and expectations as well.
Saville-Troike (1978)

Chapter 4 examines the impact of social dynamics on the education of African American and Hispanic children in the United States, and the failure of the schools to meet their needs. The implications for Deaf African American and Hispanic children are discussed, and recommendations that address the unmet needs of these children are made. The term *ethnic* is used when referring to African American and Hispanic persons as well as other cultural group members.

THE PROBLEM

Despite modest gains in recent years, African American and Hispanic children on the average continue to score far below their white peers on standardized tests and other educational measures. They are much more likely than whites to drop out of high school, or, if they remain in school, to be tracked into vocational rather than academic programs. African American and Hispanic children who graduate from high school are also less likely to enroll in college than white graduates are.

Current and Projected Demographics

Today we are a nation of 245 million people, about 79 percent of whom are white. By the year 2050: The proportion of whites will drop to 60 percent: the African American population will expand slightly to about 16 percent (it was 12 percent in 1980); the proportion of Hispanics will more than double (from 6.4 percent in 1980 to 15 percent); and the proportion of Asians/Pacific Islanders will jump from 1.6 percent in 1980 to as much as 10 percent (Kellog, 1988). Immigration is a significant issue affecting public school education. For example, California now has a "majority of minorities" in its elementary schools; therefore, it is no longer valid to refer to blacks, Hispanics, and Asians/Pacific Islanders as minorities. In Texas, 46 percent of students are black or Hispanic. In the nation's twenty-five largest urban school systems, furthermore, the majority of students are ethnic, racial, or linguistic minorities; and in the fifteen largest school systems, ethnic student enrollment levels now range from 70 percent to 96 percent (Kellog, 1988).

The Schools' Response

How effectively are the schools, especially inner city schools, responding to the pressure of accepting immigrant ethnic children, thereby determining to a large extent their education and future role in society? A bleak picture is reflected in the 1988 report of the New York State Education Commissioner's Task Force on the Education of Children and Youth At-Risk:

> Two different systems of education have been created in our State. One encompasses effective schools holding high expectations for their students and located in affluent or stable communities; the other, ineffective schools which communicate low expectations and aspirations for their students, who are not given full opportunity to succeed. . . . Our society's acceptance of two unequal educational systems is putting us at risk of creating a permanent underclass in New York and our nation. The existence of this underclass will ultimately erode the foundations of our democratic society. We are on our way to becoming two nations—one of the rich and privileged and the other of the poor and disadvantaged.
>
> Racism clearly underlies much of the problem. . . . In education, racism is expressed in a variety of ways: inadequate resources to those most in need; perpetuating segregated schools; and in some schools, the tracking of ethnic students into less rigorous academic programs without regard for individual abilities, interests and potential. (p. 2)

Schools' Role in Reinforcing the Low Status of Underrepresented Groups

Ogbu (1978) has described immigrant groups in this society as having a status similar to caste-like minorities. According to Ogbu, members of caste-like minorities are perceived by the majority group as inherently inferior in all aspects of intelligence and ability to carry out the tasks associated with high status jobs. Historically, individuals from racial and linguistic ethnic groups have tended to occupy low status positions in our society. Accordingly, members of caste-like minorities do not compete freely with majority group members but, instead, are summarily excluded from certain jobs solely because of their caste status. Children of caste-ethnic parents may therefore be socialized for inferiority on the basis of their parents' and their own perceptions of the adult statuses open to them.

Historically, groups that have performed very poorly at school have been discriminated against and regarded as inherently inferior by the dominant group (Ogbu, 1978). This underachievement may in part result from the way in which schools traditionally have reinforced the ambivalence and insecurity that many ethnic students tend to feel with regard to their own cultural identity (Cummins, 1986). Feelings of inferiority can result from the following:

negative teacher attitudes and expectations toward these children;

teachers recruited from the majority group who are isolated from the ethnic community;

inhibiting of parent–teacher interaction and collaboration in the children's education;

biased education testing;

misclassification of students as learning disabled;

ability group tracking;

biased textbooks and curricula; and

use of clinical definitions of caste-ethnic academic problems that place the blame on the ethnic family for producing "inferior" children. (Cummins, 1984; McDermott, 1976; Ogbu, 1978)

Hilliard (1989) speaks of the need to reject certain "killer assumptions" when it comes to talking about expectations for ethnic youth. These assumptions, which Hilliard feels color much educational thinking, suggest that students either are born with educational aptitude or they aren't. They also suggest that low achievers (a) need remedial drills of "more of the same," (b) are incapable of high order thinking, and (c) take years to catch up once they fall behind.

HISPANICS IN THE UNITED STATES

It is important to note that Hispanics are a very diverse population. Although Puerto Ricans constitute the majority of Hispanics in New York City (60 percent), Dominicans, Colombians, Cubans, and Central Americans also represent a significant percentage of New York's population. Unlike the other Hispanic groups, there is a population of Puerto Ricans that is constantly renewing itself in its immigrant character, and this presents a particular problem to educators.

In general, Hispanics are poor. In 1980 the median income was about $8,000 per household for Puerto Ricans and $11,700 per household for other Hispanics, compared with the median income of $14,000 per household for the city as a whole. The Hispanic population is also undereducated, largely because of an immigrant population from countries where education is not widespread. The severe lack of education among Hispanic parents is a serious problem facing Hispanic youth. Only 42 percent of Hispanic adolescents have parents who are high school graduates, compared with 66 percent of African American adolescents and 80 percent of white adolescents.

Hispanic adolescents are twice as likely as their white counterpart to have a parent younger than thirty (young parents contribute to the prospect of living in poverty). There are also more female-headed households among Hispanics, compared with the city as a whole.

Forty-four percent of Puerto Rican households and 32 percent of other Hispanic households are headed by females. A female-headed household with several young children is likely to discourage that female's participation in the labor force, further contributing to low income levels (Children's Defense Fund, 1990).

Hispanics in New York City tend to be fairly young and have larger families and a higher birth rate than the rest of the city's population. The median age of Hispanics in New York City is 26.7; the median age of the general population is 32.6. Approximately 60 percent of Hispanic families have children under the age of 18. The fertility rate among New York City Hispanics is about 1.9 per woman twenty-five to thirty-four years of age, and 1.5 per non-Hispanic woman in that age range. This results in a disproportionately large Hispanic population in the schools and greater economic difficulties of Hispanic families. In fact, the high fertility rate contributes to Hispanic youth being the fastest growing school-age population in the United States. By the year 2000 the number of eighteen- to twenty-four-year-old workers will decline by more than 4 million, and the Hispanic proportion will almost double. By 2030 about one in five youths—and probably the same proportion of young workers—will be Hispanic (Children's Defense Fund, 1990).

Factors Affecting School Performance of Hispanic Children

Hispanic children do not function well in our schools, and the schools do not function well for Hispanic children. Poor functioning refers to dropout rate, discipline problems, disproportionate nonacademic curriculum, and parents' relative unresponsiveness to teacher and school requests. The following factors should be considered by teachers and school administrators:

Daily Stress.   Because Hispanics are generally in the lower and working classes of the population, their daily lives may entail many stressful situations, which take the Hispanic child away from the activity of learning and prevent the Hispanic parent from seeing that the child is learning.

Teacher Expectations and Family Values.   Teachers' expectations about how a child will use education and what kinds of education are suitable for a child are influenced by the child's socioeconomic status. According to the concept of *generational transmission of values*, parents and school authorities collaborate so that the parents' occupation tends to be transmitted to the child. Certain occupations are considered appropriate; others are often perceived as beyond the means or ability of the child. Educational courses that lead to upward mobility are viewed as unrealistic because they are believed to be beyond the child's ability. Parents also foster this transmission of values by their definition of what it means to "do well" in school (for example, for working class parents, this means to be obedient; for middle class parents, in contrast, this means to be inquisitive and competitive).

Immigration is a process of acculturation—the learning of new ways of behaving. It is a slow process that unfolds over a lifetime and an anxiety-provoking process that places great strains on families. The children are at a pivotal point in this process because they are pulled in opposite directions by teacher and immigrant parent. The teacher's gain is the parent's loss of the "old ways." The resulting anxiety is focused mainly on the child. The school is one of the major areas in which the process of acculturation plays itself out, and the teacher is one of the main factors.

The immigrant parent who is poorly educated and isolated from American culture, the host society, often sees the school as just one more alien institution that is sometimes frightening, sometimes puzzling, and often difficult to deal with—not unlike the courts, the police, and the municipal government. Education for the immigrant parent, therefore, is not a cooperative relationship between parent and teacher. In the immigrant parent's world-view, a child is the sole responsibility of the school authorities while he or she is in school (Rodriquez, 1989).

Culture.   A third factor influencing schooling for the Hispanic child is cultural values. The Hispanic family generally has a pronounced gender division of labor. The father is considered the main source of authority and the final arbiter; the mother is the chief executive, conducting the daily business of running the family. As the primary broker of services to the family, the mother conducts relations with institutions, including the school. A teacher who wishes to discuss either a problem or something good with a parent must deal with the mother. However, any major decision requires the father's approval. The teacher who fails to understand this subtle distinction cannot communicate effectively with the family.

Furthermore, different expectations frequently are held for male and female children in Hispanic families. Traditionally, Hispanic males are thought to be driven by inborn malice and sexual energy. Females are viewed as helpless and needing protection and often are disciplined by parents in a way that teachers consider overly punitive. Arriving home twenty minutes late, for example, may result in the child's being grounded for a week. The opposite happens with males; a teacher may think that it is time to "clamp down" on the child, while the parent feels the behavior is acceptable and that "boys will be boys." Children are also viewed within the traditional Hispanic context as being dependent on the parents far beyond the age that Americans would consider appropriate. There is often unspoken conflict between a teacher and a Hispanic parent regarding the age of independence. The tendency for parent overprotectiveness, at least as perceived by the teacher, may contribute to school-related problems (Rodriguez, 1989).

Language is a unifying cultural characteristic of Hispanic life. Hispanics hold a unique emotional attachment to their language, and it is crucial for educators to be aware of this. Therefore, whether or not schools have interpreting and translation services to facilitate communication between Hispanic families and the school has particular relevance to a Hispanic child's status in the school setting.

THE AFRICAN AMERICAN COMMUNITY

Like Hispanics, African Americans do not fare well compared with whites in the United States. It is important to note that blacks in America are a diverse group representing Caribbean cultures, African cultures, and the American black experience. Although the discussion that follows may be useful in promoting certain understandings, it should be understood that rarely are generalizations entirely accurate.

Educational Achievement

Nearly two African American children out of five are growing up in a family whose head did not complete high school, which is twice the rate for white children. White children are almost four times more likely than African American children to live in families headed by college graduates.

According to standardized test results, African American students at all ages are poorer readers than white students. The older they are the worse they score. Although significant reading and math gains were made by many African American children during the 1970s, the gap remains. Today there is approximately a 19 percentage point gap between the reading scores of African American and white seventeen-year-olds.

African American seventeen-year-olds are three times more likely than white seventeen-year-olds to be two years or more behind the modal grade for their age. Almost half the African American seventeen-year-old males are either behind in school or have dropped out. In 1982, about one African American eighteen- to twenty-one-year-old in every four had dropped out of school. Forty percent of African American female dropouts give pregnancy as the reason for leaving school. African American students are twice as likely as white students to be suspended from school, to be corporally punished, or to be out of school (Children's Defense Fund, 1985).

Factors Affecting School Performance of African American Students

Traditional education has emphasized the shaping of African American children to fit into an educational process designed for Anglo-Saxon middle class children (Hale-Benson, 1982). One reason for the high failure rates of some minorities is the mismatch between the school culture and the social, cultural, and experiential background of ethnic children. This mismatch can be attributed in part to the failure of the school to take into adequate consideration that learning style is an important dimension of a child's school experience— in other words, that learning style can be defined as a way of perceiving, conceptualizing, and problem solving (Polce, 1987).

Second, schools have long neglected the effects of culture on cognition, attitude behavior, and personality (Hale-Benson, 1982; Pine & Hilliard, 1990). A third factor is the failure of schools to recognize that African Americans are strongly influenced by their African heritage and culture (Hale-Benson, 1982). Finally, educators have resisted strongly the notion that the differences between black and white children's cognitive functioning and learning styles are simply "differences," not deficits (Pine & Hilliard, 1990). Therefore, an improvement in the school performance of African American and other culturally different children in schools will occur if the school curriculum and environment are made to reflect more closely the particular learning styles and cultural backgrounds of the students. Paradoxically, the African American home environment has been labeled "pathological," and African American parents have been accused of failing to prepare their children adequately for school. The cultural orientation of the African American home and community is different from that of the school, and educators need to understand that orientation and its relationship to the school performance of African American children (Hale-Benson, 1982).

The issue for African Americans of the 1980s and 1990s seems to have been education for survival. Hale-Benson notes that African American children grow up in a distinct culture and therefore need an educational system that recognizes their strengths, their abilities, and their culture, and which incorporates them into the learning process. The necessity to make continual adaptations to the American social order has destroyed their orientation to opportunity and their trust in nonblack people (Johnson & Sanday, 1971).

The social system in America sustains African American culture. The system, with its forces of racial, mental, physical, and social isolation, allows minimal contact between the races. African Americans live, study, work, and socialize together because of the way housing, school, employment opportunities, and social stratification have been designed (Hale-Benson, 1988). Childrearing practices by African American parents are shaped by their conceptions of the realities, including racism and economic oppression, that they and their children face in the United States. The African American mother must prepare her child to take on the appropriate gender and age roles as well as the racial role, which, by social and political definition, are of resistance, suspicion, and caution (Nobels, 1974). Fordham (1988) suggests that for some African American students, school success may contradict an identification and solidarity with African American culture; adaptation to the dominant (white) culture involves the development of a strategy of "racelessness."

The conflicting expectations between African American parents and white teachers present a dilemma. African American parents have had to ignore white childrearing norms, which are perceived as irrelevant to African American children. White teachers are amazed when they teach children not to fight only to have African American children report that their parents have told them to hit anybody who hits them. The white teacher usually has no conception of the kind of reality that African American children face (Hale-Benson, 1982). A different kind of socialization is required of African Americans. African American children have to be prepared to imitate the "hip," "cool" behavior of the culture in which they live and at the same time take on those behaviors that are necessary to be upwardly mobile in the larger society. The use of black English is another example of this duality of socialization. For African Americans, as for other ethnic children, the socialization process increasingly becomes a dual one: an attempt to live both within and outside of the group (Levine, 1977). African American children who are also Deaf have a third cultural identity with which to deal.

Socialization of African American Males

African American males rank poorest in every important demographic statistic (Glasgow, 1980). For example:

African American males make up 3.5 percent of the college population but 46 percent of the prison population.

An African American male has a one in twenty-three chance of being murdered before he reaches age twenty-five.

Between 1976 and 1986, college enrollments for African American males aged eighteen to twenty-four declined from 35 percent to 28 percent.

Between 1973 and 1986, the percentage of African American males aged eighteen to twenty-nine employed full-time, year-round fell from 44 percent to 35 percent; and average real earnings for African American males fell by 50 percent (Children's Defense Fund, 1985).

To some extent these statistics become a self-fulfilling prophecy: Society points to the numbers as justification for the low regard and fear with which it holds African American men, and many African American youths are trapped into playing the destructive roles into which society has cast them.

The African American male is encouraged to become street-wise. Part of street-wise behavior is police avoidance. Nobels (1974) found that African American preschool males tended to associate white people with the police. It is noteworthy that African American mothers and fathers are keenly aware that policemen watch African American children more than they watch white children. Therefore, the socialization given to African American children must include attitudes and strategies that enhance their survival in a hostile environment.

Socialization of African American Females

African American females have a strong motherhood orientation. Girls are given substantial household responsibility. Style—how one does something—is also very important. In the African American community, one is admired for personal attributes such as wit, personality, strength, intelligence, and verbal ability rather than status or office. The high valuation of the person may be an adaptation, in part, to conditions of marginality and powerlessness within the dominant society (Hale-Benson, 1982). African American females also consider bearing children to be a validation of being female. Consequently, a positive attitude is shown toward childbearing. This validation may provide an explanation for the disproportionate number of births by girls in their early teens.

Childrearing

African American childrearing practices are generally authoritarian in nature; their objective is the development of toughness and self-sufficiency. However, these practices may result in cultural dissonance when teachers behave differently from the way that African American children expect authority figures to behave. African American mothers tend to be more firm and physical in their discipline than white mothers are. Consequently, when African American children encounter a white teacher practicing techniques learned in college, which happen to be based on the values and mores of the dominant culture, the children "run all over" the teacher and are labeled discipline problems (Hale-Benson, 1982). Henderson and Washington (1975) found that many school practices were inappropriate for treating the educational needs of African American children because their unique cultural attributes have not been taken into account. They indicated that a network of significant adults firmly corrects undesirable behavior whenever it occurs and reports such behaviors to the parent. The significant feature of the control system is that it seems to operate external to the child, and the child seems to develop an external locus of control.

In the school situation, adults seem to behave as if the locus of social control exists within the child. They do not function in ways that are consistent with the child's expectations of how adults should behave toward him or her in situations that require the enforcement of social controls. Henderson and Washington (1975) also discovered that parents and teachers almost never communicated, and few parents participated in the school's parents' association. In short, the social control apparatus of the school functioned in a way that was quite different from that of the community and did not immediately include parents in its operation.

As a result, teachers find that African American children do not behave as "good little children should," and the children find that teachers do not act in the same way adults do in their community, and that only acts of gross impropriety are reported to parents. Hence, children and teachers have mutually incompatible expectations of each other. The teachers conclude that a child is incorrigible, and the child concludes that the teachers are inconsistent and capricious (Henderson & Washington, 1975).

RESPONSE OF EDUCATORS TO THE NEEDS OF AFRICAN AMERICAN AND HISPANIC DEAF STUDENTS

Social, economic, and political factors have also created population changes throughout the country affecting schools and programs for hearing impaired children. African American and Hispanic children represent nearly a third of the hearing impaired children and youth in the United States. In many programs for the Deaf, especially those in urban settings, the majority of children are from diverse racial, linguistic, and ethnic backgrounds (Center for Assessment and Demographic Studies, 1985–1986). Given these current demographic trends, the numbers of African American, Hispanic, and other ethnic hearing-impaired children will continue to grow. There is every indication to believe that the plight of hearing impaired African American and Hispanic children and youth parallels that of their hearing brothers and sisters. The poor educational performance of African American and Hispanic hearing students seems to be paralleled by similarly depressed achievement levels of African American and Hispanic deaf students. Holt and Allen (1989) found that "ethnicity was a significant negative predictor of integration, placement, and exposure to reading content. Students who were members of ethnic groups were less likely than white, non-Hispanic students to be placed in integrated settings" (p. 557). Although there are some potentially negative psychosocial and sociocultural effects of integration for Deaf students, integration is nevertheless associated with higher academic achievement; but it is apparently an experience that few ethnic students are afforded. Holt and Allen (1989) also found that "students who are members of focus-group ethnic groups . . . are likely to be exposed to less curriculum content [and] are also likely to be placed at a lower level in school" (p. 557).

Delgado (1981) documented that Deaf students from non-English-speaking families were three to four times more likely to be classified as "learning disabled," "mentally retarded," "or emotionally disturbed." This was more likely related to the lack of specialized programs, lack of trained native language personnel, misunderstanding of culture, and diminished expectations, than to characteristics of the children themselves.

Poor educational performance of Hispanic Deaf children seems to parallel that of Hispanic hearing children. The significant cultural differences that exist between Hispanic and other linguistic ethnic Deaf students are seldom understood or addressed in the curriculum process. Hispanic parents are generally excluded from, or exclude themselves from, the educational program of their Deaf child. There are very few Hispanic professionals in the field. These truths unfortunately appear to hold for African American Deaf students, their parents, and professionals as well.

Factors such as the ones just described appear to be key contributors to the lower levels of achievement by African American and Hispanic deaf and hard-of-hearing students. For example, Allen (1986) found that "the 50th percentile reading comprehension scores for Hispanic 12-year olds is 11 scaled points less than the 50th percentile for white 8-year olds" (p. 197). At the three age levels compared—ages eight, twelve, and sixteen—African American and Hispanic students demonstrate significantly poorer achievement patterns in both reading and math comprehension.

In addressing the needs of racial, linguistic, and ethnic Deaf students, all of the preceding issues related to cultural values, childrearing practices, and varying value systems apply. *Deafness makes one no less a member of a racial, linguistic, or ethnic group*. However, educators of the Deaf have been either unaware, hesitant, or slow to respond to this proposition, often insisting that deafness in some way precludes ethnic, racial, or linguistic ethnic group membership or status. Where there has been a response, it has often been to assume that ethnic status constitutes a disability within a disability, which wrongly defines ethnic status and to a large degree denies the cultural implications of deafness.

Ogbu's (1978) castelike minorities model and the school's role in socializing ethnic people into low status jobs and strata of society appear to apply to Deaf people. The Deaf in the United States have experienced discrimination, alienation, and oppression throughout history. Notwithstanding the importance of Deaf culture as a culture in its own right, this chapter's focus in on the ethnic membership of ethnic Deaf people because these are the people whose lives are adversely affected not only because they are deaf, but even more so because they are members of underrepresented ethnic groups. The dynamic of *Deaf culture*, albeit significant, is not elaborated on in this chapter because the term, at least in the United States, unfortunately often refers to white Deaf culture, a phenomenon that has created a form of apartheid within the Deaf community itself.

Relatively few attempts have been made to address the needs of Deaf children from diverse racial, ethnic, and linguistic backgrounds. Until this text, *The Hispanic Deaf* (Delgado, 1984) and *Black and Deaf in America* (Hairston & Smith, 1983) were the only books that addressed the needs of Hispanic and African American Deaf people.

One program specifically designed to address the needs of African American Deaf children is the Black Families' and Children's Project at the Lexington School for the Deaf in Jackson Heights, New York. That project is looking at achievement, tracking, dropout rates, school suspensions, substance abuse, parent–school relations, and other factors that may influence school success for African American Deaf children. A federally funded demonstration project, Projecto Oportunidad (Rhode Island School for the Deaf, 1980–1983), developed a program specifically for language ethnic Deaf students. It was funded by the Office of Bilingual Education and Ethnic Language Affairs, not by the Office of Special Education. No such project addressing the needs of African American deaf students has ever been funded.

The Hispanic Resource Team at the Lexington School for the Deaf works with Hispanic students and families using a bicultural and bilingual model. And the Franco-American Children's Educational Team (F.A.C.E.T.), Governor Baxter School for the Deaf in Maine, works with French American students and families. The federally funded program at Lamar University in Beaumont, Texas, trains Asians/Pacific Islanders, African Americans, and Hispanics to become teachers of the Deaf.

These programs serve approximately 300 students. Yet Delgado's 1981 survey identified more than 7,000 students from non-English-speaking families. The lack of attention given to the needs of racial, linguistic, and ethnic Deaf students is a systemic shortcoming that pervades the field of deafness. For example, there are few professional school personnel, especially administrators, who are native speakers of Spanish. Despite the vast needs demonstrated in New York City alone, a Teachers College, Columbia University, proposal submitted to the U.S. Department of Education Office of Special Education Programs, Division of Personnel Preparation, to specifically recruit and train ethnic educators of the Deaf has been continually rejected.

Twenty-eight years after the Civil Rights Act of 1964 and nineteen years after the Bilingual Education Act, Hispanic resource team members at the Lexington School for the Deaf—where there is a well-developed program addressing the needs of Hispanic Deaf students—are routinely asked to conduct introductory level sensitivity and awareness workshops at schools and programs for the Deaf throughout the East Coast on the bicultural, bilingual needs of Hispanic children and their families as well as problems facing teachers and other professionals.

Although the rationale and model now exist to support a bilingual approach (Fischgrund, 1982; Delgado, 1984), schools for the Deaf continue to resist providing "home language" instruction, usually on the grounds that the children are deaf, have "no language" upon school entry, or that they must learn English. Those arguments have no validity or foundation in the literature addressing the language or educational needs of ethnic children. Translation and interpretation services, even when required by regulation, are still hard to obtain for most non-English-speaking parents of Deaf children.

School Policy

Three models of ethnic and cultural awareness present themselves:

Positive hostility was found when laws forbade the use of any language except English in the schools, when children were punished for not speaking English, and when ethnically diverse children and their backgrounds were ridiculed (Glazer, 1980). Although policies of positive hostility are officially outlawed in the United States, such practices undoubtedly survive. The effects of the positive hostility model on children have been described by one of its products, a hearing person from a regular school.

> I was consistently reminded of my "differences" through the absence of experiences that reflected my language, culture, values, and most important, being accepted in my own right. I believe it was this process, the process of having to abandon "self" and change my differences, that caused the low self-esteem, alienation, dissonance, and a most difficult and unpleasant school experience. (Benavides, 1980, pp. 8–9)

Although beyond the scope of this chapter, perhaps an example closer to home is the Deaf child of Deaf parents being denied the opportunity to use American Sign Language (ASL) as his or her first language in the school setting.

Official disinterest, including indifference, seems to have strong support. The early establishment of immigrant-sponsored, non-English-speaking newspapers, schools, churches, and social organizations has been difficult to maintain into the second and third generations. Despite John Dewey's belief in cultural pluralism in public education, in which every pupil should have been made aware of the rich breadth of our national make-up, children of various backgrounds found that schools, for the most part, ignored their backgrounds. Schools taught that the heroes and fathers of the country were George Washington, Thomas Jefferson, and Abraham Lincoln, persons far from many of these children's own backgrounds and roots. Children were often placed in the dilemma of not knowing whether to take seriously the heroes talked about at home and in ethnic organizations, persons apparently barred from the American school (Longstreet, 1980).

Positive reinforcement is now the central model of ethnic and cultural awareness among educators. It may be viewed as part of a progression from prejudice to indifference, understanding, and finally true commitment to cultural pluralism. This model may also be seen as an abandonment of earlier policies promoting the melting-pot theory. This model in a school has many dimensions. To be effective, it cannot be imposed; rather, it must evolve. Initially, process is more important than content. The goal is not to plan and carry out several exciting ethnic activities in isolation, but rather to create a school environment in which ethnic diversity becomes acceptable and institutionalized in a positive and vibrant way.

Deaf people represent a variety of ethnic minorities in addition to their cultural identity as Deaf people. Therefore, Deaf children who are members of ethnic groups have dual ethnic group membership, often compounding their role confusion and identity crises. African American Deaf people, for example, may be discriminated against by white Deaf people and by hearing African Americans (Anderson & Bowe, 1972). Helping Deaf children to become aware of the ethnic and cultural differences between themselves and Deaf people of other ethnic groups or between themselves and hearing members of their own ethnic group is an important factor in their education, development, and survival.

Educators and parents, intent on teaching reading, writing, and communications skills to Deaf children, have tended to overlook cultural and ethnic experiences and values. These experiences often occur incidentally for hearing children, since much of our culture is naturally transmitted through records, movies, plays, television, religious organizations, and other institutions that rely primarily on linguistic and auditory competency. In addition, studies have shown a significant correlation between low self-esteem and prejudice. One of the most effective actions schools could take to improve intergroup relations would be to help students develop a strong self-concept (Pate, 1988). However, overreliance on such programs is not justified by recent research, which indicates that self-esteem is an effect of academic success, not the cause of it (Holly, 1987). A major effect is needed to develop appropriate materials to teach Deaf children ethnic, cultural, religious, and racial awareness. When an environment is created in which educators promote an understanding of ethnic and racial heritage, learning will become more effective (Cohen & Grant, 1981).

Parental Involvement

> If studies of school achievement have shown one thing, it is the importance of the family. And school achievement is only one element in the process of becoming an adult; the family's contribution to other elements is even more important. If an early withdrawal of family attention, interest, and involvement is to become the fate of an increasing fraction of our youth, it can be expected to have especially serious consequences. (Coleman, Hoffer, & Kilgore, 1982, p. 32)

Parental involvement in the school's program may be more important for disabled children than for most nondisabled children, because parents often must learn specific teaching and management techniques that are not required of parents of nondisabled children. As a result of language barriers as well as cultural and socioeconomic differences, ethnic parents often experience excessive discomfort, feelings of intimidation, and alienation in their relationships with their child's school. These feelings become exacerbated in a school program for Deaf children, where communication difference, and therefore strangeness, imposes an added barrier, especially for adolescents. Every effort should be made to prevent parents from feeling different and alienated. Parent–teacher meetings conducted in the parents' own language are a worthwhile initial step toward helping parents feel able to risk and make further contacts with the school. Special parent groups such as Hispanic and African American parents' organizations foster involvement by helping these parents to make effective transitions to the school culture. However, for the benefit of *all* children in the school, the ultimate goal of these subgroups should be the full integration of all parents into one school parent organization.

Parents of African American and Hispanic children may not be highly educated. As a result, they generally do not possess skills commonly required to deal effectively with bureaucratic organizations such as schools. These skills are often acquired through the process of education in the dominant culture—that is, by middle class, educated, white, hearing North Americans. But the skills are necessary when utilizing parental due process rights concerning the education of disabled children. Without them, due process tends to be meaningless. States need to explore ways to make existing due process procedures more widely accessible to parents of multicultural children.

Board and Staff Representation

The continuation of current trends will result in a national teaching force that is 5 percent nonwhite serving a student population that is about one-third nonwhite (Hawley, 1989). African American and Hispanic teachers currently comprise about 11 percent of all teachers. Forty percent of ethnic teachers say they are likely to leave teaching over the next five years, compared with 25 percent of nonethnic teachers (Hawley, 1989). The problem is not relieved when ethnic teachers make up just a small percentage of the school's teaching staff. Recent research suggests that 20 percent is the minimum rate of inclusion required to diffuse stereotypes and other negative factors affecting ethnic members of organizations (Pettigrew & Martin, 1987).

The situation is not much different with regard to teachers of the Deaf. Jensema and Corbett (1980) found that approximately 94 percent of a teacher sample surveyed reported their ethnic background as "white." The researchers concluded that a gross imbalance in the racial make-up of the teaching population exists and indicated the need to attract more ethnic members to the field.

Many reasons have been stated for the need for more ethnic teachers. Perhaps the most persuasive is the fact that racism derives from the inaccurate and overgeneralized attribution of negative personal traits to persons whose race or ethnicity is different from one's own. Ignorance is the main nutrient of racism. Racism, prejudice, and discrimination do not require intention (Pine & Hilliard, 1990). The most effective way to combat racism is to undermine the assumptions on which it rests and to arm individuals with the skills to overcome its consequences. These objectives can best be achieved by placing individuals of different races or ethnic backgrounds in situations where they have the opportunity for recurrent interaction involving cooperative and rewarding activities (Hawley, 1989; Hilliard & Pine, 1990). The disproportionately higher numbers of white hearing staff generally result in a strong and pervading white hearing, middle-class cultural orientation, thereby excluding full participation in the process of educating ethnic Deaf children.

There is also likely to be an imbalance concerning ethnic trustee (e.g., advisory board) representation in schools and programs for the Deaf. If so, school policy and sensitivity regarding ethnic Deaf children may be limited. The lack of proportionate representation of ethnic professionals and trustees may be interpreted by parents and students as insensitivity on the part of the school toward multicultural issues (Cohen, Fischgrund, & Redding, 1990).

The Special School (Residential or Day)

For many ethnic Deaf children, the school for the Deaf takes on a special importance. As noted earlier, children from diverse ethnic or racial backgrounds represent a high percentage of the foster and institutional care population. Residential schools for the Deaf are in a strategic position to provide quality residential care and treatment for profoundly Deaf children who require such care. They are also in a unique position to work effectively with the particular needs of parents of ethnic Deaf children.

Staff training in the dynamics of language acquisition of Deaf children and the elements of acculturation of ethnic Deaf children are more likely to occur in schools for the Deaf whose entire focus is the education and development of Deaf children. These schools recognize the importance of curriculum, especially in the area of language, designed specifically for Deaf children. This awareness could be expanded to address bilingual, bicultural, dialect, and other issues that affect ethnic Deaf children. The isolation and insulation from the wider society often experienced by underrepresented ethnic hearing and Deaf children and parents in the general education setting is likely to be mitigated to some degree for ethnic Deaf students attending schools for the Deaf where programs and curricula are consciously designed to meet these needs.

Deaf professionals from diverse racial and ethnic backgrounds, although presently few in number, are a source of inspiration to ethnic children and serve to bridge the cultural gap that exists between community and school.

For Deaf adolescents particularly, the school for the Deaf represents an environment where leadership and socialization skills are fostered. The Deaf adolescent rarely becomes active in the social fabric of the large, urban regular high school. Opportunities to engage in athletics, student government, drama, yearbook, and other activities, all of which are important to overall growth, are greatly enhanced in schools for the Deaf. These opportunities are especially important for inner city ethnic Deaf students. Ianni (1989) illustrates how the peer group for inner city adolescents plays a stronger force than the family does in defining and controlling conformity. This is because so much of adolescents' time is spent outside the home.

The boards of advisors or boards of education of schools for the Deaf are in a strategic position to carry out their charge of establishing policy related to the needs of ethnic Deaf children. Boards of local education authorities are less inclined to devote time, energy, and resources toward the needs of disabled children, let alone disabled African American and Hispanic children.

Professional organizations serving the Deaf, whose constituencies are primarily in schools for the Deaf, should develop ethnic concerns sections to promote awareness of ethnic issues, personnel recruitment and training, and research and development projects— and to provide leadership in areas of concern to ethnic Deaf children. Fortunately, the Conference of Educational Administrators Serving the Deaf (CEASD) has established a standing committee on Ethnic and Multicultural Concerns of Deaf Children, and the Convention of American Instructors of the Deaf (CAID) has set up a special interest group on the Needs of Multicultural Deaf Children.

RECOMMENDATIONS

Families

Families play a crucial role in the socialization and education of children. Children do better in school when their parents are involved in their schooling. As a result of poverty, stress, racism, language barriers, and cultural differences, parents of ethnic children tend to feel alienated from their children's schooling (Lightfoot, 1978).

In addition to government-sponsored research and demonstration projects related to developing model parent programs for parents of multicultural Deaf children and adolescents, a number of specific initiatives should be undertaken by administrators and teachers to recognize the value and facilitate the involvement of parents in the educational process. In 1989 and 1990, CEASD sponsored conferences on the needs of multicultural Deaf children. Recommendations that evolved concerning parents, staff, curriculum, and assessment included the following:

> Effort should be made to minimize parents' feelings of difference and alienation regarding the school environment.
>
> Family aspirations and hopes of multicultural Deaf children should be compared with school goals and expectations.
>
> Parents and school should agree to mutually acceptable goals, as well as to strategies for achieving them.
>
> Parent participation should be encouraged through facilities such as transportation, child care, and interpreters.
>
> Staff should be educated to be more sensitive to multicultural values of the family. For example, in working with Hispanic families emphasis is needed on showing respect and personal interest. It is important that the teacher present himself or herself less as a professional educator and more as a person with qualities attractive to the Hispanic parent. The educator administrator must show interest in the parent as a human being, not simply as the student's parent. Professionalism, educational skills, and authority—attributes we as professionals are taught to stand for—should be minimized in the interest of building trust and developing long-term working relationships with Hispanic families (Rodriguez, 1985).

Culturally diverse parent advisory councils should be established to advise on formulation of school policy.

Parents should be trained in ways of working effectively within education bureaucracies.

A state-supported network of child advocacy groups should serve as a significant equalizer.

Staffing

The dearth of teachers and administrators from underrepresented ethnic groups in schools in general, and in programs for Deaf children specifically, is harming African American and Hispanic children throughout the United States. Recommendations in this area include the following:

Affirmative action plans should be developed for hiring multicultural faculty and administrators and recruiting ethnic trustees and other policymakers.

Federal and state governments should sponsor teacher training institutions that specifically design teacher training programs to recruit, prepare, and train professionals from underrepresented ethnic and racial groups to work in educational programs for Deaf children.

Mentorship programs should be developed using role models including multicultural staff, graduates, and members from the community to help white staff build stronger understanding of the needs, abilities, and realities of multicultural Deaf children.

A national clearinghouse should be established to assist programs in recruiting qualified multicultural staff.

Federal and state governments should award grants for the development of model inservice staff development activities, including issues such as learning styles, family and community structures, and how attitudes of members of the dominant culture may affect teacher and administrator expectations of ethnically diverse children.

Educators should be made aware of the need to nurture multiculturalism and bilingualism in order to foster the child's ability to feel at home in different settings. It is important for the teacher to affirm the multiple aspects of the Hispanic child's identity.

Curriculum and Learning

Ethnically diverse children in general, and deaf children from diverse backgrounds in particular, may utilize learning strategies and styles related to their cultural backgrounds. Work done at the Lexington School for the Deaf suggests that an African American Deaf person is neither an African American person who is deaf nor a Deaf person who is African American, but rather someone with his or her own persona: an African American Deaf person. It would be helpful for professionals to understand the nature of learning from a multicultural perspective in order to formulate appropriate teaching interventions. Research is needed to investigate the nature of learning of multicultural deaf children and adolescents in order to develop appropriate teaching strategies.

There is growing evidence that bilingual and bicultural, or trilingual and tricultural, activities are appropriate interventions for many Deaf children from non-English-speaking homes. The federal government should sponsor research and demonstration projects related to developing model multicultural programs and curricula for Deaf children from non-English-speaking families.

Pine and Hilliard (1990), the National Association of School Psychologists (1985), and others have developed convincing arguments for the "different, not deficient," assumption concerning African American children's learning. They present a compelling picture of schools as they could be as opposed to what they are in general, which would allow for acceptance of more diverse learning styles and strategies. Pine and Hilliard (1990) and Boykin (1983) speak of the expectation for nonwhite children to be bicultural, bilingual, and bicognitive; to measure their performance against a Euro-American yardstick. The need exists to prepare African American children to become culturally bistylistic and to learn to discriminate when one mode of expression might be more effective than the other. These recommendations are particularly appropriate for Deaf ethnic students. Further recommendations include the following:

> Development of current and accurate demographic profiles of students in each school and program for deaf students;
>
> formulation by each school program of a mission statement that embraces developing the academic and vocational achievement and personal growth and esteem of multicultural children, incorporating respect for their culture and heritage;
>
> identification, and incorporation into the curriculum, of African American and Hispanic culture as well as African American Deaf culture and Hispanic Deaf culture;
>
> development of procedures for the selection of books and other instructional materials to institutionalize ethnic and cultural sensitivity;
>
> career education from the earliest grades throughout the school years; and
>
> education of staff to appreciate the value of integrating ethnic and multicultural activities into the curriculum.

As indicated earlier, assessment of children and perception of abilities and strengths are matters not often understood or appreciated sufficiently. Accordingly, we must continue to question assumptions about children who are not from the dominant culture in order to develop a better understanding of the "different, not deficient" model (Willis, 1989). Included with this questioning would be the following recommendations:

> Evaluations of children reflect an understanding of the culture of the family;
>
> student evaluations be conducted regularly;
>
> I.Q. tests be only one of several measures of student abilities;
>
> every child be assumed capable of excellence;
>
> assessment instruments include multicultural tests and ethnographic tools;

multicultural teams be utilized in student evaluations;

programs be individualized for each student; and

equal opportunities be made available to African American and Hispanic Deaf children for valid and appropriate assessment and placement procedures and practices.

Implications

Despite Ogbu's (1978) theory of the need for schools to socialize certain groups into low-status work positions for the good of the economy, it is becoming clear that there is a growing need for employees with high-order thinking skills. The challenge to schools is to educate all students with the higher order skills that only 10 percent received in the past (Carnegie Foundation, 1986). The business community is concerned about the decreasing numbers of workers that will enter the labor force during the next decade. In 1989, there were 300,000 fewer students graduating than there were ten years prior, but 250,000 more than anticipated for the graduating class of 1994. The only source of new growth in the labor force through the year 2000 will be among women, underrepresented ethnic members, and immigrants. The greatest job growth in the next decade will be in occupations requiring some postsecondary education. The economy, basically, has closed the door on high school dropouts seeking jobs with a future (Lewis, 1989).

CONCLUSION

The current picture concerning the education of children from underrepresented ethnic groups in the United States is bleak. It is no different for African American and Hispanic Deaf children. In fact, a Deaf African American or Deaf Hispanic child's needs often exceed those of a white Deaf child for reasons that go beyond poverty. Ethnic Deaf children live in a multicultural world. They are members of their respective ethnic or racial culture, the culture of the Deaf community, and the predominant Anglo-Saxon culture in the United States. Too much attention may be focused on needs imposed by deafness, as important as they are, and too little on cultural background and the concomitant forces at play in the home and within the community.

The picture can be hopeful if trustees, teachers, administrators, and government officials are encouraged to become aware of ethnic concerns. In addition, curricula must be assessed, resources made available, diverse ethnic staff recruitment aggressively pursued, intake and placement procedures reviewed, parent and home relations analyzed and revamped, and a spirit developed that focuses on the strengths of ethnic Deaf children and their families.

Until now, neither local education agencies nor, with exceptions, schools for the Deaf have risen to the challenge presented by multicultural Deaf children and their families. It is also unlikely that "local education agencies" will do so in the near future, because of the low incidence of deafness and the enormous general education concerns with which they are beset. The opportunity exists for schools for the Deaf to develop programs for ethnically diverse Deaf children, as the proportion of these children increases, with excellence and equity as goals. The meteoric rise in numbers of children from diverse ethnic backgrounds in schools throughout the country is not debatable. The reality is that the population continues to increase. We must be ready to meet its needs.

BIBLIOGRAPHY

Allen, T. E. (1986). Patterns of academic achievement among hearing impaired students: 1974–1983. In A. Schildroth & M. Karchmer (Eds.), *Deaf children in America.* San Diego: College-Hill.

Allen, T. E., & Osborn, T. (1984). Academic integration of hearing impaired students: Demographic, handicapping, and achievement factors. *American Annals of the Deaf, 120,* 67–73.

Anderson, G. B., & Bowe, F. G. (1972). Racism within the deaf community. *American Annals of the Deaf, 118,* 617–619.

Banks, J. A. (1987). *Teaching strategies for ethnic studies* (4th ed.). Boston: Allyn & Bacon.

Benavides, A. (1980). *Cultural awareness training for the exceptional teacher.* Reston, VA: Council for Exceptional Children.

Boykin, A. W. (1983). On academic task performance and Afro-American children. In J. R. Spencer (Ed.), *Achievement and achievement motives.* Boston: W. H. Freeman.

Carnegie Foundation. (1986). *A nation prepared: Teachers for the 21st century.* Task Force on Teaching as a Profession of the Carnegie Forum on Education and the Economy. New York: Author.

Center for Assessment and Demographic Studies. (1985–1986). The annual survey of hearing-impaired children and youth, 1985–1986 school year (unpublished report). Washington, DC: Gallaudet University.

Children's Defense Fund. (1985). *Black and white children in American: Key facts.* Washington, DC: Author.

Children's Defense Fund. (1990, January/March). Hispanic youths at a crossroads (monograph). Washington, DC: Author.

Cohen, O. P. (1987, May). *Current and future needs of minority hearing impaired children and youth.* Testimony presented before the Congressional Commission on the Education of the Deaf on behalf of the Conference of Educational Administrators Serving the Deaf.

Cohen, O. P., Fischgrund, J. E., & Redding, R. (1990, April). Deaf children from ethnic and racial minority backgrounds: An overview. *American Annals of the Deaf, 135,* 67–73.

Cohen, O. P., & Grant, B. (1981, June). Ethnic heritage and cultural implications in a school for the deaf. In *Focus on infusion* (Vol. 2). 50th Biennial Meeting, Convention of American Instructors of the Deaf, Rochester, NY.

Coleman, J. S., Hoffer, T., & Kilgore, S. (1982). *High school achievement: Public, Catholic and private schools compared.* New York: Basic Books.

Cummins, J. (1984). *Bilingualism and special education: Issues in assessment and pedagogy.* San Diego: College-Hill.

Cummins, J. (1986). Empowering minority students: A framework for intervention. *Harvard Educational Review, 56,* 18–36.

Cummins, J. (1989). A theoretical framework for bilingual special education. *Exceptional Children, 56.*

Delgado, G. (1981). Hearing impaired children from non-native language homes. *American Annals of the Deaf, 126,* 118–121.

Delgado, G. (1984). *The Hispanic deaf: Issues and challenges for bilingual special education.* Washington, DC: Gallaudet College.

Fischgrund, J. (1982). Language intervention for hearing-impaired children from linguistically and culturally diverse backgrounds. *Topics in Language Disorders, 2,* 57–66.

Fischgrund, J., Cohen, O., & Clarkson, R. (1987, September). Hearing impaired children in black and Hispanic families. *Volta Review, 89*(5), 59–67.

Ford Foundation. (1989) *The common good: Social welfare and the American future.* Ford Foundation Project on Social Welfare and the American Future. New York: Author.

Fordham, S. (1988). Racelessness as a factor in black students' school success: Pragmatic strategy or pyrrhic victory? *Harvard Educational Review, 58.*

Glasgow, D. (1980). The Black underclass: *Poverty, unemployment and entrapment of ghetto youth.* San Francisco: Jossey-Bass.

Glazer, N. (1980). Ethnicity and education: Some hard questions. *Phi Delta Kappan, 62.*

Grace, C. (1989). Increasing staff awareness and sensitivity toward the needs of black Deaf children—A Training Manual. New York: Lexington School for the Deaf, New York State Education Department.

Graham, P. (1987). Black teachers: A dramatically scarce resource. *Phi Delta Kappan, 68.*

Gregory, J., Shanahan, T., & Walberg, H. (1984). Mainstreaming of hearing impaired high school seniors: A re-analysis of a national survey. *American Annals of the Deaf, 129.*

Hairston, E., & Smith, L. (1983). *Black and deaf in America.* Silver Spring, MD: T. J. Publishers.

Hale-Benson, J. E. (1982). *Black children: Their roots, culture and learning styles* (rev. ed.). Baltimore: Johns Hopkins University.

Hawley, W. (1989). The importance of minority teachers to the racial and ethnic integration of American society. *Equity and Choice, 5,* 31–36.

Henderson, D. H., & Washington, A. B. (1975). Cultural differences and the education of black children: An alternative model for program development. *Journal of Negro Education, 44,* 353–360.

Hilliard, A. (1989). Update. *Association for Supervision and Curriculum Development, 31*(3), 2.

Hilliard, A., & Pine, G. (1990). Rx for racism: Imperatives for America's schools. *Phi Delta Kappan, 71,* 593–600.

Holly, W. J. (1987, November). Students' self-esteem and academic achievement. *Research Round-up.*

Holt, J., & Allen, T. (1989). The effects of schools and their curricula on the reading and mathematics achievement of hearing impaired students. *International Journal of Educational Research, 13,* 5.

Ianni, F. (1989). *The search for structure: A report on American youth today.* New York: Free Press.

Jensema, C. (1978). *The relationship between academic achievement and the demographic characteristics of hearing impaired children and youth (Series R No. 2).* Washington, DC: Gallaudet College.

Jensema, C. J., & Corbett, E. E., Jr. (1980). A demographic overview of teachers of the hearing impaired. *American Annals of the Deaf, 125,* 1.

Johnson, N. J., & Sanday, R. R. (1971). Subcultural variations in an urban poor population. *American Anthropologist 73,* 128–143.

Kellog, J. (1988). Forces of change. *Phi Delta Kappan, 69,* 199–204.

Levine, L. W. (1977). *Black culture and black consciousness.* New York: Oxford University.

Lewis, A. (1989). *Restructuring America's schools.* Arlington, VA: American Association of School Administrators.

Lightfoot, S. L. (1978). *Worlds apart: Relationships between families and schools.* New York: Basic Books.

Longstreet, W. S. (1980). *Aspects of ethnicity: Understanding differences in pluralistic classrooms.* New York: Teachers College.

McDermott, R. P. (1976). Achieving school failure: An anthropological approach to illiteracy and social stratification. In H. Singer & R. B. Russell (Eds.), *Theoretical models and process of reading,* Newark, DE: International Reading Association.

National Association of School Psychologists. (1985). Advocacy for appropriate educational services for all children. *Communique, 9.*

New York State Education Commissioner's Task Force on the Education of Children and Youth At-Risk. (1988, October). *The time for assertive action.* Albany, NY: Author.

Nobels, W. W. (1974). African root and American fruit: The black family. *Journal of Social and Behavorial Sciences, 20,* 52–63.

Ogbu, J. (1978). *Minority education and caste.* New York: Academic.

Pate, G. N. (1988). Research on reducing prejudice, *Social Education, 52.*

Pine, G. J., & Hilliard, A. (1990). Rx for racism: Imperatives for American schools, *Phi Delta Kappan, 71,* 593–600.

Pettigrew, T. F., & Martin, J. M. (1987). Shaping the organizational context for black American inclusion. *Journal of Social Issues, 43.*

Polce, M. E. (1987). Children and learning styles. In A. Thomas & J. Grimes (Eds.), *Children's needs: Psychological perspectives.* Washington DC: National Association of School Psychologists.

Rodriguez, J. R. (1989). Hispanic culture. *Coalition Quarterly, 6,* 12–14.

Rodriguez, O. (1985). *Hispanic families and children.* Paper presented at the Urban Ethnic Minority Deaf Child Conference, Teachers College, Columbia University, New York.

Saville-Troike, M. (1978). *A guide to culture in the classroom.* Rosslyn, VA: National Clearinghouse for Bilingual Education.

Simon, R. (1989). Where were you when I was trying to get help for my child? *Coalition Quarterly, 6.*

Wallace, N., & Fischgrund, J. (1985). Minority deaf students: An overview. *ASHA* (American Speech Language Hearing Association Journal), *27*(6), 28.

Willis, M. G. (1989). Learning styles of African American children: A review of the literature and interventions. *The Journal of Black Psychology, 16.*

RESOURCES

Literature, Art, Organizations and Research Institutes

Atlanta, Georgia
Clark Atlanta University
Southern Center for Studies in Public Policy
Brawley and Fair Streets, SW
Atlanta, GA 30314
(404) 880-8085

Herndon Home
587 University Place, NW
Atlanta, GA 30314
(404) 581-9813

Jomandi Productions
1444 Mayson Street, NE
Atlanta, GA 30308
(404) 876-6346

Just Us Theatre Company
1058 Oglethorpe Avenue, SW
Atlanta, GA 30303
(404) 753-2399

U.S. National Park Service
Martin Luther King, Jr.
National Historic Site and Preservation
    District
522 Auburn Avenue, NE
Atlanta, GA 30312
(404) 331-5190

Houston, Texas
Black Art Gallery
5408 Almeda Road
Houston, TX 77004
(713) 529-7900

Community Music Center of Houston
5613 Almeda Road
Houston, TX 77004
(713) 523-9710

University of Houston
African and Afro-American Studies Program
College of Humanities and Fine Arts
Agnes Arnold Hall
Houston, TX 77204
(713) 749-2900

Los Angeles, California
Afro American Cultural Center
2560 West 54th Street
Los Angeles, CA 90058
(213) 299-6124

Brockman Gallery
4334 Degnan Boulevard
Los Angeles, CA 90008
(213) 294-3766

California Afro-American Museum
600 State Drive, Exposition Park
Los Angeles, CA 90037
(213) 744-7432

Charles R. Drew University
    of Medicine and Science
Hypertension Research Center
161 East 120th Street, M.P. No. 11
Los Angeles, CA 90274

Museum of African American Art
4005 Crenshaw Boulevard, 3rd Floor
Los Angeles, CA 90008
(213) 294-7071

New York, New York
African American Cultural Arts Network
2090 Adam Clayton Powell, Jr., Boulevard
Suite 103
New York, NY 10027
(212) 749-4408

Black Research and Resource Center
253 West 72nd Street
Suite 211A
New York, NY 10023
(212) 496-2234

National Association for the Advancement
    of Colored People (NAACP)
260 Fifth Avenue, 6th Floor
New York, NY 10001
(212) 481-4100

New York Urban League
Central Administration
218 West 40th Street, 8th Floor
New York, NY 10018
(212) 730-5200

Schomburg Center for Research
    in Black Culture
515 Malcom X Boulevard
New York, NY 10037
(212) 491-2200

Washington, DC
African Cultural Foundation
731 Rock Creek Church Road, NW
Washington, DC 20010
(202) 822-2232

African Heritage Center
    for African Dance and Music
    (AHCADM)
4018 Minnesota Avenue, NE
Washington, DC 20019
(202) 399-5252

Anacostia Museum
1901 Fort Place, SE
Washington, DC 20020
(202) 287-3183

Association for the Study of
    Afro-American Life and History
Carter G. Woodson Center
1407 14th Street, NW
Washington, DC 20005
(202) 667-2822

Howard University
    African Studies and Research Program
Washington, DC 20059
(202) 806-7115

MULTICULTURAL RESOURCES

Abrahams, R. D. (1985). *Afro-American folktales*. New York: Pantheon Books.
Aptheker, H. (Ed.) (1988). *Against racism*. Unpublished essays, papers, addresses, 1887–1961, W.E.B. Dubois.
Asante, M. K. (1990). Kemet, Afrocentricity and knowledge. Trenton, NJ: Africa World Press.
Baker, C. (1981). *Work with urban black families*. New Orleans, LA: Tulane University School of Social Work, Child Welfare Training Center.
Bass, B., Wyatt, G. E., & Powell, G. (1982). *The Afro-American family: Assessment, treatment and research*. New York: Grune & Stratton.
Baughman, E. (1971). *Black Americans*. New York: Academic Press.
Boyd-Franklin, N. (1989). *Black families in therapy: A multisystem approach*. New York: Guilford Press.

Clark, R. M. (1983). *Family life and school achievement: Why poor black children succeed or fail.* Chicago: University of Chicago.

Dadie, B. B. *The black cloth: A collection of African folktales.* Amherst: University of Massachusetts.

Dodson, J. E. (1982). *An Afro-centric training manual: Toward a non-deficit perspective in services to children and families.* Knoxville, TN: University of Tennessee School of Social Work, Southeast Regional Child Welfare Training and Resource Center.

Fantini, M. C., & Cardenas, R. (1980). *Parenting in a multicultural society.* New York: Longman.

Feliming, J. (1984). *Blacks in college.* San Francisco: Jossey-Bass.

Gibbs, J. T. (1988). *Young, black and male in America.* Dover, MA: Auburn House.

Gollnick, D. M., & Chinn, P. C. (1986). *Multicultural education in a pluralistic society* (2nd ed.). Columbus, OH: Merrill.

Hale-Benson, J. E. (1982). *Black children: Their roots, culture and learning styles.* Provo, UT: Brigham Young Press.

Hampton, R. L. (1987). *Violence in the black family.* Lexington, MA: D. C. Heath.

Jewell, K. S. (1988). *Survival of the black family: The institutional impact of U.S. social policy.* New York: Praeger.

Kunjufu, J. (1986). *Motivating and preparing black youth to work.* Chicago: African American Images.

Kunjufu, J. (1988). *To be popular or smart: The black peer group.* Chicago: African American Images.

Kochman, T. (1981). Black and white styles in conflict. Chicago: University of Chicago.

Lewis, J., & Looney, J. (1983). *The long struggle: Well functioning working class black families.* New York: Brunner/Mazel.

Lynch, J. (1983). *The multicultural curriculum.* London: Batsford Academic and Educational.

Maquet, J. (1972). *Africanity: The cultural unity of black Africa.* New York: Oxford.

McAdoo, H. (Ed.). (1981). *Black families.* Beverly Hills: Sage.

Mitchell, H., & Lewter, N. (1986). *Soul theology: The heart of American culture.* San Francisco: Harper & Row.

Nine, C., & Carmen, J. (1976). *Teacher training pack for a course on cultural awareness.* Cambridge, MA: Cambridge National Assessment and Dissemination Center for Bilingual/Bicultural Education.

Nixon, J. (1985). *A teacher's guide to multicultural education.* Oxford: Basil Blackwell.

Shapiro, H. (1988). *White violence and black response.* Amherst: University of Massachusetts.

Sheilds, J. C. (1988). *The collected works of Phyllis Wheatley.* New York: Oxford.

Simonson, R., & Walker, S. (Eds.). (1988). *Multicultural literacy.* St. Paul, MN: Graywolf.

Spencer, M. B., Brookins, G. K., & Allen, W. R. *The social and affective behavior of black children.* Hillsdale, NJ: Lawrence Erlbaum.

Staples, R. (1987). *The urban plantation.* San Francisco: Black World Foundation.

Staples, R. (1982). *Black masculinity: The black male's role in american society* San Francisco: Black Scholar Press.

Takaki, R. (1979). *Iron cages: Race & culture in 19th century America.* New York: Knopf.

Taylor, C. (1987). *Guide to multicultural resources.* Praxis publications. (P.O. Box 9869 Madison, WI 53715; (608) 244-5633.)

Washington, V., & La Point, V. (1988). *Black children: An ecological review and resource guide.* New York: Garland.

White, J. (1984). *The psychology of blacks: An Afro-American perspective.* Englewood Cliffs, NJ: Prentice-Hall.

Wilson, W. (1987). *The truly disadvantaged: The inner city, the underclass and public policy.* Chicago: University of Chicago.

Wright, B. (1987). *Black robes, white justice: Why our justice system doesn't work for blacks.* Secaucus, NJ: Lyle Stuart.

CHAPTER 5

Addressing the Needs of Hispanic Deaf Children

Barbara Gerner de Garcia

Hispanic hearing-impaired children have the potential to acquire useful language, maybe even two languages. The profession must find suitable means by which the children can realize that potential and achieve academic success.

J. Grant

The challenge for the 1990s and beyond is to educate our children—hearing and deaf, English-speaking and linguistic minority—to enable them to lead happy and productive lives. However, this means more than preparing them for a far-off future. The challenge for teachers is to discover students as individuals and then teach to that individuality. Learning is a process of self-discovery for students. Children from poor communities and oppressed groups, including the Deaf, must develop their sense of self and self-worth. As a teacher, knowing how to teach skill X and skill Y is secondary to knowing how to value a child and, in turn, to enable that child to value self. This chapter is about ways in which both teachers and Deaf children can become excited about learning for today.

INTRODUCTION

At the end of the twentieth century, we are facing complex challenges in our educational system. The demographics of our school-age population are rapidly changing, reflecting increased new immigration from Latin America and Southeast Asia. Many professionals in the United States working with the Deaf will be increasingly in contact with Hispanic Deaf children and their families.

In both regular education and Deaf education, Hispanic students have not done well. In regular education, the gap for Hispanic achievement is increasing rather than decreasing. Hispanics have one of the highest dropout rates of any group in the United States, at 31 percent. Those who were traditionally high achievers, such as Cuban Americans, are showing signs of struggle (*Boston Globe,* 1990).

In schools for the Deaf, there are parallel issues, but they may be played out differently. Achievement is low for Hispanic Deaf children, who score the lowest when compared with their white and African American Deaf peers (Allen, 1986; Jensema, 1975). It appears that dropout rates are lower among Hispanic Deaf students than they are among hearing Hispanic students. Schools for the Deaf provide a unique community that young Deaf people do not have elsewhere. However, some Hispanic Deaf students may drop out of learning: They may go to school but not to class, and they may leave school with inadequate skills.

Although earlier immigrants did well with minimal literacy skills in English, lack of literacy skills is now a serious obstacle to earning a living. Since the 1960s, the United States has been transforming from a society that produced goods to a society that produces services. A fourth grade reading level is still the average achieved by Deaf high school graduates. In our society, this constitutes functional illiteracy (Johnson, 1990). Reported achievement levels (Allen, 1986) suggest that the actual reading level of many Hispanic and other multicultural Deaf children may be even lower.

THE GROWTH OF LINGUISTIC DIVERSITY

Linguistically diverse groups make up the largest segment of the multicultural population in this country. Linguistic diversity is narrowly defined by the federal government as ''non-functional English.'' A more encompassing definition includes any person whose native language is a language other than English, regardless of their proficiency in English. The overwhelming majority of linguistically different individuals—about 80 percent—are Spanish speaking (Trueba, 1989).

Schools and programs for the Deaf face an increasingly diverse body of students. Among the Deaf population, Hispanics and Asians/Pacific Islanders are the fastest growing groups. The overall percentage of multicultural Deaf students in programs and schools for the Deaf is now 36 percent. In California, the percentage of multicultural Deaf students increased from 38 percent in 1978–1979 to 61 percent in 1988–1989. (Cohen, Fischgrund, & Redding, in press). In urban schools and programs, and in states such as California, multicultural students are the vast majority. During the 1989–1990 school year, the program for Deaf students, preschool through high school, in the San Francisco Public Schools had only three white students and a majority of Asian/Pacific Islander, Hispanic, and African American students (N. Grant, personal communication, 1990).

In 1978–1979, Hispanics made up 9.4 percent of the total children enrolled in programs for the Deaf (Maestas y Moores & Moores, 1984). Ten years later, the percentage of Hispanic students had risen to 13.1 percent. In the 1988–1989 annual survey conducted by the Center for Assessment and Demographic Studies at Gallaudet University 6,020 of the 46,178 Deaf children reported were Hispanic; that is, they had Spanish surnames or their families spoke Spanish. There are no breakdowns of figures available for Hispanic subgroups, such as Mexican, Puerto Rican, or Spanish-speaking (A. Schildroth, personal communication, July 12, 1990). This population is concentrated in the Northeast and the Southwest, where Hispanics make up 24.5 percent and 40.2 percent respectively of the total school-age Deaf population (Cohen, Fischgrund, & Redding, in press).

The largest Hispanic populations in the United States are found on the coasts, with the vast majority of the Puerto Rican population in the Northeast and Mexicans and Mexican Americans in the Southwest. There is a concentration of Hispanic people in urban areas, which impacts city schools. Other areas with large Hispanic populations are Florida and cities such as Philadelphia, Washington, DC, and Chicago.

The Hispanic Deaf population is concentrated in urban areas. In two to three years, the Hispanic population at Kendall School for the Deaf, on the campus of Gallaudet University, went from a few children to over 25 percent (Jordan, 1990). In Compton, California, near Los Angeles, it is reported that 95 percent of the Deaf children entering school are Hispanic (Gonzales, 1990). At the Horace Mann School for the Deaf in Boston, over 40 percent of the students are Hispanic; meanwhile, the Hispanic population in Boston Public Schools is only 25 percent. By contrast, the California School for the Deaf, in Fremont, one of two state residential schools, only has 19 percent Hispanic students (D. Silberg, personal communication, March 1990)—reflecting the tendency of residential schools to be predominantly white (Cohen, Fischgrund, & Redding, in press).

MEETING THE NEEDS OF HISPANIC DEAF CHILDREN

At the same time that the number of multicultural Deaf children is increasing, there is evidence that educators are not well prepared to meet their needs (Gonzales, 1991). The lack of professionals prepared to work with Hispanic Deaf children was addressed as early as 1981 by the Conference of Educational Administrators Serving the Deaf (CEASD). In a resolution that noted increasing numbers of Hispanic Deaf children and their unique needs, the first recommendation called for the hiring of professionally trained Hispanics. In 1978–1979, the percentage of Hispanic teachers was only 0.6 percent. In the ensuing ten years, this percentage increased to only 1.3 percent (CEASD, 1989). During those same ten years, the population of Hispanic Deaf children increased by two-fifths—from 9.4 percent to 13.1 percent.

Teachers of the Deaf should be aware of the failure of education to succeed with multicultural Deaf students. The earliest reports of the underachievement among Hispanic Deaf students were based on 1973 results of the Stanford Achievement Test–Hearing Impaired (SAT-HI) version (Jensema, 1975). Allen (1986) studied the academic achievement of Deaf students from 1974 to 1983 and found that Hispanic Deaf twelve-year-olds scored significantly lower on reading comprehension tests than did white eight-year-old Deaf children. Furthermore, Allen found that African American and Hispanic Deaf students showed significantly poorer achievement in math and reading comprehension.

There exists clear documentation of Hispanic underachievement in schools for both hearing (Trueba, 1989) and deaf (Allen, 1986; Cohen, Fischgrund, & Redding, in press; Jensema, 1975) children. Hispanic hearing and Deaf children differ from each other in their amount of hearing, their use of Spanish or English at home, and their country of origin and culture. Despite the differences, there are also similarities.

In the school environment, during student–teacher interaction, culture and motivation in achievement affect the success of Hispanic students (Rodriquez, 1989). Hispanic hearing children reportedly function better in a cooperative learning environment than in competitive environments (Triandis, Marin, Lisansky, & Bettancourt, 1985). This approach to teaching and learning puts students in small groups to work together. It puts students in charge for part of the day. There has been an increased call for the implementation of more child-centered, cooperative, and hands-on education for Hispanic children (*Boston Globe*, 1990), including the Deaf (Davila, 1990). This comes in response to both quantitative and qualitative (Bird, 1990) research that shows Hispanic children prefer this type of learning environment.

EDUCATIONAL AND CULTURAL TRADITIONS

When dealing with Deaf children from Spanish-speaking families, schools and staff must recognize that language and culture are inextricably linked. The relationship between language and culture is so deeply entwined that it makes no sense to talk about one without the other (Erting, 1990). Yet when most professionals consider the needs of these families, they may not go much beyond providing an interpreter for the parents and meeting the requirements of Public Law 94-142 by testing a child in his or her primary language. Once a Hispanic deaf child enters school, little may be done by the school to address that child's unique needs as Hispanic and deaf. This is because of lack of information, lack of appropriately trained personnel, lack of materials, and the rapid changes in demographics that many schools are experiencing.

The first contact between family and school may result in cultural conflict. Families and school professionals may have different expectations regarding the role of parent and family, and the role of teacher and school. Spanish-speaking families may want help integrating their child into their culture and community so that the child is not an outsider at home and in the neighborhood. Schools cannot help these families if they do not have bilingual and bicultural staff available that recognize the importance of home and family culture. Not only are cultural and linguistic knowledge important, but also respect and sensitivity.

All hearing parents of deaf children need early intervention and support in order to adjust to the deafness. Unfortunately, some of the most innovative programs are inaccessible to Spanish-speaking families, who may have difficulty getting to the school or clinic because of work hours, transportation difficulties, and lack of child care, as well as linguistic and cultural obstacles (Hatfield, 1990). There may be differences of opinion among those working with hearing parents of deaf children as to the role of Deaf adults in the early intervention process. Parents may differ in their response to Deaf adults. Some professionals believe that parents may be uncomfortable or even frightened by Deaf adults (Cohen, 1990). However, Deaf adults can provide important role models to hearing parents and deaf children. Suggestions to employ Deaf adults from the same culture as the family (B. Seago, personal communication, 1990) may also be difficult to implement. Early intervention requires training and sensitivity to hearing parents, and a person's deafness or ethnicity does not automatically make that person suited to the work. Any early intervention with multicultural families must take into account a variety of factors; for example, cultural and linguistic differences, different perspectives of the school's role and the parent's role in achieving success.

Even in schools with trained staff, Hispanic parents may not be empowered. Bennett (1987), a sociolinguist and a researcher at the Center for Puerto Rican Studies at Hunter College, carried out an intensive two-year ethnographic study of the formal intake process (assessment, programming, placement, and evaluation) of Hispanic deaf preschool children at a school in New York City. In a case study of a middle-class Hispanic mother, Bennett found that, despite the fact that the mother shared the values of the school and had some rapport with the school's professionals, her input was limited. Even though her participation as a parent was guaranteed by law in the individual education plan (IEP) process, this input did not go so far as to allow an open discussion of how the classroom organization, the pedagogy, and the curriculum related to her son's perceived behavior problem.

Furthermore, Bennett found more marginalized Hispanic parents—poorer, less educated, less acculturated—when interviewed, were very critical of the school. However, in their interactions with the staff, these same parents were "passive." Their silence seemed to be a form of resistance to the building of bridges with a school that claimed to want more parent participation. Bennett concluded that this lack of involvement may have served to help Hispanic parents maintain their own cultural integrity.

When hearing parents discover that their child is deaf, they soon must decide, with the advice of various professionals, which type of program and communication they want for their child. This decision often must be made when the parents are still coping with feelings of loss and adjustment to deafness. Often, Hispanic deaf children are identified later than is typical for significant hearing losses and may go unidentified until the child enters daycare, preschool, kindergarten, or even first grade. Many reasons are given for late identification, including lack of Spanish-speaking professionals, lack of access to health care, and lack of parental awareness. However, these explanations are not sufficient. A number of parents who expressed concern that their baby or child was deaf were ignored by their doctors. These parents were told to be patient with their child's developmental delays. Some received no help or diagnosis until they immigrated to the United States. They continue to resent their treatment by medical professionals and feel guilty and upset for years afterwards that they were unable to help their deaf children sooner.

Hispanic families who have immigrated to the United States may have communication philosophies and attitudes toward special education that are different from those which many U.S. schools assume. Most of Latin America still follows a strictly oral tradition. Deaf children coming to U.S. schools from Mexico, Puerto Rico, and the Dominican Republic usually have had an oral education, if they have been in school at all. In underdeveloped countries, universal education may be a right, but it is also a privilege. Children may not be able to go to school even if low cost or free education is available. Although there may be no tuition costs, the lack of money for documents (such as birth certificates), transportation, uniforms, and books keeps children out of school. Deaf children may live in isolated rural locations far from services. Children who are not profoundly deaf may not be appropriately identified or may be denied services. The idea of educating deaf children and children with special needs may be a universal right, but poverty, lack of resources, and resistant attitudes may make it an ideal, not a reality.

Although oral education for the deaf is still common in many underdeveloped countries, the governments of Indonesia (Gunawan, 1990), Malaysia (Omar, 1990), and Zambia (Bwalya, 1990) support total communication programs. This generally is not the case in Latin America, although there are total communication programs in Costa Rica, Panama, Columbia, and Ecuador (G. Delgado, personal communication, November 1990). In Venezuela, education of the deaf has skipped the ''total communication phase'' as a kind of transition from oral education to bilingual education for the deaf.

The Venezuelan Ministry of Education has supported the implementation of the first bilingual program in the Americas (Perez & Sanchez, 1989). Using Deaf adults as assistants in classrooms, the vast majority of schools in the country now use Venezuelan Sign Language as the base for teaching Spanish. Not only are schools under the ministry of education involved. A number of private schools have become involved in the reform of Deaf education (P. Perez, personal communication, July 11, 1989).

In the rest of Latin America, change is slowly occurring. In the Dominican Republic, the move toward total communication in the national school was thwarted by a teachers' strike in 1985 that resulted in the firing of all but one of the staff (Gerner de Garcia, 1990). In Chile, in 1989, a transition to total communication was being planned (Quintela & Ramirez, 1989), and at least one school currently uses this method (Aguad, 1990). In Argentina, research on Argentinian Sign Language (LSA) is empowering the Deaf community and helping to advocate for the use of sign language in the most oral country in Latin America (Massone, 1990).

In the United States, Deaf people have made gains in political power and are increasingly recognized as a community because of the greater visibility of Deaf people as functioning, competent adults. These changes are also beginning in Latin American countries, but the Deaf communities in developing countries still lack the influence in society to change the general view of the Deaf as deficient (Atale-Aguyaro, 1990; Famularo, 1990; Gerner de Garcia, 1990). U.S. schools for the Deaf that work with parents from different cultures must recognize cultural differences in their perception of the Deaf as capable of leading independent and productive lives. In their work with Spanish-speaking families, professionals who strive to promote a cultural view of deafness rather than a pathological one must recognize that differences in experience may lead to differences in expectations. Working with culturally different families requires an understanding of these differences, recognition of their source, and a communication style that does not alienate the family in the process of working to change perceptions and attitudes.

PLACEMENT AND ASSESSMENT CONSIDERATIONS

The issue of placement and assessment of linguistically diverse children is complex, especially for deaf children. The Education of All Handicapped Children Act, Public Law 92-142, passed by Congress in 1975, provided for an appropriate education and nondiscriminatory testing for all children. This law requires that children be tested in their home or native language. It in fact lays the legal foundation for the beginnings of bilingual special education (Baca & Cervantes, 1989).

For too long, multicultural and linguistically diverse children were overrepresented in special education classes—especially in classes for ''learning disabled'' and ''developmentally delayed'' children (Ortiz & Yates, 1983). Three major causes of this overrepresentation were biased assessment practices, examiner bias, and inadequate training of the evaluators. In addition, the ethnic and language background of the evaluators was usually not the same as that of the children whom they were assessing.

A new problem has emerged for Hispanic children, and that is their underrepresentation in some special education classes. These students are being placed in bilingual regular education classes rather than in bilingual special education classes (Baca & Cervantes, 1989). Before the advent of bilingual special education, Spanish-dominant children with special needs had to be placed in a program that met either their linguistic needs or their special needs (Cummins, 1984). This is still the case for many Spanish-dominant deaf children.

Spanish-dominant deaf (hard of hearing as well as profoundly deaf) children may be inappropriately placed if the school for the Deaf has no one prepared to work with this population. Some hard-of-hearing children who are Spanish dominant may be placed in bilingual regular classes. Others may be inappropriately placed in bilingual special education classes for language delayed, learning disabled, or developmentally delayed children. Profoundly deaf Spanish-dominant students are often accepted by schools for the Deaf because their hearing loss precludes their functioning in a bilingual program. Regardless of their ability to perform higher level academic tasks in Spanish, Spanish-dominant deaf students may be forced into an English immersion situation.

LANGUAGE DOMINANCE AND LANGUAGE PROFICIENCY

When a deaf child is from a Spanish-speaking home, questions of language dominance and language proficiency in Spanish, English, and a signed language must be considered. The dominant language should be used for assessing the child, although it is important to know the child's proficiency in Spanish, English, and a signed language in order to plan a program and decide placement. If the child is Spanish dominant, then the evaluator should try to determine the child's expressive and receptive abilities in Spanish (Payan, 1989), as well as assess language proficiency or competence in English.

The first step in the assessment of a deaf child from a Spanish-speaking home should be to determine the dominant language (the term *language dominance* is used when two languages are being compared). The dominant language should be used for all assessments: audiological, psychological, language, and academic. If the child is tested in English and American Sign Language (ASL) only, it may lead to incorrectly labeling the child as having "no language." The child may know some vocabulary and concepts in one language but not both languages. For this reason, the evaluators should be trilingual or assisted by a trilingual person.

Language dominance is often difficult to determine for a deaf child. Most deaf children of hearing parents begin school with no fluency in any language (Johnson, Liddell, & Erting, 1989). Hispanic deaf children from Spanish-speaking homes who begin school in the United States vary in their language preferences. A study by Luetke-Stahlman and Weiner (1984) looked at the language preferences of three preschool deaf children from Spanish-speaking homes. They found that some Hispanic deaf children do best with signed language input alone; others benefit from the use of Spanish paired with signed language. Looking at hearing loss alone was not enough to determine whether a child would benefit from Spanish input.

Deaf children who begin their education in a Spanish-speaking country may be

Spanish dominant. However, programs for the deaf in Spanish-speaking countries vary in quality, and almost all of them are oral.

Some profoundly deaf children who immigrate from those countries read, write, and speak Spanish. Others have learned very little, and both their written and oral skills may be minimal. These children may know very little Spanish and no formal signed language.

There is also a tendency for some children to suppress their knowledge of Spanish in formal testing situations (Lerman & Vila, 1984). If a Spanish-speaking child does not use Spanish in school, then he or she has not gotten the message that that language is valued in that environment. Spanish remains the language of the home. In this situation, only observations in the home and community can help to determine the true language capacity of a Hispanic deaf child.

Determining the language dominance of a Hispanic deaf child is often difficult. Rather than focusing on which language the child knows better, it is more useful to gain insight into what the deaf child knows in each language. Hispanic deaf children may not be dominant in any language, but they may benefit from reinforcement of the home language. Some young Hispanic deaf children use very little language in school—neither Spanish, English, nor signed language. An enrichment program in Spanish has helped improve the previously unintelligible oral Spanish of these children. Once they began to use their Spanish, their other teachers noticed an increase in expressive English and ASL (Gerner de Garcia, 1989).

Assessment should tell us what a child is capable of doing, not inform us only of his or her deficiencies. Standardized assessments should not be the only type of evaluation done. It is essential, especially for deaf children from linguistically different homes, that the assessment be ongoing, dynamic, and naturalistic. Naturalistic or ethnographic assessment methods (described in detail in Cheng, 1987) include observations by teachers and speech and language specialists in the classroom, the school environment, the home, and the community. This type of naturalistic observation and assessment allows the evaluator to see the child's use of communication in context as well as how the child uses language to learn, to grow, and to experience the world.

LIMITATIONS OF FORMAL ASSESSMENT

Culturally different children may not be familiar with formal testing situations (Erickson, Anderson, & Fischgrund, 1983). Children who have recently immigrated to the United States may have little or no prior formal education. Nor do formal assessments provide much information when used with young deaf children, who are unaccustomed to testing situations. Ethnographic and ongoing methods of assessment are crucial for both young students and immigrant children who lack school experience.

A serious limitation of formal testing is that it is decontextualized or context reduced. Deaf children depend on context to access the knowledge they have. Decontextualized tasks can be very unfair to a child with a different cultural background and different experiences (Cheng, 1987). Evaluators who do not share the culture of the child cannot adequately interpret his or her performance. It is difficult to judge whether individual test items are unclear or confusing to a culturally different child. If the evaluator is neither bilingual and bicultural, nor assisted by someone who is, then the results of the evaluation are likely to be biased (Cummins, 1984; Erickson, Anderson, & Fischgrund, 1983; Figueroa, Delgado, & Ruiz, 1984).

If a formal test instrument in Spanish is used, then it is vital that dialectal differences be taken into consideration. Many tests are adapted with a specific Spanish-speaking population in mind. Many are designed using vocabulary common among Mexican Americans—the largest subgroup of Hispanics in the United States. However, from region to region in the United States, and from country to country, dialects of Spanish vary widely. Word lists can be created for specific tests with the help of native speakers who have experience with a variety of Spanish dialects. In the testing situation, the term that one expects the child to know should be used first. If the child does not respond, then an alternative term should be offered. Young children are especially unaccustomed to variations in vocabulary if they lack preschool experience and exposure to varieties of Spanish that differ from their home dialect.

Many instruments widely available for use with English-speaking children have been translated into Spanish. However, the quality of translation varies (Erickson & Omark, 1981; Gelatt & Anderson, 1983). The appropriate use of these Spanish instruments requires more than straightforward administration of a test and subsequent scoring. Norms that exist for English versions of the test often are unavailable for Spanish versions. In testing Hispanic deaf children, Spanish language norms are not applicable. Deaf norms developed for non-Spanish-speaking deaf are not valid either. Formal instruments can be used as a point of reference for individual children and for children of a particular area as a group. Schools can develop local norms and adaptations of formal assessment, based on their Spanish-speaking deaf population, although these too are problematic (Gelatt & Anderson, 1983; Erickson & Omark, 1981).

A TEAM APPROACH TO ASSESSMENT

Despite their limitations, formal instruments are commonly used in assessing Hispanic deaf children. Schools need some type of closed-ended assessment to expedite their intake process and to compare a student with others in the school. A team approach to assessing Hispanic deaf children, preferably involving a native Spanish speaker, is essential.

One possible approach pairs a Spanish-speaking but nonnative evaluator with a native speaker whenever possible. The native speaker acts as the language model, working with the evaluator to present, elicit, and record the child's performance. Although both members speak Spanish, a team approach helps one to complement the other. The two can corroborate to record what the child produces and analyze those productions. A native speaker is better able to understand the nonstandard Spanish and articulation of a Deaf child, as well as regional variations.

A team approach is highly desirable in all assessment situations—language, academic, audiological, psychological—of Deaf children from language-different families. The lack of Spanish-speaking professionals in deafness means that schools and programs for the Deaf should collaborate to assure the most appropriate evaluation of a Hispanic Deaf child. It is important for schools for the Deaf to be in contact with all available community resources and develop a coordinated approach to ensure that Hispanic Deaf children receive the best possible services.

An audiological evaluation by a Spanish-speaking audiologist is often preferable to using an interpreter. In urban areas with large Spanish-speaking populations, it is likely that the school for the Deaf can collaborate with Spanish-speaking professionals. It is also important to know Spanish-speaking professionals who are likely to come in contact with deaf children, because these children might not otherwise be identified. If deaf and hard-of-hearing children are placed in bilingual programs, either regular or special education, then they may not receive the full range of services and support that they need. Spanish-speaking audiologists and speech and language pathologists are valuable contacts for help in identifying deaf children who may not be served adequately.

It may be more difficult to determine the best psychologist to do an assessment of a Spanish-dominant deaf child. Experience with deaf children and good nonverbal communication skills are essential in the psychological evaluation of deaf children. The choice is often between a psychologist experienced with the deaf and a Spanish-speaking psychologist. If the psychologist does not speak Spanish, then it may be difficult to administer fairly even nonverbal portions of tests. Possible solutions include using an interpreter to help a psychologist skilled in evaluating deaf children or using a trilingual teacher of the deaf to assist a Spanish-speaking psychologist. In addition, some of the psychological tests available in Spanish may be less appropriate for deaf children, which again may indicate a need for collaboration. It is important for psychologists working with the deaf and the Hispanic population to familiarize themselves with the best instruments to use with the deaf population that are available in Spanish, such as the WISC–R (Wechsler Intelligence Scale for Children–Revised).

LANGUAGE ASSESSMENT INSTRUMENTS

The Rhode Island Test of Language Comprehension has been translated and adapted for use with Spanish-dominant deaf children (Santiviago, 1981). This test consists of 100 items— 50 simple sentences and 50 complex sentences—that test receptive knowledge of a variety of grammatical structures in Spanish. It can be used with Hispanic Deaf children who are five to six years old and older with receptive language comprehension at the sentence level. There are Deaf norms for the English version of the test, but no norms for the Spanish version. This test is used with children who are Spanish dominant and know ASL. Used this way, it measures the child's receptive language ability in the stronger language. This tests language proficiency and assumes that the child requires Spanish to maximize comprehension.

If a child is trilingual, then this test can be used to determine the extent of the child's knowledge of Spanish, that is, his or her receptive language ability in Spanish. It can be administered orally with the help of a native speaker, without the use of a signed language. Used this way, it measures the child's ability to understand Spanish only through lipreading and auditory input. The test is most appropriately administered orally to children who have a lot of residual hearing and appear to use spoken Spanish functionally with their families. The results then indicate to what extent this child understands simple and complex sentences in oral Spanish. The test is also administered without ASL if the child doesn't know ASL. Administering the test orally helps the evaluator understand to what extent that child has understood the oral-only input at home and in the prior placement.

The Rhode Island Expressive Language Test can be used even though there is no Spanish adaptation. Children are shown pictures—50 in all—which they describe in a sentence. The elicited language is then evaluated for range of vocabulary, sentence structure, and general length of utterances. This assessment is limited because a child may not be motivated to demonstrate his or her full range of expressive abilities in this kind of testing situation. However, if this test is generally used to assess the expressive language of the other deaf students, then it can provide for limited and cautious comparison of the Spanish-dominant deaf students with their deaf peers.

PROGRAMMATIC CONSIDERATIONS

Once assessment is completed, placement and program recommendations must be made. The first decision that must be made is whether placement in a school for the Deaf or a bilingual program is most appropriate. This determination should depend on the resources available in each setting, as well as how easily the needs of the child will be met in any particular setting. American Sign Language (ASL) should not be considered important for the profoundly deaf student only. Many hard-of-hearing Spanish-dominant children can benefit from the receptive use of ASL. The expressive use of ASL may not be a goal for them, but often these students learn to use it to communicate with Deaf peers and staff.

The notion of least restrictive environment has been debated in the field of deafness, with greater focus since the report by the Commission on Education of the Deaf (CED), *Toward Equality*, issued in 1988. For all disabled children, mainstreaming was considered less restrictive than substantially separate education. This notion has been effectively dismantled in the case of deaf children, whose access to communication and to a peer group requires an environment where communication is accessible. This usually means the use of ASL, but an oral classroom for Deaf students would still use communication differently than a classroom for hearing children.

BILINGUAL CLASS PLACEMENTS

Hispanic deaf children in bilingual classrooms often fail to achieve their potential. No matter how moderate their hearing loss, they are often unable to take full advantage of the classroom situation. They may benefit from the use of auditory trainers, but in a regular classroom, this practice has limitations. The deaf student is isolated from normal classroom discourse. All of the limitations and problems that exist for deaf students in regular mainstream classes exist for the Hispanic deaf child in a regular or special education bilingual class.

Bilingual teachers rarely receive support from professionals trained in speech and language or deafness. Teachers are not always informed that they have a student with a hearing loss, or, if it appears on the IEP, they don't know exactly what it means. Sometimes the deaf student's classmates aid in the deception of the teacher, which they perceive as helping the survival of the deaf student. This situation not only leads to academic failure for the deaf student, but it also creates an emotional burden, with the deaf student blaming him or herself for failure, deafness, and the inability to understand. In some cases, the student's failure may be blamed on inconsistent use of amplification—either hearing aids or FM system. However, teachers usually neither have training in how to handle and work with hearing aids, nor understand their limitations. The deaf student bears the burden of failure.

Even with an accommodating and hard-working teacher, the Spanish-speaking deaf child may not have his or her needs met in the bilingual (Spanish–English) program. Deaf children often begin to experience failure at the fourth grade level. This is the point in traditional curricula when children no longer are learning to read, but reading to learn. In such an environment, the deaf child's language deficits begin to catch up with him or her, and the spiral of failure accelerates. Professional support for teacher and student in this situation may help. However, it still may be difficult for the deaf child to realize his or her potential in this setting.

LIMITATIONS OF SCHOOLS FOR THE DEAF

Although most teachers of the Deaf have a background in language acquisition, they often lack training in second language acquisition. Second-language-acquisition theory applies to the education of all Deaf children. It is essential that teachers of the Deaf know more in order to understand the situation of deaf children from homes where a language other than English is used. It is also vital that teachers in the field learn more about second language learning because of the recent development of bilingual and bicultural programs for Deaf students using ASL and English.

Deaf children are seen as children who should learn English as a second language after acquiring ASL as a first language (Hoffmeister, 1990; Johnson, Liddell, & Erting, 1989; Strong, 1988; Supalla, 1990). Deaf children of Deaf parents (DCDP), like hearing children of language different parents, come to school with a first language other than English. Deaf children of hearing parents (DCHP), however, are different from both DCDP and hearing second language learners. Deaf children of hearing parents do not share the language of their parents; they arrive at school with minimal language skills unless their parents provided early comprehensible language input.

In order to evaluate the progress of Spanish-dominant Deaf students, teachers must understand the second-language-acquisition process. Teachers may underestimate the task. The Spanish-dominant student may be learning two new languages at the same time: ASL and English. The usage of these two new languages may differ within the school environment.

Hearing second-language learners often acquire peer-appropriate conversational skills after about two years of exposure to English (Cummins, 1989). In school, ASL is used by Deaf children for face-to-face communication with their Deaf peers. Spoken English may be used by some children with hearing teachers and hearing children. Some deaf students learn to sign fairly rapidly, and others take more time.

For hearing learners, face-to-face competence in communication does not indicate that a second language learner is ready to handle academic tasks in the second language. The level of language proficiency needed for academic learning takes from five to seven years to acquire (Cummins, 1989). In schools for the Deaf, academic content is taught using both English and a version of ASL. Much of the academic content is provided to students through the air. Students' ability to take advantage of signed academic content will depend on the ASL competence of the teacher as well as the use of additional visual and hands-on experience to provide context for the signed content.

LANGUAGE MAINTENANCE

The process of learning two new languages should not mean substituting the new languages for the original language, if one exists. The right of children to maintain and grow in their first language should be asserted also for Deaf children from all linguistic environments. The Massachusetts Department of Education adopted a policy statement on the education of language minority children in June, 1989: "Language and cognitive development . . . should be continually stimulated in both (or all) the languages spoken by the linguistic minority pupils."

A Spanish-literate deaf child should continue to get support and instruction in Spanish while learning English. Such a student may learn a signed language more quickly than hearing children learn conversational English, but his or her academic progress may depend on continued support in Spanish. Competence in ASL doesn't eliminate the importance of reinforcing academic content in Spanish. English as a second language (ESL) classes can help build English vocabulary.

Literacy does not simply depend on knowing static facts. Students must know how to reason, think critically, and gain new information (Literacies Institute, 1989). Teachers may believe, erroneously, that students are functioning because they perform well on the kinds of tasks that merely require the memorization of facts. Schools may have lower expectations of Deaf students (Johnson, Liddell, & Erting, 1989) and of linguistically different students. When schools and teachers fail to provide opportunities for cognitive experimentation and growth, they perpetuate the cycle of illiteracy.

THE HISPANIC DEAF PROGRAM

In Boston, the Hispanic Deaf Program was established in the fall of 1988 at the Horace Mann School for the Deaf, in response to increasing referrals of Spanish-speaking Deaf and hard-of-hearing children. Children who were profoundly deaf and Spanish-language dominant had been accepted previously, but only limited support in Spanish had been available. Children with more moderate losses had remained in bilingual regular and special education programs, due to an inability to serve them in the school for the Deaf.

The Hispanic Deaf Program has three aspects: (1) to provide direct service to Spanish-dominant Deaf and hard-of-hearing students in the school for the Deaf, (2) to provide support and enrichment to Hispanic Deaf students who previously had received only English and ASL, and (3) to do outreach and provide support for Hispanic Deaf students in other Boston public school programs.

The staff consists of a teacher of the Deaf, also certified in bilingual education; a paraprofessional, who is a native speaker of Spanish, with training in deaf education and signed language; and a parent liaison, who is a native speaker. All members of this staff assist with assessments, interpretations, and parent outreach. The teacher works primarily in a resource room, and the paraprofessional provides support in other classrooms. In addition to her direct responsibilities to the Spanish-speaking parents, the Hispanic liaison assists the parent educator for the early intervention program in her work with Spanish-speaking parents. She interprets signed language classes, IEP meetings, and any other meetings involving parents, as well as written information sent from home to school. Her accessibility to parents makes her invaluable, as she is available to parents at all hours by phone.

LITERACY FOR HISPANIC DEAF CHILDREN

Many Deaf students fail to achieve adequate literacy skills by the time that they leave school. A recent proposal for remedying this lack of success is to use a bilingual and bicultural approach to educating Deaf children with ASL as the first language (Johnson, Liddell, & Erting, 1989). The question for Hispanic Deaf children is: Can we expect them to be trilingual or multilingual and biliterate or multiliterate? Children, including deaf children, can become multilingual. They can learn to read multiple languages, as well as to do various kinds of reading.

Ewoldt and Israelite (1990) suggest that, in order to enable deaf students to become literate in English, schools for the Deaf must do more than change the language of instruction from signed English to ASL. The substitution of one language for another is merely a mechanistic approach. In order to succeed with Deaf children, a radical change in philosophy of learning and teaching must occur. This philosophy must include not only providing Deaf children with a first language of ASL, but also using a "holistic" approach to educating deaf children. A holistic approach would empower them not only by using their language, ASL, but also by making learning and teaching child centered rather than teacher centered.

There are a variety of names for this holistic approach, such as "whole language," "whole learning," "humanistic education," and "cooperative learning." Early pioneers in using holistic approaches include Sylvia Ashton-Warner's work with Maori children in New Zealand, Paulo Freire's adult education efforts in Brazil, and Celeste Freinet's unique methods with children in the French Alps. This approach has been used successfully with Spanish-speaking children, as described by Carolyn Bird in *Becoming a Whole Language School* (1989) and Carole Edelsky in *Writing in a Bilingual Program—Habia Una Vez.* (1986). Alma Flor Ada describes the use of children's literature in Spanish in *A Magical Encounter* (1990).

Holistic education is not a method, but a philosophical orientation to children and learning. It is characterized by teachers giving up some control to their students and taking risks. It values the individual child and assumes that every child is a learner. It builds on success rather than failure, because children who succeed want to go on learning. In contrast, children who experience failure early in their education feel defeated, incapable of learning, and without worth.

A reason why teacher-centered, traditional methods have dominated education of the deaf may be related to "hearing centeredness." Maxwell described the way in which teachers of the Deaf structure their lessons so that they will not have to understand "free communication" addressed to them by the students. It is not uncommon for hearing teachers to have difficulty understanding their Deaf students (Maxwell, 1985). If teaching is formulated with the teacher seen as the transmitter of knowledge, then the teacher's only job is to put information out there. The unsuccessful student is seen as the one who has failed, not the teacher.

There are many teachers who recognize a need to change. They know that perhaps if they presented lessons in another way, their students would learn. These teachers individualize lessons, prepare separate tests for different children, and vary their language, yet still have only limited success. Because teachers are required to rely on standardized tests to measure the student progress through a prescribed curriculum, they are unable to make use of the various experiences and interests that individual children bring with them to school. Teachers may try to accommodate individual differences by varying how they teach, but they may not be allowed much latitude to do this.

A LITERATURE-BASED APPROACH

In the past few years there has been growing recognition of the value of using literature with children in school. Some school systems and states, such as California, have endorsed the central role of children's literature in teaching reading. It is recognized that literature provides children the opportunity to discover worlds they may never see and voices they do not hear in their everyday life. It embraces the use of a complete book over the reduction of stories often encountered in basal reading. It recognizes the individual preferences, interests, and experiences of children by allowing them the freedom to read about what interests them rather than the predetermined content of the basal reader.

The use of multicultural literature is one means of ensuring that all children are included. It is vitally important that multicultural children see themselves and their experiences reflected in school. A child's sense of self-esteem is diminished if the child doesn't see familiar images in books and in the school environment. What is left unsaid or untapped can cause the greatest psychological damage to multicultural students (Kokkino, 1990).

Deaf children need guidance in order to discover the world of children's books. They may not have the experience of reading with a family member before coming to school. They may not know classic stories such as "Goldilocks and the Three Bears." In order to prepare Deaf children for reading, they should be exposed to a variety of stories in many forms. Teachers may read to them. Deaf adults may tell them stories. Stories may be acted out. There are many quality videotapes of classic fairy tales, in both ASL and signed English versions. All of these experiences are a part of literacy development (see Strong, 1988, for an example of a bilingual ASL–English approach).

Experiences for Hispanic Deaf children may include a reading class and enrichment in Spanish, as well as the introduction of traditional stories, poems, and songs in ASL. The use of literature that portrays life in the Hispanic culture is especially important. This literature may be in either English or Spanish.

Whole language approaches often use songs and poetry to awaken children's interest in reading. The rhythm and regularity of the verses help hearing children to "read" versions of the song or poem often written by the teacher in chart form. With some adaptation, Hispanic poetry and songs may be used with Hispanic Deaf children (see the resource list at the end of this chapter). Some hard-of-hearing children from Spanish-speaking homes enjoy learning to sing simple songs in Spanish. This is an enjoyable vehicle for developing Spanish language as well as teaching songs familiar within the community. The songs should be written on charts and accompanied by illustrations to aid comprehension. Even children who are not yet reading benefit from the exposure to printed Spanish. It adds to their metalinguistic awareness and prepares them for potentially becoming biliterate in English and Spanish.

In the Hispanic Deaf Program, children who read Spanish, but not English, have reading instruction in Spanish. These children began their education in either a Spanish-speaking country or a bilingual program in the mainland United States. In introducing Hispanic Deaf children to English, it is important to use a variety of approaches that allow them to continue growing in Spanish literacy skills. One approach is to read aloud to students in English. When done with a group, one adult reads and another interprets. Students who are hard of hearing often choose to follow the text in a book, although some prefer to alternate between following the text and watching the signed interpretation. Deaf students follow the interpreter. Once the students understand the text after hearing or seeing it, they can use the text to find specific information to back up their answers to teacher questions.

Although there are many materials available in Spanish, there are still many more available in English. Students are never too old to "listen" to stories. Even high school teachers read to students with good results. Reading to Hispanic Deaf students in English allows them to be exposed to books that may be too difficult for them to read independently. It allows them to encounter something that their English-literate peers are reading. It also provides access to books about their experiences as Hispanics that may be available only in English.

This exposure produces unexpected but positive results. For example, a story entitled "The Christmas Secret," about a Puerto Rican mother and her two sons in New York, was read to a fifth grader. Soon after beginning the story, the child asked why the book was written in English and who had written it. When she learned that the author was not Hispanic, she asked, "Why would this lady want to write about us?" In this case, the fact that the experience of a Puerto Rican family was something an Anglo would write about made this girl realize that urban and poor Puerto Ricans, like herself, were not invisible.

Some books, such as Nicolasa Mohr's stories of Puerto Rican girls in New York are available only in English. Reading Mohr's stories "Felita" and "Coming Home" gives Puerto Rican children the message that they are of two languages and two cultures. Other stories, such as M. Stanek's "Speak English for My Mom," allow children to share their experiences. Some hard-of-hearing children do interpret for their parents—from ASL to Spanish, or from Spanish to English. Reading this story can lead students to share their own experiences in dealing with three languages.

Children who speak Spanish at home benefit from enrichment with books in Spanish. The fairy tales they read with their class are reinforced in the resource room in Spanish. This allows the parallel development of vocabulary and language in both English and Spanish. These children are also often exposed to ASL versions of fairy tales, giving them a true trilingual approach. Many children's books are now available in Spanish. By letting the regular classroom teacher know that stories such as "Where the Wild Things Are," "Corduroy," and "The Very Hungry Caterpillar" are available in Spanish, coordinated approaches are worked out. Making these books available in Spanish to parents also helps establish reading at home.

Deaf children can develop literacy in both Spanish and English. If they enter the school for the Deaf in preschool, then English literacy is the goal from the beginning. However, no one, including the deaf child, has to be taught to read more than once. Once a child knows how to decode print, that child can decode print in other languages by transferring what he or she already knows to the other language. This makes it possible for any child, deaf or hearing, to become biliterate. Hispanic Deaf children also feel empowered as they realize that the language they use at home is also something that they can read.

One Hispanic Deaf ten-year-old came to understand the relationship between English and Spanish, in that both languages are written and spoken, when he read a story in English about a little boy who spoke only Spanish (''My Dog Is Lost,'' by Ezra Jack Keats). He exclaimed after the story was read to his class, ''You mean what my mother talks is in a book!'' This new metalinguistic awareness enabled him to go on to learn to read and write simple Spanish. The approach used to foster literacy in Spanish was to read simple Spanish-language books to him as practice so that he could read the book at home to his younger siblings. After he discovered that he could read Spanish, he began writing. He wrote on the computer, dictating initially. As he realized he knew how to write more and more words, he did most of the writing himself with help in spelling.

CONCLUSION

As demographic changes affect more and more schools for the Deaf, it will be vital that teachers accept the challenge of learning new methods, using new materials, and understanding cultures that differ from their own. If multicultural Deaf children are going to have successful school experiences, then their schools must adapt to them. Schools must recognize the cultural and social experience that each child brings. Most of all, in order for multicultural children to learn, all teachers must feel responsible for all children. Special programs, such as programs for Hispanic Deaf children, provide a partial solution. Schools for the Deaf can better meet the needs of the growing number of Hispanic Deaf children by doing the following: (1) promoting a positive attitude toward diversity at all levels of the school by embracing a multicultural curriculum; (2) providing inservice and other training opportunities for staff on topics such as bilingual education, English as a Second Language, multicultural literature, cross-cultural communication, Spanish for educators, and whole language; and (3) working to involve and empower parents of Hispanic deaf children by providing ASL classes taught in Spanish and setting up parent groups for Spanish-speaking families. By involving all staff and the linguistically different parents, a partnership is formed in which all participants become responsible for the education of Hispanic Deaf children.

BIBLIOGRAPHY

Aguad, J. A. (1990, July 31). *The participation of Chilean Deaf people in society.* Paper presented at the International Congress on Education of the Deaf, Rochester, NY.

Allen, T. E. (1986). Patterns of academic achievement among hearing impaired students: 1974–1983. In A. Schildroth & M. Karchmer (Eds.), *Deaf children in America.* San Diego: College Hill.

Allphin, L. (1990, Fall). Researcher Sam Supalla says we must protect Deaf kids' access to ASL. San Leandro, CA: DCARA (Deaf Counseling Advocacy and Referral Agency) newsletter.

Anderson, P. (1990, July 17). Study finds Hispanics least educated. *Boston Globe,* p. 69.

Andrews, J., & Gonzales, R. (1991, July). *Training Hispanic, Afro-American and Asian Americans to work with minority hearing-impaired children.* Paper presented at the convention of American Instructors of the Deaf, New Orleans, LA.

Atala-Aguyaro, J. (1990, August). *The participation of Chilean Deaf people in the hearing community.* Paper presented at the International Congress on Education of the Deaf, Rochester, NY.

Baca, L. M., & Cervantes, H. (1989). *The bilingual special education interface.* Columbus, OH: Charles E. Merrill.

Bennett, A. (1987). *Schooling the different: Ethnographic case studies of Hispanic deaf children's initiation into formal schooling.* Final report to the Office of Special Education and Rehabilitation. Washington, DC: U.S. Department of Education.

Bennett, A. (1988). Gateways to powerlessness: Incorporating Hispanic Deaf children and families into formal schooling. *Disability and Society, 3,* 119–151.

Bird, L. B. (1989). *Becoming a whole language school: The Fair Oaks story.* Katonah, NY: Richard Owens.

Bwalya, A. L. (1990, August). *Communication for the deaf in Zambia.* Paper presented at the International Congress on Education of the Deaf, Rochester, NY.

CEASD (Conference of Educational Administrators Serving the Deaf). (1989). *National survey of teachers of the deaf.* Unpublished paper. Gallaudet College, Washington, DC.

Center for Assessment and Demographic Study. (1989). Annual survey. Washington, DC: Gallaudet College.

Cheng, L. (1987). *Assessing Asian language performance: Guidelines for evaluating limited-English proficient students.* Rockville, MD: Aspen.

Cohen, O. (1990, August). *Students from culturally and ethnically diverse backgrounds.* Panel at the International Congress on Education of the Deaf, Rochester, NY.

Cohen, O., Fischgrund, J., & Redding, R. (1990). Deaf children from ethnic, linguistic and racial minority backgrounds: An overview. *American Annals of the Deaf, 135,* 67–73.

Commission on Education of the Deaf. (1988). *Toward equality: Education of the Deaf.* Report to the President and Congress of the United States.

Cummins, J. (1984). *Bilingualism and special education: Issues in assessment and pedagogy.* San Diego: College Hill.

Cummins, J. (1989). *Empowering minority students.* Sacramento, CA: California Association for Bilingual Education.

Davila, R. (1990, April). *The Hispanic-American child and the school experience.* Presentation at Multicultural Deaf Children: Is the System Meeting Their Needs? San Diego State University, San Diego, CA.

Edelsky, C. (1986). *Writing in a bilingual program.* Norwood, NJ: Ablex.

Erickson, J. D., Anderson, M. P., & Fischgrund, J. (1983). General considerations in assessment. In J. Gelatt & M. P. Anderson (Eds.), *Bilingual language learning system.* Rockville, MD: American Speech and Language Association.

Erickson, J. D., & Omark, D. R. (1981). *Communication assessment of the bilingual bicultural child.* Baltimore: University Park.

Erting, C. (1990, July). Plenary session, American Society for Deaf Children Convention, Vancouver, British Columbia.

Ewolt, C., & Israelite, N. (1990, August). *Holistic perspectives on bilingual-bicultural education for the deaf.* Paper presented at a meeting of the International Congress on Education of the Deaf, Rochester, NY.

Famularo, R. (1990, July). *Conscience and promotion of the deaf community.* Paper presented at Deaf Way, Washington, DC.

Figueroa, R., Delgado, G., & Ruiz, N. (1984). Assessment of Hispanic children: Implications for Hispanic hearing-impaired children. In G. Delgado (Ed.), *The Hispanic Deaf.* Washington, DC: Gallaudet College.

Flor Ada, A. (1990). *A magical encounter*. Compton, CA: Santillana.

Gelatt, J., & Anderson, M. P. (Eds.). (1983). *Bilingual language learning system*. Rockville, MD: American Speech and Language Association.

Gerner de Garcia, B. (1989, June). *Educating Spanish-dominant hearing-impaired children*. Paper presented at the Conference of the American Instructors of the Deaf Convention, San Diego, CA.

Gerner de Garcia, B. (1990). The emerging Deaf community in the Dominican Republic: An ethnographic study. In C. Lucas (Ed.), *Sign language research: Theoretical issues*. Washington, DC: Gallaudet College.

Grant, J. (1984). Teachers of Hispanic hearing-impaired children. In G. Delgado (Ed.), *The Hispanic Deaf*. Washington, DC: Gallaudet College.

Gunawan, I. A. (1990, August). *Plans to develop a sign language system as part of a total communication program in an Indonesian school for the Deaf*. Paper presented at the International Congress on Education of the Deaf, Rochester, NY.

Gonzales, M. (April, 1990). Personal communication.

Hatfield, N. (1990, July). *Unlocking the curriculum: One parent–infant program's search for keys*. Paper presented at the American Society for Deaf Children Convention, Vancouver, British Columbia.

Hoffmeister, R. (1990). ASL and its implications for education. In H. Bornstein (Ed.), *Manual communication: Implications for education*. Washington, DC: Gallaudet College.

Jensema, C. (1975). *The relationship between academic achievement and the demographic characteristics of hearing impaired youth*. Washington, DC: Gallaudet College Office of Demographic Studies.

Johnson, R. (1990, July), Plenary session, American Society for Deaf Children Convention, Vancouver, British Columbia.

Johnson, R., Liddell, S., & Erting, C. (1989). *Unlocking the curriculum: Principles for achieving access in Deaf education*. Gallaudet Research Institute working paper. Washington, DC: Gallaudet College.

Jordan, I. K. (1990, July). Pre-convention lecture. American Society for Deaf Children Convention, Vancouver, British Columbia.

Kokkino, E. (1990, March). *Literature and the education of language minority students: An alternative*. Paper presented at conference of Teaching English to Speakers of Other Languages (TESOL), San Francisco.

Lerman, A., & Vila, C. (1984). A model for school services to Hispanic hearing-impaired students and their families. In G. Delgado (Ed.), *The Hispanic Deaf* (pp. 38–56). Washington, DC: Gallaudet College.

Literacies Institute (September, 1989). *The Literacies Institute: Its mission, activities and perspective on literacy (Technical Report No. 1)*. Newton, MA: Education Development Center, Inc.

Luetke-Stahlman, B., & Weiner, F. (1984). Language and/or system assessment for Spanish/Deaf preschoolers. In G. Delgado (Ed.), *The Hispanic Deaf*. Washington, DC: Gallaudet College.

Maestra Y Moores, J., & Moores, D. (1984). The status of Hispanics in special education. In G. Delgado (Ed.), *The Hispanic Deaf*. Washington, DC: Gallaudet College.

Massachusetts Department of Education. (1989). Guidelines for the education of deaf and hard-of-hearing students. Quincy, MA: Author.

Massone, M. I. (1990). News from Argentina. *Signpost—The Newsletter of the International Sign Linguistics Association*, No. 3.

Maxwell, M. (1985). Ethnography and the education of deaf children. *Sign Language Studies, 47*, 97–108.

Omar, M. (1990, July 30). *Current trends in special education provisions for the deaf in Malaysia*. Paper presented at the International Congress on Education of the Deaf, Rochester, NY.

Ortiz, A., & Yates, J. R. (1983). Incidence of exceptionality among Hispanics: Implications for manpower planning. *NABE Journal, 7*, 41–54.

Orum, L. (1986). *The education of Hispanics: Status and implications*. Washington, DC: National Council of La Raza.

Payan, R. (1989). Language assessment of the bilingual exceptional child. In L. Baca & H. Cervantes (Eds), *The bilingual special education interface*. Columbus, OH: Charles E. Merrill.

Perez, C., & Sanchez, C. (1989, July). *Recent advances in Deaf education in Venezuela*. Paper presented at Deaf Way, Washington, DC.

Quintela, D. A., & Ramirez, I. C. (1989, July). *The present status and future direction of research on Chilean sign language*. Paper presented at Deaf Way, Washington, DC.

Rodriquez, C. (1989). *Puerto Ricans: Born in the U.S.A*. Boston: Unwin Hyman.

Santiviago, M. (1981). *The Rhode Island Test of Language Comprehension: Spanish version*. Unpublished manuscript. Rhode Island School for the Deaf, Providence.

Strong, M. (1988). *Language, learning and deafness*. New York: Cambridge University.

Triandis, H., Marin, G., Lisansky, J., & Bettancourt, H. (1985). Simpatica as a cultural script of Hispanics. *Journal of Personal Social Psychology*.

Trueba, H. (1989). *Raising silent voices—Educating the linguistic minorities for the 21st century*. Cambridge, MA: Newbury House.

RESOURCES FOR TEACHERS

Suggested Readings

Culture and History

Lopez, A. (1987). *Dona Licha's Island: Modern colonialism in Puerto Rico*. Boston: South End.

Orum, L. (1986). *The education of Hispanics: Status and implications*. Washington, DC: National Council of La Raza.

Oster, P. (1989). *The Mexicans: A personal portrait of a people*. New York: Harper & Row.

Rivera, E. (1982). *Family installments: Memories of growing up Hispanic*. New York: Penguin Books.

Rodriquez, C. (1989). *Puerto Ricans: Born in the USA*. Boston: Unwin Hyman.

Bilingual Special Education

Baca, L., & Cervantes, H. (Eds.). (1989). *The Bilingual Special Education Interface* (2nd ed.). Columbus, OH: Charles E. Merrill.

Cummins, J. (1984). *Bilingualism and special education: Issues in assessment*. San Diego: College-Hill.

Delgado, G. (Ed.). (1984). *The Hispanic Deaf: Issues and challenges for bilingual special education*. Washington, DC: Gallaudet College.

Erickson, J., & Omark, D. (Eds.). (1981). *Communication assessment of the bilingual bicultural child*. Baltimore: University Park.

Gelatt, J., & Anderson, M. P. (Eds.). (1983). *Bilingual language learning system*. Rockville, MD: American Speech–Language–Hearing Association.

Linguistic Diversity

Cummins, J. (1989). *Empowering minority students*. San Diego, CA: California Association for Bilingual Education. (Available through Dormac.)

Trueba, H. (Ed.). (1987). *Success or failure? Learning and the language minority student*. Cambridge, MA: Newbury House.

Trueba, H. (1989). *Raising silent voices: Educating the linguistic minorities for the 21st century.* Cambridge, MA: Newbury House.

Williams, J. P., & Snipper, G. C. (1990). *Literacy and bilingualism.* White Plains, NY: Longman.

Using Whole Language and Literature Based Approaches

Allen, A. A. (Ed.). (1987). *Library services for Hispanic children: A guide for public and school libraries.* Phoenix, AZ: Oryx.

Bird, L. (1989). *Becoming a whole language school: The Fair Oaks story.* Katonah, NY: Richard Owens.

Costigan, S., Munoz, C., Porter, M., & Quintana, J. (1989). *El Sabelotodo: The resource book for bilingual education.* Carmel, CA: Hampton Brown.

Edelsky, C. (1986). *Writing in a bilingual program: Habia una vez.* Norwood, NJ: Ablex.

Flor Ada, A. (1990). *A magical encounter: Spanish-language children's literature in the classroom.* Compton, CA: Santillana.

Heard-Taylor. (1990). *Whole language strategies for ESL students.* San Diego, CA: Dormac.

Hudelson, S. (1989). *Write on: Children writing in ESL.* Englewood, Cliffs, NJ: Prentice-Hall.

Navarez, S., Mireles, R., & Ramirez, N. (1990). *Experiences with literature: A thematic whole languge model for the K–3 bilingual classroom.* Reading, MA: Addison-Wesley.

Children's Literature in English about Hispanics

*Mexican or Mexican American focus
**Puerto Rican focus

Kindergarten through Third Grade

Belpre, P. (1969). *Ote.* New York: Pantheon.

Belpre, P. (1969). *Santiago.* New York: Frederick Warne. Grades 1–4.

*Bierhorst, J. (1984). *Spirit child: A story of the nativity.* Translated from the Aztec. New York: Mulberry Books. Grades K–5.

Bunting, E. (1988). *How many days to America: A Thanksgiving story.* New York: Clarion Books. Grades 3–5.

Ets, M. H. (1959). *Nine days to Christmas.* New York: Viking. Grades K–2.

Ets, M. H. (1987). *Gilberto and the wind.* New York: Puffin Books. Grades K–1.

**Keats, E. J. (1960). *My dog is lost.* New York: Crowell. Grades K–3.

Martel, C. (1976). *Yagua days.* New York: Dial. Grades K–3.

Sonneburn, R. (1987). *Friday night is papa night.* NY: Puffin Books. Grades K–3.

*Tomperts, A. (1988). *The silver whistle.* New York: Macmillan. Grades 2–5.

Grade Three and Up

Cisneros, S. (1985). *The house on Mango Street.* Houston: Arte Publico.

Cobb, V. (1989). *This place is high.* New York: Walker.

Cobb, V. (1989). *This place is wet.* New York: Walker.

Ekare, E. (1985). *The streets are free* (Kurasa, Trans.). Toronto: Annick.

Lexan, J. (1963). *The Christmas secret (Jose's Christmas secret).* Jefferson City, MO: Scholastic. Grades 3–5.

Mohr, N. (1986). *El Bronx remembered: A novella and stories.* Houston: Arte Publico. Grade 6 and up.

Mohr, N. (1986). *Nilda.* Houston: Arte Publico.

Mohr, N. (1989). *Going home.* New York: Bantam. Grade 4 and up.

Mohr, N. (1990). *Felita.* New York: Bantam. (Original work published 1970.) Grade 4 and up.

Stanek, M. (1989). *I speak English for my mom.* Whitman. Grade 3 and up.

Poetry and Songs in English or Spanish
Aron, E. (1988). *Cantame en Espanol*. Carmel, CA: Hampton Brown. Grades K–3.
**Delacre, L. (1989). *Arroz con leche: Popular songs and rhymes from Latin America*. New York: Scholastic. Grades K–3.
**Delacre, L. (1990). *Las Navidades: Popular Christmas songs from Latin America*. New York: Scholastic. Grades K–5.
Cronan, M., & Mahoney, J. (1985). *Teach me Spanish*. Minneapolis: Teach Me Tapes (P.O.Box 35544, Minneapolis, MN 55435). Grades 1–4.
Cronan, M., & Mahoney, J. (1989). *Teach me more Spanish*. Minneapolis: Teach Me Tapes. Grades 1–5.
*Griego, M., Bucks, B., Gilbert, S., & Kimball, L. (1981). *Tortillitas para mama and other nursery rhymes: Spanish and English*. New York: Holt, Rinehart & Winston. Grades K–2.
Montanez, M. (1981). *Canciones de mi isla: Songs from my island* and *Juegos de mi isla: Games from my island*. New York: A.R.T.S. (32 Market Street, New York, NY 10002; cassette available from same address). Grades K–2.
Navarez, S., Mireles, R., & Ramirez, N. (1990). *Experiences with literature: A thematic whole language model for the K–3 bilingual classroom*. Reading, MA: Addison-Wesley.

Materials

Addison-Wesley Publishing Company
ESL and Bilingual Catalog
Jacob Way
Reading, MA 01867
(800) 447-2226

Children's Press
5440 North Cumberland Avenue
Chicago, IL 60656-1469
(800) 621-1115

DDL Books
6521 NW 87th Avenue
Miami, FL 33166
(800) 635-4276

Dormac
P.O. Box 270459
San Diego, CA 92128-0983
(800) 547-8032

Hampton Brown Books
    for Bilingual Educators
P.O. Box 223220
Carmel, CA 93922

Lectorum
137 West 14th Street
New York, NY 10011
(800) 345-5946

Santillana Publishing
901 West Walnut Street
Compton, CA 90220
(800) 245-8584

Maria Santiviago
(for information on the Rhode Island Test–
    Spanish version)
Coordinator, Hispanic Resource Program
New York School for the Deaf
555 Knollwood Road
White Plains, NY 10603

Mexico and the United States: A Cross-Cultural Perspective on the Education of Deaf Children

Donna Jackson-Maldonado

Language is a symbolic, generative process that does not lend itself easily to formal assessment.

Erickson & Omark (1981, p. 7)

The cultural and economic aspects of life in Mexico that affect the development of Deaf children are described in this chapter. Cross-cultural observations compare educational practices in Mexico and the United States. Valuable information regarding nonbiased assessment is presented. Portions of the data presented were supported by the John B. and Catherine T. MacArthur Foundation Network and the University of California Consortium on Mexico and the United States (UCMEXUS).

Mexico and the United States represent two very different realities. Different languages are spoken in the two countries, and the cultural heritage of each is quite distinct—not to mention differences in economic and political issues. Their educational systems emphasize different values and use very distinct techniques. Despite the many discrepancies, the two countries share a very important border; they also share a very large population. Most of the Hispanic population in the United States is Mexican.

According to the 1980 U.S. census, 6 percent to 7 percent of the U.S. population is Hispanic. If undocumented workers are taken into consideration, then this number could easily reach 10 percent. This is also one of the fastest growing segments of the population, with a growth rate of 61 percent from 1970 to 1980 while the general population grew only 11 percent. One-third of the Hispanic population is under fifteen, and 10 percent of the general U.S. population under five is Hispanic (Maestas y Moores & Moores, 1984; Walker, 1987).

The fact that the Hispanic population, as a whole, is younger than the general population means that very soon there will be more Hispanics in the schools. The representation of this group in the hearing impaired, school-age population is even more significant. The data vary considerably from state to state, but it has been reported that 40 percent of the New York Deaf population and 75 percent of the Texas and California Deaf population is Hispanic (Delgado, 1984; Grant, 1983). Of these, a high percentage are considered to have multiple disabilities. Many times children with more than one disability are misplaced because of misdiagnosis, test bias, or insensibility of the examiners (Baca & Cervantes, 1989; Mercer, 1973; Mercer & Lewis, 1979). This is true in classrooms both for the mentally retarded and learning disabled as well as for the hearing impaired (Delgado, 1984; Grant, 1983). These data have an important meaning for people involved in education in the United States.

This significant population in public school programs for Deaf children requires careful and appropriate assessment that takes into consideration Hispanic cultural differences. It is both a legal issue and a moral one. Children have the right to be placed in the correct educational setting. This requires understanding of their cultural reality and their value system, and knowledge of the language spoken in the home. The specialist needs specific information about the children in order to identify correctly cultural differences that may be projected erroneously as disabilities.

CULTURAL VARIABLES

Many studies have shown that educational achievement in Deaf children depends on the degree of hearing loss, the age of hearing loss detection, the type of schooling, the hearing status of the parents, the attitude of the parents toward their child's impairment, and the language used in the home (Schildroth & Karchmer, 1986). Several reports suggest that Deaf children from homes where American Sign Language (ASL) is the first language are more likely to succeed educationally than other children are. In the same spirit, children from English-speaking homes in the United States are more likely to succeed than are children from homes where languages other than English are spoken. Both of these groups of children received their early education in the home language, be it ASL or English.

Studies have tried to explain achievement in various ethnic groups based solely on language variables, but the fact is that language is only one of many cultural variables that affect the schoolchild. Firstly, the educational process is at least twofold: as seen from the perspective of the child or the teacher. Each part is made up of a complicated set of cultural variables that can affect the flow of the process. There needs to be a state of harmony between both sides in order for learning to take place, and that harmony depends on a balance between teaching and learning strategies, beliefs, and attitudes. It is important for the teacher to understand the whole cultural array of the child in order to adjust his or her own strategies, beliefs, and attitudes to make the "learning machine" work.

The factors that may affect the Hispanic's child's achievement can be seen from two perspectives: one structural and one cultural. First, it must be understood that Hispanics form a homogeneous group on some accounts, but vary considerably on others. Most of the internal differences are more structural than cultural per se. As a group they share some structural characteristics, most specifically a language and an early influence of Spanish culture from the period of the conquest of America in the sixteenth century. This early influence imposed both the Spanish language and Catholicism on a multitude of indigenous cultures, religions, and languages. This has led to a unique identity and solidarity between countries in Latin America. At the same time, these characteristics may mark the Hispanic child in U.S. schools because the child will speak a different language and will not identify so closely with peers from other cultures.

Despite these common aspects, there are other structural characteristics that the group does not share as a whole. Although the majority of the Hispanic population in the United States is of lower income levels, there is a significant group (mostly Cuban and Mexican, but including persons from other Latin American countries) that falls in the highest income scales. Although a majority of the U.S. Hispanic population may be undernourished and have low levels of education and occupation, this higher income group does not share these important aspects. They do not suffer from malnutrition, which, in turn, causes irreversible brain damage. Most parents in the high income group are from higher educational levels, and this too has been shown to affect development (Laosa, 1980). In the higher income groups there is no barrier, in this sense, to achievement.

On the other hand, the educational system that both lower and higher income Hispanic children go through is structurally different in the United States. Teaching methodologies differ because teachers' strategies are different. Put in a cognitive-style dimension, Hispanic teachers stress field-dependent strategies, whereas, traditionally, U.S. teachers stress field-independent strategies (Jackson & Espino, 1983).

The higher income group may be a different ethnic group, but it is not marginal. They most probably have not immigrated for political or economic reasons. They share many cultural traits with their U.S. counterparts both because they have similar access to information from the media and because their life style is the same. Structurally, then, higher income immigrants have two barriers: language and educational style. Through education both barriers will soon disappear. Under situations of assessment, however, they will always be at a disadvantage as compared with English-speaking peers because their mother tongue is different.

Contrary to this small, higher income group, the majority of the Hispanic population not only is structurally different, but also suffers because of cultural variables. In the case of the larger Hispanic group, many cultural variables affect adequate educational assessment and achievement within the classroom situation. Taking into consideration the structural differences, which in themselves are limiting, this group may be seriously affected by the different values, attitudes, and strategies with which they are confronted. This group (and the higher income group, as well), contrary to U.S. standards, is not instilled with the need to compete or succeed educationally. As Delgado-Gaitan (1987) found in interviews of Mexican families regarding attitudes toward schooling, parents want their children to be respectable, to learn a profession, to study, to listen to the teacher, to behave, to earn enough to be able to eat, to learn English, to work, to be happy, to do something useful. This is in opposition to U.S. standards, where children are told to do their best, to be successful, maybe even to be rich. U.S. children are inherently geared to compete at a very young age. It is difficult for a teacher to understand that Hispanic children are taught to listen, not to speak out; to work, not to do their best; to do anything for a friend, and to work in a cooperative mode.

Another cultural characteristic that is important to the Hispanic is physical contact.

People always touch one another. When close contact is not established, it is a sign of distance and difference. Within U.S. classrooms, more and more teachers are told to keep physical contact down because of possible lawsuits. Hispanic children who are not touched, hugged, and talked to close-up may interpret the distance as rejection.

Timing is a definite cultural variable that may influence the teacher's understanding of the child. In Hispanic culture being on time or even early is not necessarily respected. As a group (this definitely is not true for every individual), the pace of life is slow and priority is not placed on promptness. Therefore, when Hispanic children do not return permission slips on time, it may be a cultural issue. Timing is not the only factor that is involved, however. The need to fill out forms for everything is not consistent with Hispanic culture, and many lower income families may not be literate enough to understand the forms. The timing factor may make parents think that they can turn the forms in anytime. In most of Latin America, the telecommunications systems do not work efficiently. This means that most people do not have confidence in the mail or the telephone system, and, by projection, they do not necessarily believe what they see on television. Therefore, Hispanic parents may not think of calling on the phone to verify appointments or send forms by mail.

Deeply rooted in Hispanic culture are different attitudes toward health, death, and fear. The Hispanic does not live fearing death and trying to be secure every step of his life. Children, therefore, are left unattended by U.S. standards, and health problems may not be solved immediately due to economic reasons. Along the same line, precautions in the home are infrequent; excessive hygiene is not a custom; and, although sorrow follows death, life is not spent trying to avoid death. The teacher may meet with unanswered pleas for better personal hygiene and removal of "dangerous" objects. Stories of how children are left alone may be shocking to an Anglo teacher.

Generally stereotypes are different. Children look at McDonald's as a place where Daddy works; shopping is not something that is done on Saturday; not everyone owns a car; not everyone has his own bed, his own toy, or different kinds of clothes. Many times, when teachers mention stereotypic items and the Hispanic children do not react automatically, it may not be that they are slow. It may mean that they just do not understand.

Last but not least, the family is the basic structure of the Hispanic culture. This means that there is an extended family that may live together or at least participate together frequently in social activities. Children are often cared for by siblings. Authority is well established in the adult figure (usually in the father), and many times even formal modes of communication are used when children speak to adults. Children do not speak back to parents. Therefore, if teachers are figures to be seen with respect, it is important that their values and attitudes coincide with those of the parents. When this is not possible, at least respect and knowledge for the parents' culture and values should be shown.

This list of cultural differences is by no means extensive nor complete. It simply gives examples of elements that may cause conflict between teacher values and student values, which in turn may cause dysfunction in the teaching situation. Teachers in U.S. schools use teaching strategies that do not coincide with Hispanic styles (Jackson & Espino, 1983). This in turn may affect the harmony of the classroom, and the Hispanic child may be taken aback and "freeze" or turn off when receiving negative input with regard to cultural traditions (Suarez-Orozco, 1987; Walker, 1987).

All of the above characteristics apply to both the hearing child and the hearing impaired child. There are two structural aspects that need to be underlined when dealing with the Deaf population: the type of schooling that the child received before entering the U.S. school and multilingual considerations. In Mexico, and in most of Latin America, most educational programs for the deaf are auditory/oral or oral only (some programs are called "multisensory methods"). Total communication programs, when available, lack theoretical background. Little information is available about Mexican Sign Language (Bickford, 1989; Jackson-Maldonado, 1979; Smith-Stark, 1986). Teachers have not been fully prepared in total communication methods, and materials are simply "translated" to signed language from oral programs. Very few teachers are even nearly proficient in any form of signed language. The auditory/oral programs are lacking, too, because many children do not have hearing aids. For those who do, the majority are not in working condition (Salomon, Vega, Friedman, Amigo, & Lara, 1991).

Most children cannot benefit from oral programs, because their hearing loss is usually detected well past four years of age. Many remain undetected well into their childhood years, which is past the critical age for language acquisition. Most oral programs are not successful because children's language is contextually dependent and cognitively undemanding (Cummins, 1979). Their speech is usually unintelligible and quite limited in both vocabulary and structure. Their academic achievement is low: Many finish their elementary school years with less than a second-grade reading level. A very small percentage of the deaf population attends private clinics and is mainstreamed. Many teachers are not specialists in education of deaf children. Those who are have been trained mostly using methodologies from the 1950s and earlier, such as the Fitzgerald Key and McGinnis method. It is obvious, from the characteristics described above, that these children will acquire very limited oral linguistic skills. Some children will have access to some form of signed language in the school playground. Many times signed language is acquired late in life through contact with the Deaf community. As a consequence of the limited oral skills and the late acquisition of signed language, the general knowledge of these children will also be impoverished.

Most of the children who have recently arrived from Mexico and enroll in the schools in the United States will have gone through this system or no system at all. Many children will not even have access to an educational program because they do not live in or near a community that has a school for the Deaf. It is no surprise that their limitations will go far beyond the lack of language. The linguistic differences will be very influential on the child's academic achievement, as many studies have shown. When the home language is not the same language used in the school, children are at an academic disadvantage (Cummins, 1989; Omark & Erickson, 1983).

The Hispanic deaf child is in an even harder position because the home language is not the language most spoken in the United States. The language is taught at school, if it is American Sign Language (ASL), is not the main language spoken in the United States, either. If the child becomes oral and learns English, then he or she will have the advantage of learning the language most spoken in the United States. This will not ensure the ability to communicate at home, however. If the child learns ASL, then he or she will be able to communicate with Deaf peers, but, again, not with the family.

Although it may seem optimal for the child to learn English, there is a structural problem. In programs in which English is taught, oral skills are emphasized. This in turn requires a hearing aid in working condition. Many Hispanic families cannot afford hearing aids. It is no wonder that studies comparing Hispanic children's achievement with that of other groups rank Hispanic children so low. They are struggling to learn a language (be it English or ASL) that is not used in the home. The teacher of the Deaf in the United States cannot change this structural educational past or any other of the structural differences that separate this ethnic group. The teacher cannot change the parent's educational level, economic status, level of nutrition, or language. Where the teacher can empower the child is with an understanding of the child's own culture. The teacher must understand that the child who arrives at school with little academic knowledge and language probably does not lack ability, but rather has never had the opportunity to show potential. It therefore is imperative that assessment and treatment be carried out with the utmost care, taking into consideration not only structural differences but also cultural variables. This chapter addresses the issue of assessment in a culturally unbiased context.

LANGUAGE ASSESSMENT

As a result of the growth of bilingual Spanish/English education programs in the 1970s, many English tests were translated (and sometimes adapted) to Spanish, and efforts were made to obtain norming data on various Hispanic populations within the United States. Many, if not most, of these tests were created to determine the language dominance or preference of bilingual children. There are differences between language dominance, language preference, and language proficiency. Both *dominance* and *preference* refer to conditions in which two or more languages are used. In most cases, bilingual tests are assessing dominance of one language over another. This measure implies a comparison of the proficiencies in two or more languages. *Preference* refers to an individual motivation rather than to the proficiency in the language. Language *proficiency* refers to the control of language use and includes all skills (Payan, 1989).

Most of these measures were discrete point tests that only observed a limited part of the child's linguistic capacity and were not directed to the functional use of language (Mattes & Omark, 1984). Most of the tests compared the two languages, English and Spanish, on the basis of linguistic structures. Content validity was not carefully monitored in the Spanish versions; standardization procedures were not always reported or completed; and validation data was lacking (Baca & Cervantes, 1989; Merino & Spencer, 1983).

A careful review of several of the most-used tests in the California schools will show some of these validity and norming issues. Three frequently used tests are the Test of Auditory Comprehension of Language (TACL; Carrow, 1973), the Del Rio Language Screening Test (Toronto, Leverman, Hanna, Rosenzweig, & Maldonado, 1975), and the Screening Test of Spanish Grammar (STSG; Toronto, 1973). Some schools are beginning to use the Prueba de Expresión Oral y Percepción de la Lengua Española (PEOPLE; Mares, 1980). Of these, TACL is a direct translation of the English version and was normed on a small population. It has been reported elsewhere that no norming information is available (Mattes & Omark, 1984).

The fact that all items in both the English and Spanish versions appear in the same order suggests that all adaptations were not taken into account. Syntactic structures are acquired at different rates in different languages. This means that a structure of late acquisition in English may be earlier in Spanish. Consequently, the same syntactic structures should not appear in the same order in a language test.

The Del Rio Language Screening Test assesses both English and Spanish and was normed on children in Texas. PEOPLE—still in its experimental version—is a Spanish language assessment. It has been normed, and validity and reliability measures have been done. The Screening Test of Spanish Grammar is based on an English version, but adapted to Spanish. Norms were obtained on Mexican and Puerto Rican children. Of these tests, only PEOPLE was created for Spanish. The others use English structures as a basis for determining acquisition rates in Spanish. Although norming information is available, this initial error of using English as a basis is carried over to all other tests. It must be noted that in the Del Rio test the authors specify that their items were collected through "brainstorming sessions within the Texas community. PEOPLE used the same technique in a southern California community. Mares (1980) used language specialists, the playground, and classrooms for obtaining items. Nonetheless, no formal study of Spanish was used as a basis for any of the tests.

This problem was addressed by Merino and Spencer (1983), who carefully analyzed five bilingual tests: the Basic Inventory of Natural Language (BINL; Herbert, 1980), the Bahia Oral Language Test (BOLT; Cohen, Cruz, & Bravo, 1977), the Bilingual Syntax Measures I and II (BSM; Burt, Dulay, & Hernandez-Chavez, 1976), the Language Assessment Battery (LAB; Board of Education of the City of New York, 1976), and the Language Assessment Scales I and II (LAS; DeAvila & Duncan, 1981). They considered three types of validity (criterion, content, and construct), four types of reliability (test–retest, interscorer, internal consistency, and inter-examiner), and the population on which the test had been normed. Based on these psychometric criteria, they analyzed the strength of each test.

Of special interest was whether language and cultural differences were considered in the creation of the test. This would be reflected mostly in the content validity measures and in the norming studies. The results of the Merino and Spencer study showed that content validity was not carefully monitored in the Spanish versions of the tests. Rather, the Spanish versions seemed to reproduce the English versions. The few cases that tried to obtain relevant vocabulary samples did not use strict procedures. Therefore, with this initial validity error, the test was applied and norms were obtained that may not truly correspond to the Spanish-speaking child's potential. It may only reflect how the child did as compared with the English version of the test. Of the tests reviewed by Merino and Spencer, none gave adequate or appropriate norming information. Nor were dialectal versions available.

The issue of the effectiveness of language tests should not be limited to an analysis of reliability, validity, and norming. Although the measure may be appropriate in those terms, it is still highly probable that tests contain irrelevant items, culturally irrelevant images or contexts, and, many times, even linguistic errors. The above-mentioned tests may not perceive these important subtleties. Many are so involved in duplicating the English test version that they do not consider structures relevant to the second language—Spanish. Some have included items that are lexically, grammatically, or structurally inappropriate.

One of the most common grammatical misfortunes is the use of passive sentences. Most, if not all of the tests reviewed included assessment of the production or comprehension of passive sentences. As has been stated elsewhere (Jackson-Maldonado, 1988), this type of construction occurs under very limited circumstances in Spanish. The most common type of passive is constructed with a form of the pronominal *se*. This was not the form selected for the language tests.

Another grammatical aspect that is addressed erroneously is the oral command. In the Del Rio test, oral commands consist of structures such as *pones este libro* and *vas a la ventana* instead of using the most correct forms of either the imperative or the subjunctive (for negative commands). The imperative is an early form to be acquired in Spanish, which reinforces the idea that imperatives should be included in sections dedicated to commands.

One of the major issues has been trying to decide which morpheme should be used for isolated verb forms. In English, the progressive has been used based on Roger Brown's studies (1973). In Spanish, the progressive or gerund corresponds to different function and content. It seldom appears isolated, and it is not one of the first morphemes to be acquired (see Jackson-Maldonado, 1988, for an ample discussion of this problem). The use of the third person past or present would be more appropriate. Most tests, however, use the gerund in Spanish. Other tests, such as TACL, use the infinitive form, which is not appropriate for similar linguistic reasons.

Another verb tense that is used somewhat erroneously is the future. Although the grammatical form for the future in Spanish is with the suffix *-ra*, the most commonly used form is *ir* plus verb in infinitive. Tests such as the STSG use the *-ra* form, which may be unfamiliar to children.

Not only have grammatical problems been encountered, but lexical errors are also present. The Del Rio and the Toronto Tests of Receptive Vocabulary (Toronto, 1972) use the word *transportacion*, which is an Anglicism for *transporte*. The Toronto tests use *nutrimiento*, which correctly is *nutricion*; the Del Rio test uses *calefaccion* (heating) to refer to a campfire, *vestuario* (wardrobe) to refer to clothing, and *protegiendo* (protecting) to refer to a soldier. It is only fair to say that there seems to be a bias in the proficiency tests as they consider Spanish structures based on English concepts, and they sometimes fail even to change the order of the elements. A verb form should usually refer to an action, not to an object or person. If linguistic items are not carefully monitored to be lexically, grammatically, and pragmatically appropriate, then the problem is even worse.

Another problem in translating and adapting tests from one language into another is that test materials are seldom transformed. Research has shown that most tests reproduce middle class values (through vocabulary and types of illustrations) and many times include culturally irrelevant materials. These aspects of the tests could have negative effects on the child's ability to relate to the test and, therefore, affect the child's score of communicative ability (Jackson-Maldonado, 1988; Labov, 1972; Walker, 1987).

Most of the tests that have been reviewed present another problem. They measure syntax, vocabulary, and articulation in children K–12. Very few can be used on children as young as three years of age. Two tests, the Prueba de Desarrollo Inicial de Lenguaje (Hresko, Reid, & Hammill, 1982) and Sequenced Inventory of Communication Development (Hedrick, Prather, & Tobin, 1979) cover this age range. Of these, only the first has available norms. It is problematic, however, in that parts of it are direct translations of the English version and more validity information is needed. It also is applicable only to children three years and older; therefore, early communications skills are not assessed. The last test is especially interesting. Its English version was normed on children from four to forty-eight months of age. It includes a range of linguistic behaviors and has been used with diverse language disordered populations. Many of the items that are applicable to infants and young toddlers are done through parental report. Unfortunately, although the test has been adapted to Spanish, norms are not available. Its strength lies in that it is one of the few tests available for very young children. Although the authors report that some items had to be changed for Spanish, some materials were not changed for cultural relevance and norms are not available.

Most of the tests that have been reviewed here share basic methodological and theoretical problems:

1. Very few tests have been created for Spanish, and most are translations with inappropriate adaptations.
2. Little, if any, adequate content-validity development processes exists.
3. Very little norming information is available. Usually English norms are used, as most Spanish items are translations of the English ones.
4. The tests have not been adapted to be culturally and linguistically relevant.
5. Most tests are of language dominance, not proficiency, and they do not deal with complete communicative domains.
6. Most target the school-age population.

When we confront the task of assessing hearing impaired children, many complications arise. Assessment must begin at an early age so that adequate placement and programs can be created. Furthermore, several studies (Figueroa, Delgado, & Ruiz, 1984; Fischgrund, 1984; Grant, 1984; Mattes & Omark, 1984) have shown that hearing impaired children do not test well on instruments created for normal populations. Fischgrund emphasized that the use of psycholinguistic instruments with deaf children ''is a questionable practice because the correlation between the specific abilities tested and those abilities that underlie language acquisition has not been established'' (p. 100). He further asserted that the language tests may not focus on the aspects of language that represent the hearing impaired child's linguistic ability. In the case of children from other cultures, the problem becomes deeper, because they may be unfamiliar with the tasks and the type of testing situation. Furthermore, the available Spanish language instruments are not normed or adapted to the Spanish-speaking population; therefore, this population is not assessed to the best of its ability. To top off this disadvantage, the Hispanic deaf child is not only from a Spanish-speaking family, but is also deaf. If studies are correct, then assessment instruments are even less applicable to this group because of their hearing impairment.

This disadvantage may have several solutions. First of all, there are alternatives to the use of biased tests with the Hispanic population as a whole. Mattes and Omark (1984) have stressed that, although normed referenced and discrete-point language tests have major limitations, an effective and common alternative is to use natural communication samples in conjunction with some form of standardized test (Christensen, 1988; Mattes & Omark, 1984; Prutting, 1983). The natural communication sample is meaningful only in light of language acquisition information. Although there are very few studies about Spanish language acquisition (Clark, 1985; Jackson-Maldonado, 1988; Lopez-Ornat, 1988), the few studies that have been done, along with observations in each community, can provide a basis on which to compare the language sample obtained from the hearing impaired child.

The advantage of a natural communication sample is that ''the assessment of communication in context allows one to examine an individual's communication in terms of its effect on the behavior of the listener'' (Mattes & Omark, 1984, p. 73). It also allows observations of the speaker's behavior alone. This observational procedure is especially pertinent when considering Deaf children in the early stages of language development when little formal language may be present. A natural communication sample, then, allows the observation of all communicative behavior. It is also appropriate for hearing impaired subjects because they are seen in their natural context rather than measured against unfamiliar contexts and situations. The outcome of a descriptive language sample is that the results can be used to create an appropriate language program for the child. If this sample is then contrasted with a comparable measure to ascertain language dominance and proficiency, then a more complete language picture will be available for the teacher to begin instruction at the child's level of language development.

Two procedures have been developed to fulfill both needs: a natural observation format and a scale of language development in Spanish (which is being normed at present). Both have been based on Mexican Spanish. The natural observation guidelines consist of a system for considering contextually relevant features and a list of eighteen *communicative intents*. The model was the outcome of a study of Mexican middle class children observed in the natural home setting in Mexico (Jackson, 1989). The list of intents is based solely on the utterances of Spanish-speaking children. Although the categories resemble, by name, previous English classifications of communicative intents (Bates, 1976; Dore, 1974; Halliday, 1975), many categories had to be redefined or created for Spanish (see Table 6.1). This model is based on observing children in natural situations and registering utterances according to the communicative intent that they represent. It is especially important that no previous English model per se was used to develop the Spanish categorization of utterances. The English models served as theoretical guidelines. Therefore, the model can only be treated with Spanish interpretation of the items.

The second model is a translation and adaptation of the MacArthur Communicative Development Inventory: Infant and Toddler. It is the *Inventario del Desarrollo de las Habilidades Comunicativas* (Jackson-Maldonado & Bates, 1989). In this case, the original English version of the MacArthur inventory was used to develop the Spanish version. Special care was paid to modifying the English version to ensure cultural and linguistic relevance for the Spanish-speaking population in the United States. Modifications of the English version included changing or adding large numbers of words in each category based on Spanish diary studies, language tests, and a few published articles. Most of the grammatical sections of the MacArthur inventory had to be completely modified or made more extensive. In general, the Spanish version contains more words than the English version. The preliminary set of data were obtained from Spanish-speaking families in southern California. The most significant portion of the families were of Mexican origin, although many other Hispanic nationalities were represented.

The data gathering technique was also modified. Most families were recruited through some personal means (church, family, social reunions, and community organizations), rather than through public notices in newspapers, as was done for the English version. Currently, preliminary norms have been obtained for the Spanish inventory (Jackson-Maldonado, Marchman, Thal, & Bates, 1992). They are presented in Figure 6.1 along with norms of the MacArthur Communicative Development Inventories.

As can be observed, the instruments are not mere Spanish versions of a test. They were carefully adapted or developed for the specific purpose of capturing a different language and culture. They represent the two systems for observing very early language development

TABLE 6.1 Spanish Communicative Intents

Code	Definition and Example
PROTOI	*Proto-imperatives* are contextually dependent intentions whose form is nonconventional. They usually are nonverbal, such as gestures or vocalizations. They are requests by nature: an extended hand or "eee" vocalization asking for a ball.
PROTOD	*Proto-declaratives* are also contextually dependent. They are assertions by nature: a point of "aaa" vocalization to show a ball.
DESC	*Descriptions assert,* describe or name: *"mamá," "leche."*
RDESC	*Descriptive responses* answer descriptive requests for information: *Qué es? "pato," Dónde esá? "kita."*
RYESN	*Yes/no responses* answer yes or no to requests for information: *Quieres leche? "ti," Es de Papá? "Papá."*
REQACC	*Requests for action* seek for the hearer to perform an action (nonvolitional): *"abre," "más"* (do more of something).
REQINS	*Instrumental requests* show volitions or exchange: *"dame," "mío"* (wants something).
REQINF	*Requests for information* seek information or confirmation from the hearer: *"Éste?" "Aquí?"*
NEG	*Negations* refute or negate actions or information, or show inexistence: *"no," "nada."*
IMIT	*Imitations* repeat a previous utterance without changing the intention: *ca-ma, "cama," Es de mamá, "Mamá."*
ATENT	*Attention to objects* solicit attention to events or objects: *"mira."*
VOCAT	*Vocatives* seek attention from a hearer: *"Mamá," "Pepe."*
BOUND	*Boundary markers* announce the beginning or end of an utterance: *"a ver...."*
RECOG	*Recognitions* maintain contact in a conversation: *"mhm."*
EXCL	*Exclamations* express emotions such as surprise, effort, pleasure: *"a!," "mm!"*
PROT	*Protests* manifest strong negations or demands: *"MIO!"*
COURT	*Courtesy markers* express politeness: *"gracias," "hola."*
PRACT	*Practices* seek to repeat sounds with the sole objective of vocal exercise: *"tatatitataká..."*

Adapted from D. Jackson, 1989.

that take into account both natural observation with backup data about normal language acquisition and norm-based instrument. As mentioned earlier, natural observation is especially pertinent for assessing hearing impaired children, because the data obtained demonstrate their abilities rather than disabilities.

WHY TWO INSTRUMENTS?

A study was carried out to show the effectiveness of the two aforementioned instruments. Four children with profound or severe to profound bilateral hearing losses were studied. Two of the children were students in the Deaf and Hard of Hearing Infant program in a southern California school. The other two attended a clinic for hearing impaired children in Mexico City. Both children from California used hearing aids and were in programs where

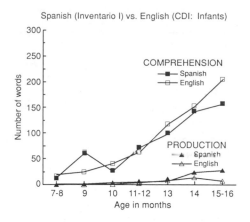

Spanish (Inventario I) vs. English (CDI: Infants)

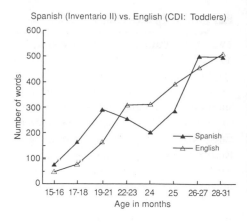

Spanish (Inventario II) vs. English (CDI: Toddlers)

FIGURE 6.1 Median comprehension and production scores of the Spanish and English inventories

SOURCE: D Jackson-Maldonado, V Marchman, D Thal, E Bates, & V Gutiérrez-Clellen. (1992). *Early lexical acquisition in Spanish speaking infants and toddlers.* Unpublished manuscript. Used with permission.

both signed and oral language were used. In contrast, the Mexican children were in a strictly auditory environment. Table 6.2 gives general information about each child.

The children were seen under two conditions: (1) a home visit in which a 30- to 45-minute videotape was made, and (2) a parental report was filled out. In the case of Rosa and Julio, parents filled out a Spanish inventory and the teacher filled out an English inventory. Parents indicated, as well, if the child signed some of the words. In the home visit, children were observed interacting with their parents or friends. They were seen in free play and eating situations with no previous script. The videotapes were transcribed and the Spanish communicative intent checklist was completed.

Frequency and types of utterances were registered. Utterance form was also noted. Vocabulary counts were done on both inventories, and frequencies per word group were registered. Most frequently used words were also noted. Both word counts and types of words were compared against the preliminary Spanish norms.

The data obtained reflect a general panorama of the language of each child. Several tendencies can be noted for each child. Most important, the results demonstrated the strength of using two instruments to describe early language. Several factors may be observed from these case studies: language preference (in Rosa and Julio only), vocabulary types and norms, and communicative ability. Each factor will be addressed in turn.

TABLE 6.2 General Information on Selected Children

Name	Age	Hearing Loss	Program	Language	Residence
Rosa	3.6	sev.-prof.	sign/oral	Spanish/English/ASL	United States
Julio	2.1	sev.	sign/oral	Spanish/English/ASL	United States
Blanca	3.2	sev.-prof.	oral	Spanish	Mexico
Teresa	2.6	prof.	oral	Spanish	Mexico

Language Preference

Two of the children, Rosa and Julio, live in a multilingual situation. Spanish is spoken at home; English and American Sign Language (ASL) are used at school. Rosa's family is learning English and ASL in order to communicate with her. Julio's family does not know English or ASL. Both children present very different language pictures. As Table 6.3 shows, Rosa comprehended a total of 153 signs and produced 48, as reported by the teacher (or produced 167, as reported by her parents; see Table 6.4). The teacher reported no oral English. The parents reported 24 spoken Spanish words. A similar tendency is observed in Rosa's language sample. Of a total of 165 utterances, 74.5 percent were signs, 13.3 percent were oral Spanish, and 7.3 percent were oral English across a variety of communicative intents (see Table 6.5).

Julio, on the other hand, was reported to produce 33 English words and 16 signs (by his teacher) and 113 Spanish words (by his parents). In his language sample, with a total of 73 utterances, 71.2 percent were Spanish words and 11.0 percent were English words. Julio

TABLE 6.3 Number of Words Comprehended and Produced in English and Sign (Teacher Report)

| | Rosa | | | | Julio | | | |
| | Comprehension | | Production | | Comprehension | | Production | |
	EN	SG	EN	SG	EN	SG	EN	SG
Sounds	–	–	–	–	na	na	1	–
Animals	–	15	–	9	na	na	–	–
Vehicles	–	4	–	4	na	na	3	1
Toys	–	3	–	–	na	na	4	–
Food	–	12	–	8	na	na	4	–
Clothing	–	6	–	3	na	na	1	1
Body parts	–	3	–	2	na	na	4	4
Furniture	–	–	–	–	na	na	–	–
Small household items	–	5	–	1	na	na	1	–
Outside	–	6	–	3	na	na	1	1
Places	na	na	na	na	na	na	2	–
People	–	5	–	3	na	na	–	2
Games	–	8	–	5	na	na	4	2
Action	–	21	–	5	na	na	1	3
Descriptive words	–	12	–	3	na	na	7	2
Time	–	–	–	–	na	na	–	–
Pronouns	–	–	–	–	na	na	–	–
Questions	–	2	–	1	na	na	–	–
Prepositions	–	2	–	–	na	na	–	–
Quantifiers	–	1	–	1	na	na	–	–
Helping verbs	na	na	na	na	na	na	–	–
Connectives	na	na	na	na	na	na	–	–
TOTALS	–	153*	–	48			33	16

*The comprehension score is the sum of production and comprehension. Any word reported as produced is considered to be comprehended as well.

TABLE 6.4   Number of Words Comprehended and Produced (Parent Report)

	Rosa		Julio		Blanca		Teresa	
	Comp	*Prod**	*Comp*	*Prod*	*Comp*	*Prod*	*Comp*	*Prod*
Sounds†	−	5	na	6	1	10	−	11
Animals	−	(26)	na	8	−	20	−	19
Vehicles	1	(6)	na	3	−	6	−	5
Food	2	1(11)	na	21	1	27	12	10
Clothing	1	(12)	na	5	2	11	5	3
Body parts	−	(8)	na	9	3	17	5	14
Toys	1	(3)	na	3	1	7	2	4
Small household items	1	2(11)	na	6	−	23	8	5
Furniture	3	(2)	na	5	−	9	4	1
Places	1	(10)	na	1	na	na	na	na
Outside	na	na	na	−	−	13	1	7
People	−	3(8)	na	7	−	10	−	7
Games	−	5(9)	na	10	−	14	4	9
Actions	8	6(25)	na	9	1	44	25	8
Statements	−	−	na	−	1	1	1	−
Descriptions	−	1(22)	na	4	9	20	7	10
Time	−	(1)	na	1	−	3	1	−
Pronouns	−	(2)	na	8	−	5	4	6
Questions	−	(2)	na	−	1	3	−	1
Articles	−	−	na	na	na	na	na	na
Prepositions	−	(1)	na	2	1	2	−	1
Quantifiers	−	1(1)	na	3	−	6	2	3
Locatives	−	(7)	na	2	−	7	1	7
Connectives	na	na	na	−	3	−	−	−
TOTALS	42‡	24(167)	na	113	282‡	258	213‡	131

*Numerals in parentheses denote ASL on the Spanish form.
†Category names and numbers differ on the English and Spanish versions of the Inventory.
‡The Comprehension score is the sum of Production and Comprehension. Any word reported as produced is considered to be comprehended as well. Any word in the Production column is counted in the Comprehension score.

also used 17.8 percent gestures. He used no signs, and most of his English words were imitations.

The data show that, although they are in similar educational settings, Rosa had a marked preference for ASL both in her vocabulary and in her communicative intents, and Julio was predominantly Spanish speaking. It must be noted, too, that Rosa's parents made an effort to learn English and ASL and used them to communicate with her, whereas Julio's family used Spanish only. This information is important in considering educational programs for both children, as will be discussed further on.

Vocabulary Types and Norms

Through the language inventories, different kinds of information may be obtained: word class preference, language styles, relative developmental lags, and specific word frequencies. Results from the inventories may also be compared with language samples in order to obtain more qualitative information. Tables 6.3 and 6.4 show frequencies of words per word class for each child. Total number of words are also given.

If the total word frequencies for each child are compared with the preliminary

TABLE 6.5 Percentage of Utterances

Communicative Intent*	Rosa				Julio				Blanca		Teresa	
	NV	*EN*	*SP*	*SG*	*NV*	*EN*	*SP*	*SG*	*NV*	*SP*	*NV*	*SP*
PROTOI	2.4		4.8		16.4		5.5		4.5		2.6	.6
PROTOD	2.4		4.2		1.4				11.5		2.3	2.0
DESC			3.6	31.0		1.4	15.0			19.5		20.0
RDESC		1.2		9.1			6.8			16.7		7.4
RYESN			.6	.6			2.7			6.3		3.8
REQACC				3.0			5.5			4.5		3
REQINS		.6		4.8			5.5			8.0		3.2
REQINF		.6		3.6						2.0		.6
NEG		3.0		2.0			1.4			5.2		1.3
IMIT		.6		16.3		9.6	27.4			12.1		46.1
ATENT		1.2		.6						1.0		.3
VOCAT				1.2						2.0		
BOUND										2.0		1.3
RECOG				.6						1.0		
EXCL				.6						2.0		3.5
PROT		.6										.3
COURT		.6		.6			1.4			.7		2.0
PRACT												2.3
Total Percentages	4.8	8.4	13.2	74.0	17.8	11.0	71.2		16.0	83.0	4.9	95.2
Total Utterances		165				73				287		310

Key: NV, Nonverbal; EN, English; SP, Spanish; SG, Sign.
*Communicative intents are defined in Table 6.1.

inventory norms of hearing children (Fig. 6.1), it can be readily observed that all subjects fall well behind their hearing peers. Rosa produced 167 English signs, which falls within the range of a nineteen-month-old. In Spanish, she produced 24 words (fourteen-month level). She also comprehended 153 English signs (fifteen-month level). She comprehended only 42 Spanish words (nine-month level).

Julio produced 113 Spanish words, which corresponds to an eighteen-month level. He was reported to produce 16 English signs (fourteen-month level). His oral English production was 33 words (fifteen-month level). Only production scores are available for Julio because the Toddler forms were used and they do not include comprehension. Blanca produced 258 Spanish words (twenty-four-month level) and comprehended 282 (fifteen-month level). Teresa produced 131 Spanish words (eighteen-month level) and comprehended 213 (fifteen-month level).

It might appear that Teresa was doing quite well, considering her hearing loss, when only the inventory measure is taken into account. But if this is compared with her language sample, which shows three times more imitations than any other communicative intent, then it is questionable that the inventory alone could describe her true communicative ability. It is most probable that Teresa's parents considered parroting to be language and therefore reported any word that the child could imitate as known. Therefore, although Teresa did not lag behind her hearing peers drastically, it is likely that most of her reported language is unspontaneous. This example shows the importance of using both measures before making conclusions about a child's language.

Frequency of total words alone only illustrates how the child functions as compared with hearing peers. For therapeutic purposes, a more qualitative description of vocabulary types is necessary. A word class frequency gives a more complete picture of what kind of language the child uses. As Tables 6.3 and 6.4 show, each child showed preference for certain word groups. The general panorama of word classes per child is quite similar to the distribution shown by hearing children. That is, most children show lower frequency in function word classes.

The preliminary norming study also has shown that certain children have tendencies for certain types of words. Some children use more nouns; others use more functional words. Hispanic children also show high frequencies in game routines, and similar tendencies can be observed in these four children. All four presented high frequencies in most noun classes: animals, toys, body parts, food, qualities, people. Games and routines also ranked high, and both Rosa and Blanca had high frequencies of action words.

Specifically, the word class description gave important information about weak areas in each child as well as strong areas that need other types of stimulation. Blanca, for example, was quite constant in her frequency of word classes. She even produced states. When this information is compared with her language sample, it is apparent that although she knew and produced a great number and variety of words, she produced all of them within an unintelligible form that was narrative in nature. Therefore, her parents could understand her, but she would not be understood out of her home or school context. This indicates that, therapeutically, most work should be concentrated on correcting the form of her utterance as well as increasing her vocabulary.

Julio, on the other hand, demonstrated a need for work with action and descriptive words and, most important, an increase in overall vocabulary. Although he evaluated low in Spanish, English, and ASL, he is predominantly Spanish speaking and therefore needs more stimulation in English if he is to function within a classroom where only English is used. Rosa's language covered a variety of classes, but was very weak in quantifiers, questions, time, furniture, and pronouns. Most of these classes are not object oriented. She, therefore, needs stimulation in more function-oriented classes.

The analysis of each child per word class can give valuable information as to weak language areas that need to be strengthened. In combination with the language sample, the form of expression can also be observed. In these three children, total vocabulary was quite below the preliminary norms. The distribution across word classes, although quite even in many ''noun'' categories, requires specific attention to individual weak areas.

Another factor that can be readily observed using the vocabulary information is a relationship to normal developmental trends. Whereas normal developmental trends show that comprehension exceeds production at every age level, in these data the trend goes in the opposite direction. When their raw vocabulary scores are compared with age percentiles, they all have higher production levels than comprehension levels.

Communicative Ability

The use of the language sample to reinforce vocabulary interpretation has been mentioned in several of the above areas. The use of the sample to note both the form of expression and the use of imitation is most enlightening. The language sample, as well, can give an overall picture of the way the child communicates. Does the child mostly label? ask for things?

answer questions? use communication devices in conversations? The communicative intent checklist demonstrates which intents the child uses in general. A frequency count of intents shows which functions predominate. By transcribing the utterances in the checklist, an example of the form of expression can be obtained.

An overview of the four children shows that Rosa is the most able communicator. She uses all communicative intents in proportions similar to hearing children. The only ones not present are conversational devices—practice and boundary—which may be more characteristic of Spanish or oral language. It is significant that Rosa has made a successful linguistic adjustment. It is also interesting that she even has examples of self-correction with ASL.

Julio, on the other hand, communicates with only a restricted number of communicative intents. Most of his utterances are related to the same event. He does not express petitions, attention to object, vocatives, exclamations, or most conversational devices. Most of his imitations are of English words. In general, both his vocabulary and his communicative ability are weak. He needs growth in both areas.

Blanca is highly conversational. She is one of the few children who consistently use conversational devices such as boundary markers and recognition. Nonetheless, when the form of her utterances is observed, her weakness becomes apparent. She produced long sequences of alternating repetitive syllables, which sometimes resembled some of the specific words she intended. She also produced intelligible utterances, such as: *"Ete e babayo"* (*Este es un caballo*) to show a horse, *"Mama"* to call her mother, or *"po tao"* (*por favor*) to ask for an object. Blanca also showed a typical sign of language development—the ability to recognize that a question has been asked and an answer is required—but without matching the content to the question. She therefore answered yes-or-no questions with long descriptive narrations (in prosodic form) and answered descriptive questions with a yes or no.

One of the most powerful uses of the communicative intent guidelines can be observed in Teresa. Although a general view shows that she knows how to communicate with most intents, what is most important is the proportion of types. Out of a total of 310 utterances, 46.1 percent were imitations and 20.0 percent were descriptions. She also used few requests. In most children, a significant number of utterances tend to be descriptive, but in none of the previously analyzed cases of Spanish-language acquisition (Jackson, 1989) was such a high percentage of imitations present. It becomes quite apparent that although Teresa knows how to describe, request objects, and respond to questions, her language is mostly imitative. As mentioned before, this would probably indicate that the vocabulary report of the inventory may be inaccurate. It explains, as well, why she demonstrated such a low percentage of action words, since her parents asked her to imitate mostly object words. This child needs to break repetitive patterns and begin to generate her own spontaneous utterances.

This brief summary of the data obtained from four case studies has shown the strength of using two instruments to describe Deaf Hispanic children's language. Children were compared using norms taken from their own culture, as well as their family language. The use of the inventory has also proved effective in determining strengths and weaknesses within vocabulary groups in order to suggest possible language goals. The combination of the inventory with the communicative intent checklist has permitted a projection of words into functions. It has shown that children are using the words in different manners. Some are more descriptive, some request more, some control conversational strategies, some are mostly imitative. In lieu of demonstrating communicative abilities rather than deficits, both instruments have shown that the children are communicatively able. However, Julio needs to broaden his use of language, and Teresa needs to de-emphasize imitations.

Another important outcome of using both instruments with teachers and parents is apparent in the cases of Julio and Rosa. In both cases the language reported by teachers and parents was different. In both cases teachers had underestimated language use. Julio's teacher reported the production of 33 English words and 16 English signs, and the parents reported the production of 113 Spanish words. The teacher did not (and probably could not) know the child's full communicative potential because she lacked the Spanish information. In Rosa's case another issue is present. Both parents and teacher reported the use of ASL. The teacher reported 48 English signs, whereas the parents reported 167. Not only did the number vary, but the words that two parties indicated were quite different. They did coincide, though, in the preference of word classes. This information brings to light the necessity of parent–teacher communication and, most important, the need for teachers to acknowledge the child's communicative abilities.

The use of the inventory also underlined an interesting issue. As indicated earlier, these children's developmental trends are contrary to normal hearing children. When data were available, all produced more words than they comprehended.

Both of the instruments presented in this chapter were created to take into consideration cultural and linguistic differences. Their use in this study has also been carefully monitored. The application of both measures requires cultural sensitivity on behalf of the person who does the assessment. Language samples cannot be interpreted using the communicative intent checklist unless they were obtained in culturally relevant ways. Parental reports cannot be considered accurate if the appropriate previous explanation and support are not given. The optimal way to assess Hispanic children is for the evaluating person to share the cultural identity. If this is not possible, then every effort to understand cultural and linguistic differences must be made before reaching any conclusions about behavior and language.

CONCLUSIONS AND RECOMMENDATIONS

Two Spanish-language measures have been proposed as alternatives to previously created language tests that have not monitored content validity appropriately and, most important, have not covered early child language. Both measures have been designed for Spanish-speaking children. The inventory is in the process of being normed on a Spanish-speaking population. The strength of both measures has been shown based on case studies of four Hispanic Deaf children, two who reside in the United States and two who reside in Mexico. The combination of two instruments that tag both strengths and weaknesses of the children allows for objective language descriptions to be obtained. Although they are compared with norms based on hearing children, the emphasis has been on showing their abilities and specific strategies for strengthening weak areas. Language assessment of children whose language is not English is a delicate matter. Explanations need to be found for why Hispanic children are lagging behind other groups of children in school achievement.

It is well known that children will not test well under conditions where cultural identity is not respected (Labov, 1972). Not only does this mean that they will not function to the best of their ability, but also implied is that the interviewer will also show bias toward the child. If we add to these human factors the fact that most tests contain middle class values of a different culture, then it is clear that from the start these children will not receive adequate assessment. In turn, it is most probable that they will be met with biases in the classroom.

The underachievement may be due not to their inability to learn, but more likely to their incapacity to adapt to a different system. These students need an identity in the educational environment. They need to know that their language and culture are respected. DeVos (1980) and Suarez-Orozco (1987) have clearly shown that "learning requires a harmonious functioning of the mechanism" (Suarez-Orozco, 1987, p. 164). The child, in the classroom, may not respond because he or she chooses not to answer or because the question was not understood because of its cultural irrelevance. Therefore, the answer is not only to create culturally relevant instruments, but to apply them, in both the testing situation and the classroom, in culturally relevant ways. A pat on the back, hand contact, a few reassuring words in the home language, a culturally relevant time frame, a gesture to make the child feel at home rather than pressured in the testing situation are just a few simple examples of important strategies.

It is possible that, with careful assessment that includes cultural identity, linguistic relevance, and sensitivity. Hispanic Deaf children may no longer constitute the majority in classrooms for students with multiple disabilities. They will be assessed and placed with respect to their heritage and their academic potential.

BIBLIOGRAPHY

Baca, L., & Cervantes, H. (1989). *The bilingual special education interface*. Columbus, OH: Merrill.

Bates, E. (1976). *Language and context*. New York: Academic Press.

Bickford, A. (1989). *Lexical variation in Mexican sign language*. Unpublished paper, University of North Dakota, Grand Forks.

Board of Education of the City of New York. (1976). *Language assessment battery*. Palo Alto, CA: Houghton Mifflin.

Brown, R. (1973). *A first language*. Cambridge, MA: Harvard University.

Burt, M., Dulay, H., & Hernandez-Chavez, E. (1976). *Bilingual syntax measure*. San Diego: Harcourt Brace Jovanovich.

Carrow, E. (1973). *Test of auditory comprehension of language*. Hingham, MA: Teaching Resources.

Christensen, K. M. (1988). I see what you mean: Nonverbal communication strategies of young deaf children. *American Annals for the Deaf, 133,* 270–275.

Christensen, K. M., and Regan, J. O. (1983). *Nonverbal and verbal communication acts: A functional analysis*. San Diego: Los Amigos Research Associates.

Clark, E. (1985). The acquisition of romance with special reference to French. In D. Slobin (Ed.), *The cross linguistic study of language acquisition* (Vol. I, pp. 687–782). Hillsdale, NJ: Lawrence Erlbaum.

Cohen, A. D., Cruz, R., & Bravo, R. (1977). *Bahia oral language test*. Berkeley, CA: Bahia Media Productions.

Cummins, J. (1979). Cognitive/academic language proficiency, interdependence, the optimum as age question and some other matters. *Working Papers on Bilingualism, 19,* 121–129.

Cummins, J. (1989). A theoretical framework for bilingual special education. *Exceptional Children, 56,* 111–119.

DeAvila, E., & Duncan, S. (1981). *Language assessment scales I & II.* San Rafael, CA: Linguametrics Group.

Delgado, G. (1984). Hearing impaired children from non-native language homes. *American Annals of the Deaf, 126,* 118–121.

Delgado-Gaitan, C. (1987). Parent perceptions of school: Supportive environments for children. In H. T. Trueba (Ed.), *Success or failure?* Cambridge, MA: Newbury House.

DeVos, G. A. (1980). Ethnic adaptation and minority status. *Journal of Cross Cultural Psychology, 11,* 101–124.

Dore, J. (1974). A pragmatic description of early language development. *Journal of Psycholinguistic Research, 4,* 343–350.

Erickson, J., & Omark, D. (1981). *Communication assessment of the bilingual bicultural child.* Baltimore: University Park.

Figueroa, R. A., Delgado, G., & Ruiz, N. (1984). Assessment of hispanic children: Implications for Hispanic hearing impaired children. In G. Delgado (Ed.), *The Hispanic Deaf.* Washington, DC: Gallaudet College.

Fischgrund, J. (1984). Language intervention for hearing-impaired children from linguistically and culturally diverse backgrounds. In G. Delgado (Ed.), *The Hispanic Deaf.* Washington, DC: Gallaudet College.

Garcia, E. E. (1983). *The Mexican American child.* Tempe, AZ: Center for Bilingual Education.

Grant, J. (1983). The bilingual hearing impaired: Teaching children and preparing teachers. In D. Omarck & J. Erickson (Eds.), *The bilingual exceptional child.* Boston: College Hill.

Grant, J. (1984). Teachers of Hispanic hearing impaired children: Competencies and preparation. In G. Delgado (Ed.), *The Hispanic Deaf.* Washington, DC: Gallaudet College.

Halliday, M.A.K. (1975). *Learning how to mean.* New York: Elsevier-North Holland.

Hedrick, D., Prather, E., & Tobin, A. (1979). *Sequenced inventory of communication development—revised.* Los Angeles: Western Psychological Services.

Herbert, C. (1980). *The basic inventory of natural language.* San Bernardino, CA: Checkpoint Associates.

Hresko, W. P., Reid, D. K., & Hammill, D. D. (1982). *Prueba del desarrollo inicial del lenguaje.* Austin: Pro Ed.

Jackson, D. (1989). *Una palabra: Multiplicidad de intenciones y funciones.* Unpublished doctoral dissertation, El Colegio de Mexico, Mexico.

Jackson, S., & Espino, L. (1983). Cultural antecedents of cognitive style variables in Mexican American children. In T. Escobedo (Ed.), *Early childhood bilingual education.* New York: Teachers College.

Jackson-Maldonado, D. (1979). Lenguaje manual: Un enfoque objetivo. In D. Jackson-Maldonado (Ed.), *Audicion y lenguaje en education especial: Experiencia Mexicana.* Mexico, DF: Secretaria de Programacion y Presupuesto.

Jackson-Maldonado, D. (1988). Evaluacion del lenguaje infantil: Enfoque transcultural. In A. Ardila & F. Ostrosky-Solis (Eds.), *Lenguaje oral y escrito.* Mexico, DF: Trillas.

Jackson-Maldonado, D., & Bates, E. (1989). *Inventario del desarrollo de las habilidades communicativas.* Unpublished document, University of California, San Diego.

Jackson-Maldonado, D., Marchman, V., Thal, D., Bates, E., & Gutierrez-Clellen, V. (1992). *Early lexical acquisition in Spanish speaking infants and toddlers.* Unpublished manuscript.

Jordan, I. K., & Karchmer, M. A. (1986). Patterns of sign use among hearing impaired students. In A. N. Schildroth & M. A. Karchmer (Eds.), *Deaf children in America.* San Diego: College Hill.

Labov, W. (1972). The logic of nonstandard English. In W. Labov (Ed.), *Language in the inner city.* Philadelphia: University of Pennsylvania.

Laosa, L. M. (1980). Maternal teaching strategies in Chicano and Anglo-American families: The influence of culture and education on maternal behavior. *Child Development, 51,* 759–765.

Lopez-Ornat, S. (1988). On data sources on the acquisition of Spanish as a first language. *Journal of Child Language, 15*, 679–686.

Maestas y Moores, J., & Moores, D. (1984). The status of Hispanics in special education. In G. Delgado (Ed.), *The Hispanic Deaf*. Washington, DC: Gallaudet College.

Mares, S. (1980). *Prueba de expresión oral y percepción de la lengua Espanola*. Downey, CA: Office of the Los Angeles County Superintendent of Schools.

Mattes, L., & Omark, D. (1984). *Speech and language assessment for the bilingual handicapped child*. San Diego: College Hill.

Mercer, J. R. (1973). *Labelling the mentally retarded*. Berkeley, CA: University of California.

Mercer, J. R., & Lewis, J. F. (1979). *The system of multicultural pluralistic assessment: Conceptual and technical manual*. New York: Psychological Corporation.

Merino, B. J., & Spencer, M. (1983). The comparability of English and Spanish versions of oral language proficiency instruments. *NABE Journal, 7*, 1–31.

Omark, D., & Erickson, J. (1983). *The bilingual exceptional child*. Boston: College Hill.

Padden, C., & Humphries, T. (1988). *Deaf in America*. Cambridge, MA: Harvard University.

Payan, R. M. (1989). Language assessment for bilingual exceptional children. In L. Baca & H. Cervantes (Eds.), *The bilingual special education interface*. Columbus, OH: Merrill.

Prutting, C. (1983). Assessing communicative behaviors using a language sample. In D. Omark & J. Erickson (Eds.), *The bilingual exceptional child*. Boston: College Hill.

Salomon, R., Vega, V., Friedman, A., Amigo, M. R., & Lara, E. (1991). *Estado de los auxiliares auditivos en Mexico*. Paper presented at the Biennial Congress of the World Federation for Mental Health, Mexico, DF.

Schildroth, A. N., & Karchmer, M. A. (1986). *Deaf children in America*. San Diego: College Hill.

Smith-Stark, T. (1986). *La lengua manual Mexicana*. Unpublished manuscript, El Colegio de Mexico.

Strong, M. (1988). *Language learning and deafness*. Cambridge: Cambridge University.

Suarez-Orozco, M. (1987). Towards a psychosocial understanding of Hispanic adaptation to American schooling. In H. T. Trueba (Ed.), *Success or failure?* Cambridge, MA: Newbury House.

Thal, D., & Bates, E. (1988). Language and gesture in late talkers. *Journal of Speech and Hearing Research, 31*, 115–123.

Thal. D., Tobias, S., & Morrison, D. (1991). Language and gesture in late talkers: A one year follow up. *Journal of Speech and Hearing Research, 34*, 604–612.

Toronto, A. S. (1972). *Toronto tests of receptive vocabulary*. Illinois: Academic Tests, Inc.

Toronto, A. S. (1973). *Screening test of Spanish grammar*. Evanston, IL: Northwestern University.

Toronto, A. S., Leverman, D., Hanna, C., Rosenzweig, P., & Maldonado, A. (1975). *Del Rio Language Screening Test*. Austin: National Education Laboratory.

Trueba, H. T. (1987). *Success or failure?* Cambridge, MA: Newbury House.

Walker, C. (1987). Hispanic achievement: Old views and new perspectives. In H. T. Trueba (Ed.), *Success or failure?* Cambridge, MA: Newbury House.

SUGGESTED READINGS

Cultural

Duran, R. P. (1983). *Hispanics' education and background*. New York: College Entrance Examination Board.

Garcia, E. E. (1983). *The Mexican American child*. Tempe, AZ: Center for Bilingual Education.

Moore, J., & Pachon, H. (1985). *Hispanics in the United States*. Englewood Cliffs, NJ: Prentice-Hall.

Professional

Bilingual Education Office. (1986). *Beyond language: Social and cultural factors in schooling language minority students*. Los Angeles: Evaluation, Dissemination and Assessment Center.

Cummins, J. (1984). *Bilingualism and special education: Issues in assessment and pedagogy*. San Diego: College Hill.

Fradd, S. H., & Weismantel, M. J. (1989). *Meeting the needs of culturally and linguistically different students: A handbook for educators*. San Diego: College Hill.

NABE (National Association of Bilingual Education) *Journal*, SIG Eda Valero-Figueroa, George Mason University, Department of Education, 4100 University Drive, Fairfax, VA 22030.

Thomas, H., & Thomas, J. L. (1982). *Bilingual special education resource guide*. Phoenix: Oryx.

CHAPTER 7

Deafness: An Asian/Pacific Island Perspective

Li-Rong Lilly Cheng

Look, it cannot be seen—it is beyond form.
Listen, it cannot be heard—it is beyond sound.
Grasp, it cannot be held—it is intangible.
These three are indefinable.
Therefore they are joined in one.

Lao Tsu

In this chapter, the history, languages, and cultures, including religious beliefs and immigration backgrounds, of the Asian/Pacific Islander populations in the United States will be discussed. The cultural attitudes of Asian populations toward disability and toward childrearing practices and the subsequent guidelines for cross-cultural communication will be examined. The cross-cultural implications for the Deaf will also be reviewed.

Asian/Pacific Island people have been immigrating to the United States for over two centuries. The first records of the arrival of the Chinese date from 1785. Large numbers of Japanese farmers came between 1891 and 1907. The Chinese and Japanese were the first groups to immigrate to Hawaii, followed by Filipinos and Koreans. Filipinos and Koreans began to immigrate to the U.S. mainland in large numbers in the 1950s. More recently, an influx of Asian/Pacific Island immigrants and refugees has occurred during the past decade. Since 1975, more than 900,000 Southeast Asian refugees have settled in the United States. Throughout this country there has been a significant growth in the Asian/Pacific Island population, from less than 1 percent in 1970 to 1½ percent in 1991 and an expected 4 percent in the year 2000—a projected growth of 400 percent in thirty years (Gardner, Robey, & Smith, 1985). In 1991, approximately 40 percent of immigrants were from Latin American countries and 40 percent from Asian/Pacific Island countries.

Despite the number of years that Asian groups have lived in the United States, it was not until the recent influx of immigrants and refugees that the special needs of all Asian/Pacific Island populations have surfaced. Prior to the recent influx, the major Asian American groups were the Chinese, the Japanese, and the Filipinos, many of whom are second or third generation who have English-language proficiency and have acculturated. The recent influx represents a diverse group from Indochina, Hong Kong, China, and other Pacific rim and basin areas. They are greater in number and have many more adjustment problems. Professionals in the field of education and in related fields are being challenged to provide appropriate services for these populations, yet many are unprepared to deal with the cultural, social, and linguistic differences that the Asian/Pacific Island populations present (Sue & Padilla, 1986). Recent studies (Stewart, Anae, & Gipe, 1989) indicate that a large percentage of Pacific Island children in the U.S. school system fail hearing screening. The enrollment of Asian/Pacific Island hearing impaired children under the age of six in the U.S. school system climbed 206 percent during the 1980s (Schildroth, Rawlings, & Allen, 1989). In order to serve these people, it is necessary to understand their background, culture, and beliefs.

BACKGROUND INFORMATION: ASIAN/PACIFIC ISLAND POPULATIONS

Numerous variables must be considered when working with individuals from Asian/Pacific Island populations: languages, religions, childrearing practices, beliefs and values, kinship systems, customs, life style, practices in medicine, reasons for leaving the homeland, educational levels, and others. Despite their many similarities, individuals from Asian/Pacific Island countries cannot be placed together in terms of common views and expectations regarding life styles, perceptions of illnesses, methods of healing, or family and community support systems. Thus, although broad similarities and differences between Asian and Western belief systems and practices may be discussed, one must always keep in mind the many similarities and differences among the Asian/Pacific Island populations themselves.

Asian/Pacific Island Americans have come from the following areas:

East Asia: China, Taiwan, Hong Kong, Japan, and Korea;

Southeast Asia: Philippines, Vietnam, Cambodia, Laos, Malaysia, Singapore, Indonesia, Thailand;

Indian Subcontinent or South Asia: India, Pakistan, Bangladesh; and

Pacific Islands: Hawaii, Guam, American Samoa, Tonga, Fiji, and other Micronesian Islands.

Languages

Over 1,200 indigenous languages are spoken among the 5 million inhabitants of the Pacific Islands; these include Chamorro, Marshallese, Trukese, Carolinian, Papua New Guinea, Korean, Japanese, Ponepean, Samoan, Hawaiian, Fijian, and Tahitian. The five *lingua francas* used by the Pacific Islanders are French, English, pidgin, Spanish, and Bahasa Indonesian. The Hawaiian language is spoken mainly on the island of Niihau, and few locals speak it or speak it well. English is spoken on Guam, American Samoa, Saipan, and many of the Pacific Islands. There are hundreds of distinct languages spoken in Pacific Asia. These can be classified into five major language families:

Malayo-Polynesian: Tagalog, Illocano;

Sino-Tibetan: Thai, Yao, Mandarin, Cantonese;

Austro-Asiatic: Vietnamese, Khmer, Hmong Papuan; and

Papua New Guinea Altaic: Japanese, Korean.

The main Asian/Pacific Island languages spoken in the United States are Mandarin, Cantonese, Taiwanese, Tagalog, Illocano, Lao, Khmer, Hmong, Hindi, Chamorro, and Samoan. These languages differ a great deal—from being tonal, monosyllabic, and logographic (a property of writing system) to being intonational, polysyllabic, alphabetic, and agglutinational. Tonal languages such as Mandarin, Lao, and Vietnamese rely on tonal differences for meaning. For example, there are four tones in Mandarin: The first is high level, the second is rising, the third if fall-rising, and the fourth is falling. The same syllable *ma* means mother in the first tone, hemp in the second, horse in the third, and scold in the fourth. People learning the language must gain a mastery of the tones both receptively and expressively. This presents a real challenge for people with impaired hearing.

Chinese is logographic, and words are represented graphically by logographs. Logographs, also called ideographs, are used singly or in combination to represent a meaningful unit. Japanese writing uses a combination of *Kanji* (Chinese characters) and *Kanas* (all possible syllables in Japanese). The Khmer and Lao writing systems are based on Sanskrit and Pali. The Hmong, as well as Vietnamese, use an alphabetical system. It is important for educators to have some background of these languages so that they will be able to understand why certain linguistic constructs are present or absent in the children's linguistic repertoire.

Religious and Philosophical Beliefs

The major religious and philosophical beliefs of the Asian/Pacific Island populations are Hinduism, Buddhism, Confucianism, Taoism, Shintoism, Animism, Protestant Christianity or Catholicism, and Islamism. Hinduism is the main religion in India; Buddhism began as an offshoot of Hinduism around the fifth century. Kindness and nonviolence were preached. Confucianism exerts a strong influence in China and Vietnam. Confucius defined the rules that dictate relationships between family members, subordinates, and others. His influence spread to Japan and Korea. Similarly, Taoism is derived from the doctrines of Lao Tzu. The basic principle of Taoism is that one must not interfere with nature but must follow its course. Those who practice Taoism display a sense of fatalism about events surrounding them because the religion promotes passivity and inaction. There is a poem that denotes some of these thoughts:

Tao is (likened to) an empty bowl, Whose function is inexhaustible; Bottomless, It seems to be the "ancestor" of the Ten Thousand Things. It blunts all sharpness, Unties all tangles, Softens all lights, And becomes one with all dust. Deep and hidden, It seems as if it were ever-present. I do not know whose child it is, It looks as if it were prior to the Lord. (Fu & Wawrytko, 1988)

The principal religion of Japan is Shintoism, with emphasis on worship of nature, ancestors and ancient heroes, and reverence for the spirits of natural forces and emperors. Animism is another common religion in Southeast Asia. It holds that there are spirits in everything, including one's body, and that demons and spirits exist. The head is where the chief spirit resides; touching it brings bad luck. *Baci*, a common ritual in Animism, is usually performed when a person is ill or going away on a trip. This ceremony represents the religious or folk belief system of a major part of Southeast Asia; such practices are often regarded as means of healing and getting rid of the evil spirits.

The Pacific Islanders have been influenced by Protestant Christianity and Catholicism, which are practiced with a mixture of folk beliefs, such as *taotaomona*/spirits (Chamorro culture), *menehune*/spirits (Hawaiian), and *suruhana*/healer (Chamorro) (Ashby, 1983). They often seek medical advice from the faith healers or "witch doctor." Natives also may prefer herb medicine. A small portion of Asians are Moslem, scattered from the Malaysian Islands to the Philippines. Ancestral worship is a prevailing theme in Asian beliefs, and it is practiced in China, Japan, Korea, and Vietnam (Cheng, 1989). Religion is an integral part of any culture; it impacts how people view life and disabilities. Educators would benefit from learning about how disability is viewed in those cultures and specifically how deafness is viewed.

Home of Origin

Some of the incoming people are immigrants; others are refugees. Although immigrants have planned to come to the United States, they differ in their education and degree of exposure to the English language and American culture. By law, immigrants must have a sponsor, either a close relative or an employer. They file for an immigrant visa and then must wait for a period of time (ranging from six months to five years) before beginning visa interviews and screening procedures. On the other hand, refugees leave their countries to escape persecution; many risk their lives and leave their families behind. They may wait in refugee camps until their sponsors can arrange passage to the United States. The conditions in refugee camps are not ideal. Medical attention is limited, and children with ear infections often go unattended. Many refugees and immigrants speak no English and have never traveled beyond their homeland (Chhim, Luangpraseut, & Te, 1989).

American Born.   Many of the Asian school-age children were born in the United States or in refugee camps. On the other hand, many Asians are *nisei* (second generation), *sansei* (third generation), and *yousei* (fourth generation) Americans. They were born and educated in the United States and may not speak the language of their parents or grandparents. For more information about the history of Asian Americans in the past decade, see Chapter 8 (also, Takaki, 1989).

Researchers in Asian studies have discussed the differences within the Asian/Pacific Island group. There is a great diversity in social class among the families of refugees and immigrants. About 95 percent of the Vietnamese and Chinese Vietnamese came from urban backgrounds, whereas 50 percent of Cambodians came from rural backgrounds. Overall, Vietnamese parents are more educated, having an average of nine years of schooling. The Hmong have an average of one year of schooling (Ima & Rumbaut, 1989). Fathers have higher educations than mothers in all groups.

There are major differences between the early immigrants and the recent ones. The early immigrants came to the United States in the late nineteenth century to work in the mines, for the railroads, and on the farms (see Chapter 8; Asian Women United of California, 1989; Chin, 1967). They experienced unfair treatment, including the Asian Exclusion Act and the internment of the Japanese during World War II. Later immigrants came after World War II to further their education, and many found employment in major industrial and academic institutions. Recent immigrants to the United States seek better job opportunities and to further their studies. Many people have had to wait for years before a visa was granted, because of quota restrictions. A large number of immigrants have come from China and Hong Kong. Many recent Asian immigrants are from Malaysia, China, India, Hong Kong, Taiwan, Korea, and Japan. Some came to get a better education and to seek better employment opportunities; others came to escape Communism. Their personal life history has significant impact on how they feel about themselves and how they view life. This directly influences how they view education. It behooves educators to be sensitive to their needs and views.

Refugees.   Most refugees never dreamed of leaving their home. For them, the journey to the United States was filled with trauma, anxiety, separation, fear, hunger, and unrest (Te, 1987). The refugees came in three waves. Those who came in the first wave, primarily Vietnamese, came between the fall of Saigon and the onset of the boat people. They were more educated and had higher-than-average social resources and professional and managerial skills. The second wave, the boat people, arrived between 1979 and 1982. This group included a wide variety of ethnic groups and socioeconomic backgrounds, mainly farmers and fishermen. Refugees from the third wave (1982 to present) continue to show diversity in terms of ethnicity and social class.

There is, however, great diversity among the Indochinese population. All bring with them a diverse mixture of customs, education, beliefs, and values (Rumbaut & Ima, 1988). The Vietnamese, Chinese, and Hmong have similar cultural traits, including sharing of patrilineal-extended family systems. Patrilineal-extended families were built on the Confucian cultural model that emphasizes family relationships, duties and discipline, filial piety, obedience, parental authority, and respect for the elderly. The Lao and Khmer people have common cultural roots, elements of which are borrowed from Indian culture, religion, and languages. The Indian languages, Sanskrit and Pali, have influenced the Lao and Khmer languages. In religion, the Theravada Buddhism is shared.

Pacific Islanders.   Pacific Islanders from Samoa, Tonga, and Guam have migrated to Hawaii and the U.S. mainland in large numbers. The Chamorro people of Guam hold U.S. passports and can travel freely to the United States. Western Samoa is under the rule of the British government; American Samoa is a U.S. territory. In recent years, more than 60,000 Samoans have left their homeland, leaving approximately 30,000 Samoans on the island.

Frequently, the Filipinos are grouped as either Asians or Pacific Islanders. The Philippines is an archipelago of more than 7,200 islands from which there has been a steady flow of immigrants since the end of World War II. In their homeland they speak a total of eighty-seven mutually unintelligible languages, but most of the Filipino immigrants speak English.

ACCULTURATION

Various degrees of acculturation are present in the immigrant and refugee populations. Some immigrants, either as groups or as individuals, totally reject the new culture into which they have come. Some adapt to the new culture, integrating some of its aspects while still retaining part of their own culture. Others become assimilated into the culture, giving up their former cultural identity (Berry, 1986). Kitano and Daniels (1988, p. 191) proposed the assimilation model for the Asian American shown in Figure 7.1.

Some people are highly assimilated and still retain high ethnic identity (Cell B), whereas others give up or reject their ethnic identity to achieve assimilation (Cell A). On the other hand, some preserve their ethnic identity but with low assimilation (Cell D), while some get lost in a low cultural identity and low assimilation situation (Cell C). Berry's model described the European American situation, since Europeans can assimilate completely into the majority, whereas Asians never quite get "swallowed up" because of their appearance.

During personal contact with an Asian/Pacific Island individual, educators should always be reminded of the cultural values associated with the individual's family background. Variables such as eye contact, physical contact, and praise and reinforcement are

FIGURE 7.1   Assimilation model

SOURCE: H. H. L. Kitano & R. Daniels (1988). *Asian Americans: Emerging minorities.* Englewood Cliffs, NJ: Prentice-Hall. Reprinted with permission.

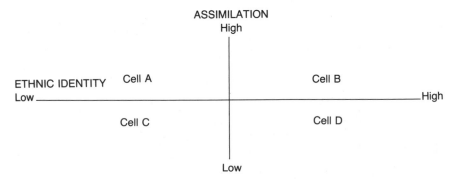

acceptable in Western culture but are viewed differently by Asian/Pacific Island people. Asian cultures in general do not encourage physical contact. Eye contact is used minimally, and open praise is reserved for special occasions.

The United Nations Educational, Scientific, and Cultural Organization (UNESCO) defined *culture* as a dynamic value system of learned attitudes, with assumptions, conventions, beliefs, and rules that permit members of a group to relate to one another and the world. Some of the many cultural constituents as identified by Kohls (1979) are general beliefs, religious beliefs, myths, values, and knowledge. Cultural beliefs such as attitudes toward illness and disability shape societal thinking. Aspects of culture, such as language, are fluid because they tend not to persist generation after generation. On the other hand, static aspects of culture such as kinship systems, attitudes, and beliefs do tend to persist generation after generation. Asians who are second and third generation still hold many of the same beliefs and values. The following section concentrates on the cultural beliefs that are prevalent in Asian/Pacific Island cultures.

CULTURAL BELIEFS ABOUT DISABILITIES IN GENERAL

The following is a synopsis of some of the primary cultural beliefs, kinship systems, and childrearing practices in many parts of Pacific Asia.

What is considered a disability? Disabilities are conditions caused by congenital physical deformities or acquired injuries, such as blindness, deafness, cleft palate, and paralysis (Meyerson, 1983).

From whom does one seek medical advice? People may seek help from a medical doctor trained in Western medicine and/or a folk medicine man or woman, faith healer, or shaman.

How is medicine used? People may choose a combination of Western and folk medicine, which at times has disastrous results; for example, they may substitute the suggested frequency for the prescribed dosage. There have been reports of overdose because the patient thought that by taking more medication, recuperation would occur sooner. Some do not understand the use of measurements such as one teaspoon or two drops.

What are the methods of healing? These include surgery, medication, physical therapy, acupuncture for ''curing deafness and other illnesses,'' massage (Chinese, Korean, Japanese), *cao gio* (coin rubbing), herbal medicine, *bat gio* (pinching), *giac* (placing a very hot cup on the exposed area), *xong* (steam inhalation), balm application, *baci* (a ritualistic healing practice among Vietnamese), or ingestion of hot or cold foods (Chamorro, Hawaiian, Hmong).

What religious or philosophical beliefs affect treatment? As mentioned above, the Asian/Pacific Island populations have a variety of religious and philosophical beliefs. For a more complete description of these beliefs, see Cheng (1987, 1989). Many Asian/Pacific Island people believe that a disability or deformity is *karma* (fate), and therefore nothing can be done about it. Some have a fatalistic attitude about any such defect and will not seek intervention.

What are the perceived causes of disabilities? These arise from a variety of spiritual and cultural beliefs, such as imbalance of inner forces; bad wind or spoiled food; gods, demons, or spirits; and hot or cold forces. Most people view a disabling condition as the result of wrongdoing by the individual's ancestors (e.g., talking about others behind their backs).

How are disabled individuals treated? Some cultures view a disability as a gift from God; the disabled individual belongs to everybody and is protected and sheltered (Chamorro culture). Other cultures view a deformity as a curse and may ostracize the individual from society (Philippines and China).

What are the attitudes toward disabilities? These vary from culture to culture. Some view deafness as dumbness and mutism. Others view deafness as a curse and children's disabilities as a personal embarrassment (Epstein, 1989).

What steps are taken in seeking a cure? Again, these vary from culture to culture and individual to individual. For those who have been acculturated, seeking medical advice from a physician is common practice. Those who have recently arrived in the United States may first seek advice from family members and take folk medicine, then see a medicine man or a clan head who may communicate with the deceased ancestors for advice. Next one may seek medical advice from a physician from the same language and ethnic group, and, finally, as a last resort, consultation from persons who are not members of the same ethnic and linguistic group.

How is illness perceived? A person with mental disorders may be viewed as healthy since there is no physical evidence of disability. On the other hand, a person with a physical difference may be regarded as sick even though he or she is otherwise in good health.

What are the childrearing practices? The Asian/Pacific Island cultures may view children as helpless, dependent, and lacking intentionality. A good baby is one that is not fussy but quiet. Views on dressing, toilet training, feeding, and self-help skills may vary a great deal among cultures. Methods of discipline also vary widely (Sue, 1986). Individuals may have mixed feelings regarding disability and the treatment of disabled individuals. For example, the cultural value of being benevolent may be taken over by the superstition that deformity brings bad luck, resulting in the abandonment of the disfigured newborns. The Asian views on education, authority figures, discipline, self-direction, parent–school interaction, parent–child interaction, parental responsibilities, and filial piety make it difficult for Deaf educators to comprehend the interrelatedness of those principles and how they relate to the ultimate success of the Deaf population.

TREATMENT OF THE DEAF IN ASIAN COUNTRIES

As described earlier, Asian Americans have been influenced mainly by Chinese and Indian philosophies, religions, and cultures. Some Asian countries have been influenced by the Indian religion of Buddhism. The Chinese, Japanese, Korean, and Vietnamese people, on the other hand, have a deep-rooted humanistic philosophy, which began with the teachings of Confucius. Confucius was born about 550 B.C., during a time of harsh rule and loss of human rights when only those in the aristocracy were allowed to be educated. Since Confucius was born into a family of lower status, he had to struggle to gain his education. Through his writings and teachings, Confucius laid the foundation for the educational philosophy of the Chinese, Korean, Japanese, and Vietnamese people. Confucius was the first person who taught all people without regard to their position or social status. He believed that everyone had the capacity to become a virtuous individual through learning and education. To him, people were the most important component in society. They were to aspire to become virtuous and to follow "the Way." A series of steps was necessary on the journey along "the Way." There were progressive degrees of achievement, each dependent on successful completion of the previous step. The attainment of the whole series constituted the knowledge for self-motivation.

The traits to be developed were humanity, benevolence, kindness, compassion, charity, courtesy, diligence, respect and deference to the elderly, filial piety, and responsibilities in relationships. Confucius stated that to attain these traits one must have loyalty (being true to one's self and being free from self-delusion) and reciprocity (loyalty to others and an appreciation of the feelings of others).

Confucius' concerns for the disadvantaged were apparent from his teachings. His principles of self-cultivation, fondness for learning, and vigor for learning remained a driving force in the education of disabled individuals. It was many years, however, before these teachings were applied directly to the educational needs of Deaf students. The official document of Li Chi, originating from China and dating to approximately 200 B.C., outlined society's responsibility for the care and education of the disabled. Specifically, society was deemed responsible for giving assistance to and meeting the special needs of widows, widowers, orphans, singles, the Deaf, the blind, the physically handicapped, and all sick individuals. Such individuals have been protected and cared for by family members because they were ostracized from society.

In China, the earliest records of treatment of the disabled were in 1870 when Pastor William Moore established the first school for the blind in Peking (Beijing). In 1887, the first school for the Deaf in China was founded by Madame Annette Thompson Mills in Shangtung province. She was an American trained at the Clark School. Later more schools were established. These schools were founded and supported by churches; they received no government funding. By 1916 there were only twelve schools for the Deaf in China.

The government of the Republic of China (Taiwan) opened its first school for the deaf and blind in 1927. During the next ten years, a few more such schools opened. At that time the government began putting emphasis on the educational opportunities for the deaf and blind, and the population's awareness of the importance of education for the disabled increased. Within ten years the number of Deaf students being served was 1,624 (Ministry of Education, 1975).

In 1890 the first privately owned school for exceptional children in Taiwan was begun. It was started as a school for the blind, but later included the deaf. As time went on, other schools were opened to serve the deaf population. In 1987 there were four schools for the Deaf with a total enrollment of 1,965 students. Other hearing impaired students attended special classes in regular schools. Today in Taiwan, most Deaf individuals receive vocational training and work in sheltered workshops. A report by Lin and Ho (1986) indicated that male students have more severe losses than female students. Another report (Chen, 1983) indicated that 76 percent of the special education population in Taiwan are Deaf. The total number of Deaf children in China exceeds 550,000. China has made progress, but currently educates less than 10 percent of its Deaf children. China also lacks preschools for the Deaf—in fact, most Deaf Chinese students do not begin school until age nine and leave to begin working at age sixteen.

In the People's Republic of China, between 1949 and 1985, the number of schools for blind, deaf, and developmentally disabled students increased from 40 to 375, as enrollments expanded from 2,322 to 41,706. From 1985 to 1988, the number of schools increased to 504 serving 52,800 students (Epstein, 1989).

Several reports referred to societal attitudes as well as current rehabilitation efforts in the Asian countries. Gokhale (1982) explained that legislation for the disabled, as well as public assistance and social security, are newly emerging concepts in most Asian countries. In the past, a child with an impairment was often denied the chance for education and intellectual stimulation. Sidel and Sidel (1982) reported that at least as far back as the 1940s, the blind in China were described as "isolated in a tangle of superstition, fear and contempt" (p. 121). People in China with disabilities were considered to be "sick" and were therefore "eliminated" before or soon after birth (Gudalefsky, 1989). Blindness was often considered a punishment for the sins of parents or ancestors, and blind children were frequently abandoned or sold into slavery (Sidel & Sidel, 1982). According to traditional Shinto beliefs practiced in Japan, illness was a state that was considered polluting, calling for temporary separation and even ostracism from the group (Lock, 1980). Such beliefs are prevalent in other parts of Asia, including India, the Philippines, and Malaysia.

Sidel and Sidel (1982) described the Shanghai Children's Welfare Institute, which provided care for approximately 500 patients. Most of the patients ranged in age between newborn and sixteen years. Many of the children had been abandoned by their families, probably because of the parents' superstitious ideas about physically disabled and retarded children. They were often viewed as monsters or ghosts, or foreign spirits that came to the parents as punishment for a sin. These views were particularly widespread in the rural areas, and even today such beliefs exist. A 1989 study on birth defects (Cheng) revealed that the Chinese people still believe that birth defects are caused by parents' wrongdoing and pregnant women looking at rabbits or using scissors.

In Japan, disabled students are mandated to attend school under the School Education Law. Mentally and physically disabled children are placed in special schools or classrooms depending on the type and degree of disability. Standardized degrees of mental and physical deficiencies are used as guidelines. The Municipal Committee for Instructions, composed of doctors, school teachers, professors, and welfare facility staff, judges the degrees of deficiency. Placement in special schools, special classes in normal schools, or regular classes in normal schools is recommended, depending on the degree of deficiency. The special schools serve 11,308 children in 110 national, public, and private schools for the deaf, ranging from kindergarten through upper secondary grades. At the level of compulsory education there are 100 schools serving 5,588 Deaf students and 467 special classes serving 2,005 hard-of-hearing students. The tendency in rehabilitation efforts made so far has been to isolate Deaf persons in terms of special institutions and special places to work (Gokhale, 1982). It is estimated that more than 6 million children in China are in need of special education. Only 6 percent of them are receiving services, leaving the rest unserved (Epstein, 1989).

In 1986, a law for special education was passed in the Republic of China (Taiwan), mandating that the disabled be served educationally. In Taiwan in 1976, 31 percent of those with hearing losses were being served by public schools. In special schools and residential schools, 52 percent were being served. The remaining portion were reported as not attending school (Kuo, Chen, & Liang, 1976). The latest trend seems to be toward integrating deaf children into the regular classroom, and utilizing other methods of teaching, such as aural-oral communication. In many programs, signed language is being used, along with other communication modes, to instruct Deaf children.

Teachers are working with deaf students in all fields in which they can achieve. One indication of this is a report stating that the conservation abilities of hearing impaired students had a significant relationship to their age and intelligence. A positive linear growth in conservation abilities was noted as they advanced in age (Chang, 1988). Also, early home training in listening skills and speech of hearing impaired children has led to better developed fine and gross motor skills, higher scores in receptive and expressive language skills, better self-help skills, situation comprehension, and personal and social skills (Hwang, 1988). Parents of disabled children are also being served through genetic counseling, which explains the disability and the availability of treatment.

EDUCATIONAL IMPLICATIONS

When working with Asian/Pacific Island populations, the following factors must be considered:

Personal life history: immigration/migration history, including the reasons for coming to the United States; war, trauma, abuse, separation.

Life style prior to immigration: Many immigrants and refugees lived an agrarian life style in which farming was the main focus. Others from the Pacific Islands may have depended on fishing and growing livestock for their living (Walker, 1985).

Prior education: length and consistency of schooling, amount and type of exposure to English, repeated moves or transfers, lack of schooling.

Home environment: social class resources (educational level, employment and income level of parents), home language, caretakers, members of the family (especially the mother's socioeconomic and emotional characteristics), roles and expectations, activities, forms of discipline.

Prior medical information: screening, examinations, surgery, medication, birth history, illnesses, or the lack of medical care.

Personal status: detached youth, accompanied minor, multiple guardians, orphan.

Family and community support systems: childcare providers, medical assistance personnel, providers of advice during crises.

Cultural beliefs: folk beliefs about medicine, birth defects, disabilities, the causes of disabilities.

School information: present school performance, strengths, weaknesses, quality of school life, and classroom behaviors.

Referral: who made it and why. Professionals face significant difficulty when they come in contact with Asian/Pacific Island populations. Interpreters may be difficult to locate, and resources are not readily available. (The question of providing adequate service to the Asian/Pacific Island population is explored further in Chapter 8.)

When working with such a culturally and linguistically diverse population, knowledge of the following may be necessary:

various languages, learning styles, values and beliefs, kinship systems, communication styles (Matsuda, 1989), and religious beliefs;

recent history (refugees, war, migration); and

family and support systems.

Furthermore, the following critical information must be gathered through home visits with a teacher and interpreter team:

number of years in the United States;

language of the parents (hearing or deaf);

prior education (disrupted, lack of schooling, repeated moves and transfers);

home environment (unsupervised minors, detached youth, single parent, parent working two jobs, multiple guardians);

education background;

languages used at home; and

childcare arrangement at home (who takes care of the children).

CONCLUSION

Professionals need to be innovative in their application of intervention strategies, since Asian/Pacific Island multicultural hearing-impaired students provide a special challenge. These individuals come from diverse cultural, linguistic, and religious backgrounds. Educators must increase their sensitivity and awareness of cultural differences in Asian/Pacific Island learning and communication styles in order to make the adjustments necessary to meet the needs of this population. We also need to have the children educate us about their world. Only as we understand them can we empower their lives through the education we offer. Furthermore, we need to engage parents in the educational process, thus maximizing the natural support system. More research needs to be done in order to understand the needs of the Asian/Pacific Island population and to further our knowledge about the culture that deaf people from a multicultural world are facing today.

BIBLIOGRAPHY

Ashby, G. (1983). *Micronesian customs and beliefs*. Eugene, OR: Rainy Day Press.
Asian Women United of California (Ed.). (1989). *Making waves: An anthology of writings by and about Asian American women*. Boston: Beacon Press.
Berry, J. W. (1986). The acculturation process and refugee behavior. In C. L. Williams & J. Westermeyer (Eds.), *Refugee mental health in resettlement countries* (pp. 25–37). Washington, DC: Hemisphere.

Chang, B. (1988). A study on conservation abilities of hearing impaired students in primary school level. *Bulletin of Special Education, 4,* 113–130. Taiwan Normal University, Taipei.

Chen, Y. H. (1983). *Welfare policies for the handicapped in the Republic of China.* Taipei: Executive Yuan Research and Development Commission.

Chen, Y. H., Seitz, M., & Cheng, L. (in press). Special education. In D. Smith (Ed.), *Modernization of education in the Republic of China.* New York: Praeger.

Cheng, L. (1987). *Assessing Asian language performance: Guidelines for evaluation of limited English proficient students.* Rockville, MD: Aspen.

Cheng, L. (1989). Service delivery to Asian/Pacific LEP children: A cross-cultural framework. *Topics in Language Disorders, 9*(3), 1–14.

Chhim, S. H., Luangpraseut, K., & Te, H. D. (1989). *Introduction to Cambodian culture; Laos culturally speaking; Introduction to Vietnamese culture.* San Diego: Multifunctional Service Center, San Diego State University.

Chin, T. (Ed.). (1967). *A history of the Chinese in California.* San Francisco: Chinese History Society of America.

Conference Proceedings of the Asian-Pacific Regional Conference on Deafness, Jakarta, Indonesia, July 31 to August 4, 1989.

Epstein, I. (1989) *Special education issues in mainland China.* Taipei: International Conference on Education in Mainland China.

Fu, C. W., & Wawrytko, S. A. (1988). *Lao Tzu: Tao Te China.* Unpublished manuscript.

Gardner, R. W., Robey, B., & Smith, P. C. (1985). Asian Americans: Growth, change, and diversity. *Population Bulletin, 40,* 1–44.

Gokhale, S. D. (1982). Rehabilitation of disabled workers in Asia and Oceania. *Indian Journal of Social Work, 43,* 27–28.

Gudalefsky, A. (1989). The China scene. *TASH* (The Association for Severely Handicapped) *Newsletter, 15*(10).

Honna, N. (1980). Cultural pluralism in Japan: A sociolinguistic outline. *Journal of the Association of Law Teachers, 2,* 5–29.

Hwang, T. (1988). A study on the guidance program for the speech development of hearing impaired infants. *Bulletin of Special Education, 4,* 97–112. National Taiwan Normal University: Taipei.

Ima, K., Khommarath, B., Le, T. T., & San, K. (1989). *A handbook for professionals working with Southeast Asian juvenile delinquent youth.* San Diego: Southeast Asian Diversion Project.

Ima, K., & Rumbaut, R. G. (1989). Southeast Asian refugees in American schools: A comparison of fluent-English-proficient and limited-English-proficient students. *Topics in Language Disorders, 9*(3), 54–75.

Kitano, H.H.L., & Daniels, R. (1988). *Asian Americans: Emerging minorities.* Englewood Cliffs, NJ: Prentice-Hall.

Kohls, L. R. (1979). *Survival kit for overseas living.* Chicago: Intercultural Network/SYSTRAN Publications.

Kuo, W., Chen, Y., & Liang, C. N. (1976). *National prevalence study on exceptional children in the Republic of China.* Taipei: National Taiwan Normal University, Special Education Center.

Lin, P. B., & Ho, M. H. (1986). Research on audiological evaluation of the hearing impaired, cerebral palsied and mentally retarded in the Republic of China. In *The modernization of special education.* Taipei: National Taiwan Normal University.

Lock, M. M. (1980). *East Asian medicine in urban Japan.* Berkeley, CA: University of California.

Matsuda, M. (1989). Working with Asian parents: Some communication strategies. *Topics in Language Disorders, 9*(3), 45–53.

Meyerson, M. D. (1983). Genetic counseling for families of Chicano children with birth defects. In D. R. Omark & J. G. Erickson (Eds.), *The bilingual exceptional children.* San Diego: College Hill.

Ministry of Education, Republic of China. (1975). *Ministry of Education report.* Taipei: Author.

Rumbaut, R. G., & Ima, K. (1988). *The adaptation of Southeast Asian refugee youth: A comparative study*. Washington, DC: U.S. Department of Health and Human Services, Office of Refugee Resettlement.

Schildroth, A. N., Rawlings, B. W., & Allen, T. E. (1989). Hearing-impaired children under age 6: A demographic analysis. *American Annals of the Deaf, 134*(2), 63–69.

Sidel, R., & Sidel, V. W. (1982). *The health of China*. Boston: Beacon Press.

Stewart, J. L., Anae, A. P., & Gipe, P. N. (1989). Pacific Islander children: Prevalence of hearing loss and middle ear disease. *Topics in Language Disorders, 9*(3), 76–83.

Sue, D. (1986). *Counseling the culturally different: Theory and practice*. New York: Wiley.

Sue, S., & Padilla, A. (1986) Ethnic minority issues in the United States: Challenges for the educational system. In *Beyond Language*. Los Angeles: California State University.

United States Navy. (1944). (Formosans). *Human Relations Area Files* (HRAFF), Section ADI, Category 732, 15: U.S. Navy.

Takaki, R. (1989). *Strangers from a different shore*. Boston: Little, Brown.

Te, H. D. (1987). *Introduction to Vietnamese culture*. San Diego: Multifunctional Center, San Diego State University.

Walker, C. L. (1985). Learning English: The Southeast Asian refugee experience. *Topics in Language Disorders, 5*(3), 53–65.

Walker, W. (1988). *An introduction to the Hmong*. Unpublished manuscript.

SUGGESTED READINGS

Choy, B. (1979). *Koreans in America*. Chicago: Nelson-Hall.

Daniels, R. (1988). *Asian America: Chinese and Japanese in the United States since 1850*. Seattle: University of Washington Press.

Kim, H. (Ed.). (1986). *Dictionary of Asian American history*. Westport, CT: Greenwood Press.

Quinsaat, J. (Ed.). (1976). *Letters in exile: A reader on the history of Filipinos in America*. Los Angeles: University of California.

Saran, P. (1985). *The Asian Indian experience in the United States*. Cambridge, MA: Schenkman.

Strand, P. & Jones, W. (1985). *Indochinese refugees in America*. Durham, NC: Duke University Press.

Tsai, S. (1986). *The Chinese experience in America*. Bloomington, IN: Indiana University Press.

Yonemura, M. (1986). Empowerment and teacher education. *Harvard Educational Review, 56*, 473–480.

CHAPTER 8

Teaching Deaf Asian and Pacific Island American Children

C. Tane Akamatsu

Stay with the ancient Tao,
Move with the present,
                    Lao Tsu

In this chapter, the reader will learn how Asian and Pacific Island Americans who are deaf or hard of hearing are viewed by their communities. The chapter begins by describing the historical, political, and cultural influences that Americans of Asian and Pacific Island descent bring to their participation in American society. Following on Chapter 7, in which the geographic, cultural, religious, linguistic, and historical variations within the Asian/Pacific Island populations found in the United States are described, this chapter examines the relationship between immigration, migration, and settlement patterns and legislation and policies that arose from U.S. ambitions for colonial expansion in the Pacific basin. All of these forces foster ignorance and distrust of Asians and Pacific Americans, which in turn prevent accurate information about this group of people from being gathered. Most of the remarks pertain to the Asian/Pacific Island population of the United States as a whole, and certain statements may not be true of Hawaii because of the large Asian/Pacific Island population there. Where applicable Hawai'i's situation is discussed separately.[1]

Next, the deaf and hard-of-hearing Asian/Pacific American population is

---

The author gratefully acknowledges the fruitful discussions she has had with Lilly Cheng, Doreen Higa, and Terry Watada in developing this chapter. Of course, all errors of interpretation are the author's alone.

discussed in light of general census information. Areas of concern when working with deaf and hard-of-hearing Asian/Pacific Americans and their families are also presented. The chapter ends with a look ahead at the next decade and century.

In simplest form, Asian Americans are Americans whose ancestry has roots in East or Southeast Asia. The U.S. Census Bureau currently acknowledges some seventeen Asian American groups. Some come from families who have been in the United States for over two centuries; others are newcomers, refugees from the Vietnam conflict. Some are highly assimilated into American culture; others retain a strong ethnic identity; and still others are alienated from both American and ethnic identities (Kitano & Daniels, 1988).

In addition to Americans with roots in Asia, there are the myriad Pacific Islanders, who were more strongly subjected to political forces driving U.S. colonial expansion during the nineteenth and early twentieth centuries. By dint of having had their governments overthrown and annexed to the United States, these peoples differ from the Asians in that they became "Americans" not through migration, but through political processes. Yet, many have left their native islands, migrated to the mainland United States, and are faced with unique cultural, linguistic, and educational challenges.

An important distinction must be made here between migrants, immigrants, and refugees. *Migrants* merely move from one part of a country to another. These moves can be triggered by demographic and economic factors. Because the Pacific basin is so large, migration among islands was fairly limited until quite recently, and so distinct cultures developed within island groups.

Like migrants, *immigrants* are viewed as being "pulled" to new places, attracted by greater job opportunities, fertile land, clean water, better education, and more freedom. In this sense, immigrants from Asia were pulled to this country by the promise of wealth and opportunity. Immigrants often plan their migration, perhaps making contact with friends or family who are already in the new country, learning the new language when possible, packing treasured belongings, and saying good-bye to loved ones. There is always the possibility of return to the old country.

Hawai'i represents an interesting mix of immigration and migration. As recently as 200 years ago, the Americans and British were foreigners to the Kingdom of Hawai'i. However, between the introduction of new diseases that wiped out nearly half the native Hawaiian population, the later overthrow of the Hawaiian monarchy by American industrialists and subsequent annexation of Hawai'i to the United States, native Hawaiians were relegated to second class citizenship. Furthermore, in the effort to develop the sugar and pineapple growing industries, which the native Hawaiians resisted, large numbers of Asians were brought in.

At the time that Hawai'i was granted statehood (1959), two-thirds of the population was made up of ethnic groups other than black or white (U.S. Department of Commerce, 1975). Therefore, what happened to Hawai'i is that a numerically small but ultimately dominant culture (white Americans) "immigrated" to a new home. More recent immigration patterns in Hawai'i differ substantially from those of the rest of the U.S. These will be treated separately in this chapter.

Refugees, alternatively, were pushed out of their homes, often with less than twenty-four-hours' notice. There was nowhere to go, only a place to *leave*. There was no time to prepare—many escaped with only the clothes on their backs—and there would often be nothing to return to, if indeed the chance to return existed.

In addition to migrants, immigrants, and refugees, there are those whose families were subjected to American colonialism. They neither immigrated nor fled their homes. Their status relative to the U.S. government simply changed. The Filipinos and Hawaiians are examples of this subjugation.

LEGISLATIVE AND SOCIAL CONSEQUENCES OF IMMIGRATION

Two major waves of Asian immigration to the United States can be found. A period of active immigration between 1850 and 1924 saw the first wave of Chinese, Japanese, Indian, and Filipino laborers. The Immigration Act of 1924 effectively halted Asian immigration (except for Filipinos). Immigration was not to resume until after World War II with the McCarran–Walter Act (1952), which dropped race as a restriction to immigration. Immigration during the 1950s and 1960s consisted of Chinese and Japanese women (wives of pre-1924 immigrants), Korean families, Indians and Pakistanis, and Southeast Asian refugees fearing communist takeover after the French were defeated at Dienbienphu, Vietnam, in 1954. The second wave of immigration followed the fall of Saigon in 1974, and consisted largely of refugees from Vietnam, Cambodia, and Laos. Immigrants from all over Asia continue to enter the United States.

Closer examination of immigration from Asia and the Pacific Islands reveals an intricate dance among world events and U.S. legislation. This is an important consideration because it highlights the difference in how people view themselves and others. These differences affect the social organization of ethnic communities, their relationship with the mainstream culture, and consequent service delivery.

The first Asian immigrants, the Chinese, arrived prior to 1850, perhaps lured by promises of the "gold mountain" and the California gold rush. Chinese men were welcomed as a cheap and abusable source of labor during the building of the transcontinental railway. They, however, were neither acknowledged at the "golden spike" ceremony, nor tolerated well thereafter.

In large part, these men had left families in China. Apparently, the U.S. government was afraid that a negative consequence of allowing these families to immigrate would be that subsequent children born in the United States would have citizenship rights. Therefore, in an attempt to prevent further immigration, the Chinese Exclusion Act of 1882, the Geary Act of 1892 and its extension in 1902 halted further Chinese immigration. This effectively stranded a "bachelor society" in the new country.

Meanwhile, in Japan, the building of a new society following the Meiji Restoration of 1869 and the opening of trade with the outside world made possible the emigration of Japanese scholars and workers. The Chinese Exclusion Act, and subsequent agreements with the United States and the Kingdom of Hawai'i, opened the doors for large numbers of Japanese laborers to enter these two countries beginning in 1885.[2] Like the Chinese before them, the Japanese were seen as good laborers, but not good neighbors. A gentlemen's agreement between the United States and Japan in 1907 limited the number of people able to immigrate. During this period of immigration, the typical pattern was for the men to arrive first, establish a home, then send to Japan for a wife. Thus, Japanese families were begun in the United States.

In 1898, two major acts of American colonialism, the conquest of the Philippines and the annexation of Hawai'i, changed the lives of the native Filipinos and Hawaiians. Both were now considered to be American nationals, with certain rights that were denied the Chinese and Japanese immigrants. Thus, the Filipinos and the Hawaiians did not immigrate, per se.

In addition, because of cultural factors, migration of native Hawaiians from the state of Hawai'i to the mainland United States has sometimes been couched as "immigration," although the term is technically inaccurate.[3] World War I, begun in 1914, was followed in 1917 with the creation of a "barred zone," which excluded immigration from China, Southeast Asia, Asian Russia, Afghanistan, Iran, part of Arabia, and Pacific and Southeast Asian islands not territories of the United States. Because of the previously mentioned gentlemen's agreement with Japan, the Japanese were not affected initially by this barred zone. However, in 1924 with the Immigration Act, Japan was added to the barred zone. The Tydings–McDuffie Act of 1934, ostensibly designed to return sovereignty to the Philippines, also came at a time when all other Asians were excluded from immigration. The only way to prevent Filipinos from immigrating was to grant them independence. Thus ended the first wave of Asian immigration.

The Asian and Pacific Islanders already in the United States continued to work mostly as laborers on plantations, as migrant workers on farms, and as small businessmen in fishing and textiles. Fear and ignorance of these visibly different people was given legitimacy through the various pieces of legislation passed by the government. Prejudice haunted the children of the immigrants, even though by law these children were full-fledged American citizens.

The Japanese attack on Pearl Harbor in 1941 plunged the United States into World War II. War creates strange bedfellows, and the United States, finding itself allied with China against Japan, repealed the Chinese Exclusion Act in 1943. Some racist elements did remain in the repeal, however. Chinese immigration resumed, this time largely of women, peaking in 1948.

In a purely racist act, and without military necessity, Executive Order 9066 was signed by President Franklin D. Roosevelt in 1942, mandating the incarceration of some 120,000 Japanese immigrants and Japanese Americans. In this act, the civil rights of a segment of American citizens and permanent residents were stripped away. Although this is not strictly an issue of immigration, it does speak to the treatment that was accorded to the immigrants and their offspring once they were in the United States. At the same time, the military conscripted young Japanese American men into service, often taking them from the U.S. incarceration camps to fight for "freedom" in Europe. It is ironic that while serving in the U.S. military, Japanese Americans freed many Jews from Nazi concentration camps while their own families were still behind barbed wire at home. It is even sadder that, although the American internment camps were closed by the end of the war, Executive Order 9066 was not repealed until 1974. Formal apology was not made until the Civil Liberties Act of 1988. Redress monies for the incarceration have been legislated, but actual payments did not begin until October, 1990.

The resulting fear, shame, and bitterness felt by many Japanese Americans led them to attempt to blend into the U.S. landscape. Many chose to marry outside the Japanese American community. "Obey the government," "don't rock the boat," and "don't do anything to draw attention to yourself or the family" were common admonishments during the postwar years. This fear, combined with the desire to be accepted, confirmed the oppressive stereotype of Asians as the "model minority." After World War II, the United States began to relax immigration laws. In 1946, Filipinos and "races indigenous to India" could be naturalized citizens, and the quota system for the Chinese was relaxed. The Displaced Person's Act of 1948 allowed immigration for refugees as a consequence of World War II and those fleeing Soviet persecution. Other Asians finally became admissible to the United States under the McCarran–Walter Act of 1952. This gave rise to the second major wave of immigration.

Hostilities in Southeast Asia set in motion a sequence of events, beginning with the French defeat at Dienbienphu, Vietnam, in 1954. The Refugee Relief Act of 1953 allowed for refugees fleeing communism, and the first wave of Southeast Asian refugees came at this time. The Migration and Refugee Assistance Act of 1962 and the Immigration Act of 1965 both made emigration from Asia to the United States easier. The fall of Saigon in 1974 was followed by a second wave of Southeast Asian refugees (the third major wave of immigration), which continues to the present. Since 1974, the U.S. government has passed the Refugee Assistance Act (1980) and the Immigration Reform Act (1986), facilitating entry of all immigrants into the United States.

Table 8.1 summarizes information on immigration patterns for various Asian and Pacific Island ethnic groups. This brief history shows that Asian and Pacific Islanders became Americans through a number of different routes, over a long period of time. Their fates in the United States were sometimes determined by the relationship of their home government with the United States, and sometimes by internal economic and demographic forces. It is clear, however, that until fairly recently, the United States pursued a policy of economic convenience with regard to Asian immigration, and a policy of colonial expansion with regard to the Pacific Islands. These policies fueled the discrimination against Asian and Pacific Americans, preventing an accurate understanding of these people and their rightful place in American society.

TABLE 8.1 Summary of Immigration History

Ethnic Group	Immigration Years
Hawaiian	Original settlers; first contact with West (British) in 1778; annexed to the United States in 1898
Chinese	Pre-1850–1882; 1943 to present
Japanese	1868–1924; 1952 to present
Korean	1882–1924; 1952 to present
Filipino	Pre-1898; migration 1920–1934; immigration 1965 to present
Indian	1947 to present
Vietnamese	1954 to present (immigration 1954–1975; mostly refugees since 1975)
Hmong, Khmer (Cambodian), Laotian	1975 to present

DEAF ASIAN/PACIFIC ISLAND AMERICANS

Neither the U.S. Department of Education nor the Office of Civil Rights collects statistics on the numbers of Asian/Pacific Americans receiving services for individuals with hearing loss.[4] Therefore, what follows are estimates of the number of Asian/Pacific Americans receiving such services, particularly within the school-age population. This problem can be approached from two perspectives. The first is to find the number of Deaf and hard-of-hearing people in the general population and then calculate the Deaf and hard-of-hearing Asian/Pacific American population according to the percentage of that group within the general population. The second is to find the number of Asian/Pacific Americans, then calculate the Deaf and hard-of-hearing population according to the percentage of Deaf and hard-of-hearing persons in the general population.

Two sources of information are the National Health and Nutrition Evaluation Survey (NHANES) and the National Health Interview Survey (NHIS), both collected by the U.S. National Center for Health Statistics (Reis, 1986). These data are only for children receiving special services through the local schools, not through residential schools. Therefore, the numbers are likely to include proportionately more children whose hearing losses are mild to moderate, and fewer children with severe to profound losses. Data from the NHANES for 1976–1980 show almost 45 million children, of whom 84,000 had hearing losses of greater than 41 decibels. Using a figure of one percent as the proportion of Asian/Pacific Americans in the general population at that time (Kitano & Daniels, 1988), the population includes 450,000 Deaf and hard-of-hearing Asian/Pacific Americans, of whom 840 had hearing losses greater than 41 decibels.

Using the data from 1971 and 1977, and collapsing them to yield a midcycle (1974) estimate, Reis (1986) estimated 841,000 Deaf and hard-of-hearing children, of whom 129,000 were Deaf. Again using the one percent proportion figure, this indicates 8,410 Deaf and hard-of-hearing Asian/Pacific Americans, of whom 1,290 are Deaf. Because of the population surveyed (which, as noted above, did not include residential schools), these figures are very likely to underestimate the actual numbers of Deaf Asian/Pacific Americans.

Furthermore, because estimates of the Asian/Pacific American population were used in these calculations, and the proportion of this population has grown in recent years, it is likely that these figures, disparate as they are, are underestimates of the size of the Deaf and hard-of-hearing Asian/Pacific American population.

A second calculation, based on research by Sontag, Smith, and Certo (1977), estimated approximately 377,000 school-age children with educationally significant hearing losses. Again using the one percent proportion, this yielded an estimated 3,700 deaf and hard-of-hearing Asian/Pacific American school children during the 1970s, and a projected 5,500 in 1980.

In 1990, Asian/Pacific Americans represented approximately 2.9 percent of the U.S. population (U.S. Department of Commerce, 1991). They are the fastest growing population in the country. Accordingly, from an estimated two million Deaf Americans (Moores, 1987), one can estimate that some 58,000 are Asian/Pacific Americans. Based on this figure, 11,600 might be born deaf or become deaf during childhood.

The annual survey collected by the Center for Assessment and Demographic Studies (CADS) at Gallaudet University, tends to sample more heavily from residential and special schools than from local schools. However, response is voluntary. The survey for 1990–1991 sampled 47,025 students, representing 60 percent to 70 percent of the total population of deaf and hard-of-hearing students (Allen, personal communication, 1992). Of these students, some 1,700 were Asian/Pacific American, resulting in an estimated total of 2,615 deaf and hard-of-hearing Asian/Pacific American students nationwide. These figures reflect 3.7 percent incidence of deaf and hard-of-hearing students, which is somewhat higher than in the general population. The data from the CADS survey will be used in further discussions because it is the only survey for which actual numbers were reported for children who were Deaf and hard-of-hearing *and* Asian/Pacific American. Therefore, in spite of the bias toward sampling from special schools, this is probably the most accurate estimate available.

Ethnic and multicultural groups as a whole are overrepresented in the Deaf and hard-of-hearing school population (35 percent). The proportion of Deaf and hard-of-hearing Asian/Pacific Americans receiving special education services is also somewhat higher than the proportion of Asian/Pacific Americans in the general population. However, it is unknown whether hearing impairment is more prevalent among Asian/Pacific Americans, whether it is more prevalent among the more recent immigrant population and therefore among the younger school-age children, or whether there are actually more immigrants than census counts indicate. The difficulty in ascertaining the size of the deaf and hard-of-hearing Asian/Pacific American population is compounded by one startling statistic: The number of deaf and hard-of-hearing Asian/Pacific American children under the age of six enrolled in the school system has increased by 206 percent (Schildroth, Rawlings, & Allen, 1989). This alone argues the necessity of finding out who these children are, where they are, what their backgrounds are, what kinds of services need to be provided, and how best to accomplish this.

Given that many deaf or hard-of-hearing Asian/Pacific American children probably are recent refugees, the higher incidence of hearing impairment could be caused by lack of adequate health care of both mother and child, especially if pregnancy, birth, and infancy were spent in refugee camps.

In addition, medical services in the United States are prohibitively expensive, and it is unlikely that many refugee families participate in any group health insurance plans. Even when low-cost or free help is available, personal problems (in particular, mental health and social problems) are not topics for public discussion. Delayed or deviant speech patterns and difficulties in social interactions caused by hearing impairment may be viewed as taboo. Even after arrival in the United States, treatable health problems that can lead to hearing impairments may go undetected and untreated until permanent damage is done.

According to CADS (Schildroth, personal communication, February 2, 1990), nearly 21 percent of the 1,700 Asian/Pacific American children they surveyed were enrolled in special schools, which is lower than the 34 percent reported in the general population. Within special schools, about 12 percent were in oral programs, and 88 percent were in total communication programs. This division is close to that represented in the general deaf and hard-of-hearing population attending special schools. Conversely, local schools serve 71 percent of the deaf and hard-of-hearing Asian/Pacific American students. Just under half were placed in oral programs; the remainder in total communication programs. This breakdown is also close to that of the general deaf and hard-of-hearing population in the local schools. The higher proportion of students in the local schools may reflect strong family ties that would mitigate against a child's being sent to a residential program. It may also result from ignorance of available social services in the communities, as well as a reluctance to use services. This point is discussed more fully in the next section.

The remaining 8 percent of the 1,427 Deaf and hard-of-hearing Asian/Pacific American population receive no services at all, although it is unclear why. Perhaps the kinds of hearing impairments that Asian/Pacific Americans have are mild and medically manageable and do not necessitate special educational services. However, the fact that Asian/Pacific Americans already appear to be overrepresented in the deaf and hard-of-hearing population suggests a problem in identifying and programming.

One final word about demographics. Moores (1987) found that, although African American, Hispanic, Asian/Pacific American, and Native American groups as a whole are overrepresented in the deaf and hard-of-hearing school population, less than 6 percent of their teachers are drawn from these populations. In 1981, Corbett and Jensema found only forty-seven Asian/Pacific American teachers of the deaf and hard-of-hearing. This represents about one percent of the total population of teachers of deaf and hard-of-hearing children. It is unknown how many of these Asian/Pacific American teachers were deaf or hard of hearing themselves. This is not to argue that only Asian/Pacific American teachers can teach Asian/Pacific American deaf children, but rather that the odds of an Asian/Pacific American deaf child being taught by someone of a different culture are very high. Effective teachers will have the ability to work effectively with diverse cultures.

WORKING WITH DEAF ASIAN/PACIFIC AMERICANS AND THEIR FAMILIES

In Chapter 7, Cheng discussed some characteristics of Asian families. Asian Americans come from cultures with long-standing roots in Confucian philosophy. The status of the family is primary, and the individual's identity is seen in relation to that group. Pacific Island Americans also have a notion of family (e.g., Hawaiian *'ohana*; see Boggs, 1985; Handy & Pukui, 1972), albeit a different one from that of Asian Americans. In both cases, however, there is a clear notion of one's identity as related to the group's identity, and individuals are seen in terms of their roles within the group.

Asian and Pacific American families display a mixture of both Eastern and Western characteristics, depending on when the family first arrived in the United States. Typically, the longer the family has been in or associated with the United States, the more Americanized they tend to be, particularly if the parents received a U.S. education. It is not known the extent to which hearing impairment overrides the family's ethnic culture. In other words, does the ethnic deaf hard-of-hearing child identify more with Deaf culture or with his or her ethnic culture? Certainly any generalizations must be taken with some caution.

It is also important to remember that not all Asian American children are raised by Asian American families. As part of the refugee assistance movement, orphaned children are commonly adopted in white (Anglo) families and grow up in that culture. Because of the common cultural and linguistic bond with the mainstream culture, these families may participate more directly in their children's educational programming than Asian American families do.

Many Chinese and Japanese American children now in the public school system are fourth and fifth generation Asian/Pacific Americans, and come from English-speaking families. Any explicit knowledge they possess about their ethnic heritage is likely to be limited to stock phrases and food names. They may carry values from their ethnic communities but be unaware of the origins of those values. Because these families are often physically integrated into suburban neighborhoods, their life styles reflect the ambiance of the neighborhood rather than anything noticeably ethnic. Outmarriage rates (to whites) in California range from 14 percent to 32 percent, depending on ethnicity (Takaki, 1989). There is also a growing number of Asian-Hispanic and Asian-African American intermarriage, particularly in southern California.

The children of families who immigrated between the end of World War II and the fall of Saigon are second or third generation Americans. The children are likely to prefer English as their native language, but they may retain considerable receptive ability in the ethnic language. This is particularly true for the second generation. There may still be fairly strong identification with both the ethnic and American cultures, leading to both internal and external conflict. On one hand, parents probably maintain certain ethnic traditions at home. On the other hand, they encourage the children to succeed in the American mainstream. This sets up an uncomfortable tension when the ethnic values at home conflict with mainstream values.

On the mainland United States, the Southeast Asian refugees represent the most recent immigrant group. The children are first generation Americans, usually bilingual in their ethnic language and in English. The extent to which they are integrated in the American mainstream probably has more to do with individual personality than with any other factor. The more gregarious children will likely make more friends, both ethnic and mainstream, and thereby have a greater "in" to the new community. These children, however, may also have been victims of tragic events in their own lifetimes, including the loss of sociocultural identity.

In Hawai'i, Asian/Pacific Americans comprise 79 percent of the deaf and hard-of-hearing student population, a proportion somewhat higher than in the general population (roughly 55 percent to 60 percent). Hawaiians and part-Hawaiians comprise between 17 percent and 20 percent of the state's population (Boggs, 1985), and about 31 percent of the deaf and hard-of-hearing children. In contrast, the Japanese account for approximately 25 percent of the state's population but only 10 percent of the deaf and hard-of-hearing children. The fastest growing ethnic group is Filipino, comprising 23 percent of the deaf and hard-of-hearing school children (D. Higa, personal communication, August 17, 1990). The remaining deaf and hard-of-hearing Asian/Pacific American students are, in descending order, "other"[5] (5 percent), Samoan (4 percent), Chinese (3 percent), Korean (2 percent), and Indochinese (1 percent) (J. Fernandez, personal communication, April 29, 1990).[6]

The disparities between the occurrence of hearing impairments among Hawai'i's various ethnic groups and in the state's general population may be partially explained by the intricate interplay among socioeconomic status of the ethnic groups. Of particular interest for Hawai'i, however, is the pervasive finding among various native populations (e.g., the Aleuts in Alaska, other Native American peoples on the mainland United States, native Hawaiians and part-Hawaiians in Hawai'i, other people native to Pacific Islands) of a higher than average incidence of otitis media (inflammation of the middle ear), which appears to be endemic to these populations (Stewart, Anae, & Gipe, 1989). Perhaps exacerbating or certainly interacting with this are certain demographic factors. Pacific Island children grow up in the tropics (high humidity), on islands (lots of swimming), somewhat isolated from sophisticated medical facilities, and under living conditions that border those of the third world. Hawaiians frequently have incomes lower than the state average (Alu Like, Inc., cited in Boggs, 1985), and are more concentrated in the rural areas of the islands.

BELIEFS ABOUT DEAF CHILDREN

Because many Asian and Pacific people believe that deafness is a disability caused by *karma* (fate), they carry a fatalistic attitude about any kind of intervention.[7] Furthermore, differences among cultures regarding the general treatment of people with disabilities lead to different reasons for accepting or declining services. For example, in cultures where deaf children should be sheltered from the outside world (e.g., Chamorro), there will be a reluctance to send the child to school in the belief that school is a challenge that the child should not have to face.

People from cultures that ostracize those who are "deformed" or "cursed" (e.g., Filipino, Chinese) may be hesitant about devoting extra time to the benefit of the deaf child, or may even question the wisdom of public specialized education. That is, the families may care for the children, but other community members will be reluctant to "taint" themselves by working with these children. Still others, who take deafness as a personal embarrassment, may be reluctant to appear in public on behalf of the deaf child. Therefore, it is extremely important to ascertain the view of the deaf child held by the family and ethnic community.

Generally, Asian and Pacific Island cultures view children as helpless, dependent, and lacking intentionality (see Chapter 7). Therefore, if a child does not demonstrate certain behaviors, it is believed that the child cannot, for whatever reason. "Disabled" children, in addition, are exempt from tackling many of the challenges of growing up because of "ill health," even though a deaf child might be in perfect health. This exemption may also include tasks of which the child is quite capable but simply has not been taught. Deaf children are no different in this regard. Therefore, parents might look askance if an educator tries to place their deaf children in schools with the intention of teaching them to read and write and perhaps eventually attend college.

Infants who show signs of development generally regarded as positive by mainstream culture, such as advanced physical and verbal abilities and increasingly independent behavior, are often viewed as "difficult" by Asian parents. Ironically, because Asian/Pacific American cultures often define "good" infants as quiet ones, the possibility of deafness may be overlooked in the Deaf infant who is, of course, exceptionally quiet—especially after the instinctive babbling stage has passed. Delays in the diagnosis of deafness, and the continued communicative interaction with the infant through the oral-auditory modality means that appropriate measures to establish communication for the purpose of linguistic and cognitive development may be delayed longer for Asian/Pacific American families than for mainstream families. Whereas the traditional Asian or Pacific Island cultural beliefs will be stronger in recently immigrated families, those who have been in the United States for several generations will be aware of Western beliefs and educational practices. An ironic twist is that Deaf children of "Westernized" Asian families are often unaware of their ethnic cultural values because of the communication gap between them and their families. Thus, Asian/Pacific American Deaf children may grow up to become Deaf adults first, and ethnic Deaf second.

HOME LANGUAGE LITERACY AND SCHOOLING CONSIDERATIONS

One must remember that although many immigrants come from societies in which mass public education is accessible, some do not. Among immigrants who come from societies where formal schooling and literacy are not common (e.g., the Hmong), the whole system of public education may be a great shock.

Even people who come from long and distinguished literate traditions (e.g., the Chinese and Japanese) may find their cultural systems at odds with the educational system. Furthermore, the local level implementation of Public Law 94-142 (Education for All Handicapped Children Act of 1975) varies from state to state and can be a confusing process even to those familiar with mass public education. Exacerbating this situation is the fact that Confucian values hold teachers in utmost respect. Parents are likely to trust educators as the ultimate authority regarding their children's educations; therefore, they may not understand their own role on the individual educational planning committee (IEPC), nor in parent–teacher conferences.

Furthermore, recent Asian refugees are by and large war refugees who have not had the luxury of attending school. Indeed, many have spent several years immediately prior to entering the United States in refugee camps and "on the run." Therefore, they may not even understand the principles of schooling, much less the principles of Western education. Therefore, depending on the particular population, the school system and the role of special education within that system will need to be explained.

If the parents come from a preliterate society such as the Hmong, or have not participated to any great extent in a public education system in their homeland, then they may not understand their rights, nor how to exercise those rights. Parents may not trust strangers to look after their children, and they may be even more wary on behalf of their deaf child. They may view the IEPC as a collection of experts who make recommendations that are so foreign as to be unintelligible, even with translators. Although in recent years teachers have been encouraged to involve parents more in their children's education by eliciting ideas from them, this style of interaction may be misinterpreted. Parents may perceive that teachers do not have the knowledge to do their jobs, and thus lose confidence in the educational system. Ironically, parents may choose to keep their deaf child in the same school that their brothers and sisters attend because that is the only familiar option.

The use of the ethnic language as the primary language of the home may present difficulties when teachers attempt to establish home–school relationships. Even families from highly literate and educated societies come from school systems that are quite different from those in the United States. For example, in Japan, classes are large, and individualized instruction is virtually unheard of (Sato, 1990b). Rather, children are taught to "learn with the head (academics), learn with the body (physical education), learn with the hands (skills) and learn with the heart (aesthetics)" (Sato, 1990a). In this way, each child's individual ability to learn in different ways is recognized. In contrast with the West, Japanese children who are physically but not academically talented are not put into special classes, but merely praised for their physical prowess and encouraged to continue trying within the academic curriculum.

INTERACTION STYLES

Typically, Asians do not perceive disabilities without some kind of physical manifestation (Matsuda, 1989). Although deafness does have a physical component, little can be done medically to create normal hearing. Deafness, as it is perceived by many Asian families, can create an additional emotional burden on the family. The educational needs of both the child and the family must be considered. Tung (1985) cautioned that, as a group, Asian/ Pacific Americans are particularly reticent in discussing emotional matters with anyone outside the family, and problems are often presented in muted, understated form.

Interpersonal relationships among Asian cultures are governed by one's relationship to others in a group. Kim (1985) observed that "verbal articulation is less important than non-verbal, contextual sensitivity and appropriateness. Eastern cultures favor verbal hesitance and ambiguity to avoid disturbing or offending others" (p. 405). As such, even if parents are uncomfortable with a recommendation, or if they disagree with an observation, they will be unlikely to state their own point of view for fear of offending the "expert" clinician or teacher. They may merely smile, nod, and proceed to ignore recommendations or not implement any changes at home.

Teachers must place all observations *within a cultural context* before evaluating their relevance. For example, spiritual beliefs and practices such as ancestor worship make seeking the advice of dead family members common. Such behavior is acceptable in some cultures.

One common practice for schools or agencies is to hold workshops or meetings for parents, during which brochures and pamphlets are passed out to be taken home and read. Although much information is available in print for parents regarding deafness, it must be presented in a form that the parents can understand. It is helpful if educators translate this information into other languages and make it available in spoken form for parents who cannot read either their ethnic language or English. For example, parents might be allowed to borrow a tape player to listen to cassettes at home.

Often, because of economic exigencies, parents have neither the time nor the money to attend community meetings, even if the meetings are free. A more personal approach is needed to work with these families. By soliciting liaisons within the ethnic community, a teacher may be able to visit the home and both observe and talk with the family. Sometimes community agencies may coordinate with the schools to provide this information. For example, in Toronto, Canada, Japanese Family Services, a nonprofit agency funded by government grants, provides monthly seminars on various family-related topics to new Japanese immigrants (Thurlow, 1990). Any questions raised by families at school–community meetings can be dealt with through follow-up meetings or home visits.

Status is very important in Asian/Pacific American families. Teachers are authority figures and may have higher status than the father, who in turn has higher status than the mother. Formal introductions among members at a meeting allow parents to understand lines of authority, and they create the context in which all remarks can be interpreted.

Matsuda (1989) has discussed several guidelines for communicating with Asian parents. For example, reaching consensus is more productive than confrontation. Parents will usually indicate how far they are willing to go in implementing recommendations. They may do this indirectly, perhaps by offering a compromise solution that addresses some but not all of the child's needs.

Indirect approaches to information gathering are best, because they allow parents to take the lead in offering information that they feel comfortable revealing. It also allows for teachers to circumvent confrontations and tread lightly on sensitive areas, and for parents to save face. The usual Western style of asking direct questions is often taken as "prying," and parents may tell teachers what they think they want to hear, rather than the truth. Although an indirect approach may take much longer to get needed information, the quality of the information will be much better.

Nonverbal cues speak volumes, but they can be misleading. In the Asian culture, it is rude to meet the eyes of one's superior. Therefore, many Asian parents will not look directly at teachers when they speak. In Western culture, this is sometimes misinterpreted as avoidance behavior, as if the parents had something to hide. On the other hand, Asian parents may misinterpret an avid, interested gaze as "hostile," and questions as "prying."

SCHOOL PLACEMENT

The range of placements, from residential schools to center programs to local public schools, places different pressures on the families. Deafness is probably the only disability area in which what is commonly taken to be the "least restrictive environment" can be the most restrictive. That is because of the communication difficulties inherent in deafness. For example, at a residential school, where a large number of people use signed language as a matter of course, role models exist in the form of older Deaf students and Deaf adults, and one has communicative access twenty-four hours a day. This is less restrictive than living at home, where maybe only one person in the family can communicate with the Deaf child with any ease, and attending school where there may be only one teacher of the Deaf and a handful of other Deaf children. Yet, the recommendation to send a Deaf child to a residential school may be taken as an attempt by the school system to disrupt the family dynamics.

Very little information is available on effective education of the Asian/Pacific American deaf and hard-of-hearing populations. However, particularly with recent immigrants, a good start might be to work on the model of bicultural and bilingual education. In the case of deafness in Asian families, a potentially trilingual and tricultural situation exists between the English-speaking mainstream establishment, the English- and/or ethnic-language-speaking family, and the American Sign Language (ASL) Deaf community. This can be accomplished by tapping community resources from *within* the Asian/Pacific American community (Cheng, 1989), as well as from within the Deaf community (Taylor, 1990).

For example, in the San Diego Unified School District, the deaf and hard-of-hearing program has worked with the second language department and various community agencies, such as social service, resettlement, and health care (MacNeil, 1985). Such a system allows community agencies to provide information about the families. Asian/Pacific American students who are receiving English as a second language (ESL) services could be paired with deaf and hard-of-hearing Asian/Pacific American students to practice English, for example. Or, at least, an ESL student's knowledge about Asian/Pacific American culture could be used in interpreting what is going on with a deaf or hard-of-hearing Asian/Pacific American student whose family does not speak English. In addition, bilingual Asian/Pacific American adults could be recruited as translators to work between home and school. English-speaking Asian/Pacific American teachers could help educate other staff members who are unfamiliar with Asian/Pacific American cultures. The success of such an approach varies widely from family to family, depending on which combinations of language and cultural identities are at work (Higa, personal communication, August 17, 1990). Clearly, various models must be tried and reported in the literature before any recommendations can be made with confidence.

University programs in teacher education need to actively recruit Asian/Pacific American students, stressing the need for role models and the value of a multicultural society. Hawai'i has no university-level program for working with deaf and hard-of-hearing Asian/Pacific American students; however, there is a Gallaudet Regional Outreach Center in Honolulu. Although a good command of English is valuable, fluency in English must not be of utmost priority in the profession. If demographics, history, and common sense serve us correctly, then most college and university Asian/Pacific American students have a strong command of English. Once in the profession, Asian/Pacific American teachers must be valued not only as sources of information about Asian/Pacific Americans, but as resources to that community at large.

SUMMARY AND A LOOK TO THE FUTURE

This chapter introduced briefly the historical, social, and legislative forces that have shaped the community of Asian and Pacific Americans. The histories of the different ethnic groups varied considerably in terms of the conditions of their arrival, the home languages used, and the kinds of legislation used to prohibit immigration. Different interaction styles must be adopted when working with Asian and Pacific American people, because of their strong identification with a group. In this respect, the priority must be to work harmoniously and achieve goals for students with a minimum of confrontation and conflict, while keeping in mind the needs of students in relation to their group identity.

The Asian/Pacific American community will continue to grow at a rapid pace, largely because of immigration. By the year 2000, they will make up 4 percent of the general population. The key to the survival and well-being of the community, nevertheless, lies in the hands of the dominant culture (Kitano & Daniels, 1988). A look at the history of immigration, prejudice, and legislation must serve as a reminder to future generations that Asian/Pacific Americans have given much to this country, in spite of legal and social barriers. One can expect no less from Asian/Pacific Americans who are also deaf or hard of hearing.

NOTES

1. The spelling of *Hawai'i* used in this chapter reflects the current drive for respect of Hawai'i's indigenous people and language. The ['] represents the glottal stop consonant in the Hawaiian language.

2. Hawai'i was annexed to the United States in 1888 and became a U.S. territory in 1900. Therefore, this gentlemen's agreement covered those laborers in Hawai'i as well.
3. Interestingly, the Hawaiians are the only "native American" group to be included in the Asian/Pacific American population rather than in the Native American population, for cultural, geographic, and historical reasons. As such, they have not enjoyed what little sovereignty the Native Americans retain over their lands. Negotiations between the U.S. government and the Native Americans over issues such as land claims have not included the Hawaiians.
4. Indeed, the very fact that neither department collects statistics on the incidence of disabling conditions among any ethnic group suggests that people of color who are also disabled in some way must choose between being a person of color or being disabled. This further implies that disabled people of color must fit whatever policies are developed for disabled people in general. The author uses the term *disabled* here reluctantly recognizing that Deaf people themselves, while counted among the disabled, do not consider themselves in that way, but rather as a separate cultural group.
5. "Other" probably means mixed ethnicity, excluding part-Hawaiians.
6. The ethnic breakdown of the rest of Hawai'i's hearing impaired population is as follows: white (including Portuguese) 17 percent, black 2 percent, Hispanic (Spanish and Puerto Rican) 1.7 percent, Native American 0 percent. These statistics were provided by the Statewide Center for Students with Hearing and Visual Impairments. The interested reader is referred to other chapters of this text for comparative statistics.
7. This fatalistic attitude is reflected in phrases still used today. For example, in Japanese, there is *"shikata ga nai"* (it can't be helped).

BIBLIOGRAPHY

Boggs, S. (1985). *Speaking, relating, and learning: A study of Hawaiian children at home and at school*. Norwood, NJ: Ablex.

Cheng, L. (1989). Service delivery to Asian/Pacific LEP children: A cross cultural framework. *Topics in Language Disorders, 9* (3), 1–14.

Corbett, E., & Jensema, C. (1981). *Teachers of the hearing impaired: Descriptive profiles*. Washington, DC: Gallaudet College.

Gardner, R., Robey, B., & Smith, P. (1985). Asian Americans: Growth, change and diversity. *Population Bulletin, 40*(4), Figure 4.

Handy, E., & Pukui, M. (1972). *The Polynesian family system in Ka'u, Hawai'i*. Wellington, New Zealand: The Polynesian Society. (Original work published 1953).

Kim, Y. Y. (1985). Intercultural personhood: An integration of Eastern and Western perspectives. In L. A. Samovar & R. E. Porter (Eds.), *Intercultural communication: A reader* (4th ed.). Belmont, CA: Wadsworth.

Kitano, H., & Daniels, R. (1988). *Asian Americans: Emerging minorities*. Englewood Cliffs, NJ: Prentice-Hall.

MacNeil, B. (1985, June–July). *The hearing-impaired Indochinese in San Diego Unified School District*. Paper presented at the Convention of American Instructors of the Deaf—Conference of Educational Administrators Serving the Deaf, Santa Fe.

Matsuda, M. (1989). Working with Asian parents: Some communication strategies. *Topics in Language Disorders, 9*(3), 45–53.

Moores, D. (1987). *Educating the deaf: Psychology, principles, and practices* (3rd ed.). Boston: Houghton Mifflin.

Reis, P. (1986). Characteristics of hearing impaired youth in the general population and of students in special educational programs for the deaf and hard-of-hearing. In A. N. Schildroth & M. A. Karchmer, (Eds.), San Diego. *Deaf children in America* (pp. 1–31). San Diego: College-Hill.

Sato, N. (1990a, April). *A different conception of "intelligence" in Japanese elementary schools—with different results*. Paper presented at the meeting of the American Educational Research Association, Boston.

Sato, N. (1990b, April). *Equity issues reconsidered: Insights from a study of Japanese elementary schools*. Paper presented at the meeting of the American Educational Research Association, Boston.

Schildroth, A., Rawlings, B., & Allen, T. (1989). Hearing-impaired children under age 6: A demographic analysis. *American Annals of the Deaf, 134*(2), 63–69.

Sontag, E., Smith, J., & Certo, N. (1977). *Educational programming for the severely and profoundly handicapped*. Reston, VA: Council for Exceptional Children.

Stewart, J., Anae, A., & Gipe, P. (1989). Pacific Islander children: Prevalence of hearing loss and middle ear disease. *Topics in Language Disorders, 9*(3), 76–83.

Takaki, R. (1989). *Strangers from a different shore*. Boston: Little, Brown.

Taylor, N. (1990, July–August). *IMPACT-ASL: Working with English-illiterate deaf adults*. Paper presented at the International Congress on Education of the Deaf, Rochester, NY.

Thurlow, S. (1990, July). Ibunka shakai in okeru kosodate [On raising children in a foreign culture]. *Nikkei no koe, 4*(6), 13, 16.

Tung, T. M. (1985). Psychiatric care for Southeast Asians: How different is different? In T. Owan (Ed.), *Southeast Asian mental health* (pp. 5–40). Bethesda, MD: National Institute of Mental Health.

U.S. Department of Commerce. (1975). *Historical statistics of the United States: Colonial times to 1970*. Washington, DC: Author.

U.S. Department of Commerce. (1991). Race and Hispanic Origin. *1990 census profile*, no. 2. Washington, DC: Author.

CHAPTER 9

American Indian Deaf Children and Youth

Sue Anne Hammond and Linda Hagar Meiners

People throughout the world are brought up to react to strange situations in different ways. The American Indian when faced with an unfamiliar situation which may be cause for anxiety will seem to freeze or become motionless and from appearances seem to show no emotion. During this time however, he is using all senses to discover what is expected of him to meet the situation or crisis. At this time he will determine which activities are proper, correct or safe.

E. Morton

American Indians* comprise one of the least understood cultural groups in the United States. Despite the historical efforts of the U.S. government to eradicate their unique languages, beliefs, and life styles, most Indian people maintain some degree of traditional cultural identity (Szasz, 1974). American Indians with hearing loss are no exception in this regard. This chapter examines the situation of American Indian Deaf children, with particular attention to tribes in Arizona.

Professionals in the field of deafness are increasingly aware of the need for additional research and training in issues affecting multicultural Deaf children (Cohen, Fischgrund, & Redding, 1990). Very little attention, however, has been given to the American Indian Deaf child as a member of a distinct cultural community. A review of the literature has produced

---

*Many terms are commonly used to label the descendants of the first Americans—*Indian, American Indian, Alaska Native,* and *Native American*—but the first two are preferred by most members of these cultural groups (Dillard, 1983). For that reason, the terms *Indian* and *American Indian* will be used interchangeably throughout this chapter.

some initial reports regarding American Indian perspectives on disability (Joe & Miller, 1987; Locust, 1985). A great deal of literature related to the high incidence of otitis media (inflammation of the middle ear) and conductive hearing loss among Indian children is also available (Gregg, Roberts, & Colleran, 1983; Leviton, 1980; McShane & Mitchell, 1979; Shaw, Todd, Goodwin, & Felman, 1981). However, no specific information exists regarding the implications of severe to profound deafness among American Indians. It is evident that further study of this population is needed in order to understand the issue of deafness as it applies to the United States' first ethnic group.

DEMOGRAPHICS OF THE AMERICAN INDIAN

The legal definition of *American Indian* is vague. Federal Indian Law of 1985 includes two central qualifications: (1) Some of the individual's ancestors lived in America before its discovery by the Europeans; and (2) the individual is accepted as an Indian by the legally constituted Indian community in which he or she lives (Dillard, 1983). Individual tribes, therefore, may vary in their determination of who is entitled to tribal membership.

According to the Native American Research and Training Center report on the needs of Indians with disabilities (O'Connell, 1987), the American Indian population nearly tripled between 1960 and 1980; and American Indians have the highest birth rate when compared with white, African American, and Hispanic groups. The 1980 census reported almost 1.5 million American Indians within the total U.S. population (U.S. Bureau of the Census, 1983).

This percentage of Indian people in the United States parallels the 6 percent American Indian Deaf population reported by the *1988–89 Annual Survey of Hearing Impaired Children and Youth* (Center for Assessment and Demographic Studies, 1989). Although this survey included approximately 60 percent of the total hearing impaired students receiving special education in the United States, the applicability of this statistic to American Indian students is questionable (A. Schildroth, personal communication, June 5, 1990). Comparison of census and annual survey figures seems to indicate that deafness does not occur with significantly greater or lesser frequency among Indians than among the general population. O'Connell (1987), however, reported that sensory impairments are disproportionately high among Indians when compared with the general population: American Indians were almost three times more likely to be hospitalized for conditions of the ear. Direct investigation of the incidence and frequency of severe to profound hearing impairment among American Indians may result in figures more definitive than those described above.

The majority of American Indians reside in the western United States; in fact, half live in California, Oklahoma, Arizona, New Mexico, and North Carolina (Snyder, 1982). This distribution is also reflected in the *1988–89 Annual Survey for Hearing Impaired Children and Youth*, in which four of the same five states are listed as having the highest numbers of Indian hearing impaired children (Center for Assessment and Demographic Studies, 1989). Tables 9.1 and 9.2 rank population totals by state for both the general American Indian population and hearing impaired Indian youth reported in the annual survey (Center for Assessment and Demographic Studies, 1989; Snyder, 1982).

TABLE 9.1 Population Totals for American Indians, Eskimos, and Aleuts—Fifteen Highest Ranking States, April, 1980

Rank	State	Population
1	California	201,311
2	Oklahoma	169,464
3	Arizona	152,857
4	New Mexico	104,777
5	North Carolina	64,635
6	Alaska	64,047
7	Washington	60,771
8	South Dakota	45,101
9	Texas	40,074
10	Michigan	40,038
11	New York	38,732
12	Montana	37,270
13	Minnesota	35,026
14	Wisconsin	29,497
15	Oregon	27,300

SOURCE: Snyder, F. (1982). *Native American Directory, Alaska, Canada, United States*. San Carlos, AZ: National Native American Cooperative. Copyright 1982. Adapted with permission.

TABLE 9.2 Annual Survey of Hearing Impaired Children and Youth, American Indians—Highest Ranking States, 1988–1989

Rank	State	Frequency of Total Identified Number
1	Arizona	58
2	New Mexico	40
3	Oklahoma	27
4	Minnesota	24
5	California	20
6	Oregon	19
7	Wisconsin	17
8	North Dakota	16
9	North Carolina	14
10	Washington	13
11	Montana	10
12	South Dakota	9
13	Michigan	7
14	Utah	6
15	Texas, Wyoming, Louisiana	5

SOURCE: Center for Assessment and Demographic Studies. (1989). *1988–89 Annual Survey of Hearing Impaired Children and Youth*. Washington, DC: Gallaudet University, Gallaudet Research Institute. Copyright 1989. Adapted with permission.

Almost half of the American Indian population resides in rural areas, in contrast to the residency patterns of the non-Indian population. Of the Indians living on rural reservation lands, 49 percent live on ten reservations: Navajo (Arizona, New Mexico, Utah), Pine Ridge (South Dakota), Gila River (Arizona), Tohono O'odham (Arizona), Fort Apache (Arizona), Hopi (Arizona), Zuni (New Mexico), San Carlos (Arizona), Rosebud Sioux (South Dakota), and Blackfeet (Montana) (O'Connell, 1987). These reservation lands can be accurately described as isolated and remote.

The isolated nature of most reservations limits the availability of resources. Transportation problems also contribute to difficulties in providing specialized services to disabled individuals. Special education and vocational rehabilitation services are often unavailable to disabled Indians on a local level (Hodge & Weinmann, 1987); Deaf Indian children and youth are no exception in this regard.

The limited resources of the reservation lands make it increasingly difficult to support the growing Indian population. Many Indian people choose to leave the reservations in search of improved economic conditions (Sorkin, 1978). As is the case with many refugees from foreign countries, large urban areas often offer the employment opportunities that many American Indians seek.

The ten metropolitan areas with the highest populations of Indians are: Los Angeles–Long Beach, Tulsa, Oklahoma City, Phoenix, Albuquerque, San Francisco–Oakland, Riverside–San Bernardino–Ontario, Seattle–Everett, Minneapolis–St. Paul, and Tucson (O'Connell, 1987). Given the shifting trend toward urbanization, increasing numbers of American Indian Deaf children will most likely be identified in these and other metropolitan areas in the years to come.

American Indian Languages

Despite the use of the general term *American Indian*, there remains a great deal of cultural diversity among the population. There are 278 reservations and 209 Alaska villages in the United States (Hodge & Edmonds, 1988), and no two tribes share identical cultural characteristics. Many native languages still exist, and, in some cases, American Indians have little or no English proficiency. Hodge and Edmonds (1988) surveyed disabled Indians from three tribes and found that over 78 percent of the respondents spoke their native language.

Indian Deaf children from such native-language-speaking families have not been studied directly. The findings regarding students from other non-English-speaking families, however, may be applicable to Indian students. Reported increased incidence of additional disabilities and lower academic achievement levels among hearing impaired students from non-English-speaking families (Delgado, 1984) may warrant increased attention to culturally sensitive assessment and educational placement of Indian Deaf children whose families speak native languages other than the majority language.

In addition, native Indian languages differ greatly from the European language background of the dominant society. Most European languages are nominally oriented, whereas American Indian languages are action oriented (Skelly, 1979). The morphology and syntax of Indian languages have been found to be similar to those of American Sign Language (ASL) (S. Supalla, personal communication, July 11, 1990).

The phonological systems of native Indian languages may incorporate features quite distinctive from those of European languages. The Navajo language, for example, includes tonality, nasality, and frequent use of glottal stops; these features are virtually unrecognizable to most English speakers and speech readers. There is a need for further study regarding the language acquisition of Deaf children from native Indian-language-speaking families.

Socioeconomic Conditions

Socioeconomic conditions are important factors to consider when discussing a specific ethnic group. Despite the prosperity of mainstream U.S. society, American Indian reservations are comparable to third world nations in many respects. The living conditions of Indians are among the least developed of any ethnic group in the nation. In 1979, nearly half of on-reservation Indian families with children lived at or below federal poverty levels (O'Connell, 1987). The rural, often remote nature of reservation land has led to unavailability of electricity, refrigeration, telephone, and running water in a significant number of Indian homes (Hodge & Edmonds, 1988). For example, in a study conducted among Navajo vocational rehabilitation clients, 71 percent reported not owning a telephone (O'Connell & Minkler, 1987).

The socioeconomic status of off-reservation American Indians has not improved greatly. In 1989, about 20 percent of urban Indian families had incomes below the federal poverty levels (Sorkin, 1978). The standard of living for urban Indians may be lower than income levels would seem to indicate, however. Unlike most reservation Indians, who receive free medical care and rent-free housing on tribal lands, urban Indians must meet the ever-increasing costs of medical care and housing in metropolitan areas (Sorkin, 1978).

Health Concerns

Health-related data on American Indians are worthy of attention when examining a specific disability group within the population. The federal government's Indian Health Service (IHS) provides health care for approximately two-thirds of the U.S. Indian population. This agency's data regarding hospitalization rates shed light on the causes and patterns of disability among American Indians. Hodge and Weinmann (1987) examined IHS hospitalization rates among Navajo, Billings, and Alaska area programs. They found that fetal alcohol syndrome, bacterial meningitis, otitis media, diabetes, accidents/trauma, alcohol and drug abuse, and mental and emotional disorders caused disabilities among Indians at significantly higher rates than among non-Indians.

Many Indians living on reservation lands must travel great distances to obtain health care at IHS clinics (Hodge & Weinmann, 1987), and transportation difficulties often limit access to timely medical treatment. Urban Indians, also, often have trouble obtaining medical care. With IHS reductions in off-reservation areas, medically indigent Indian people often are unfamiliar with the complexities of existing health care programs in metropolitan communities. This has created a serious health problem among urban Indians and has resulted in a significantly lower standard of health than that of the non-Indian urban population (Sorkin, 1978).

The leading identifiable disease in the American Indian population is otitis media. Among children in the general population, middle ear problems are estimated to occur at a rate of about 5 percent; among Indian children, estimates range from 20 percent to 70 percent (McShane & Mitchell, 1979). Although low socioeconomic status if often associated with otitis media, McShane and Mitchell (1979) concluded that American Indian children have even more middle ear disease than can be explained by their relatively low socioeconomic status.

The implications of otitis media and related conductive hearing loss during critical years of language development are well documented (Gregg et al., 1983; Leviton, 1980; McShane & Mitchell, 1979). This disease is also suspected to lead to increased rates of permanent hearing loss among Indian adults (Hodge & Weinmann, 1987). Of significance also is the association of otitis media to cases of bacterial meningitis, a leading cause of sensorineural hearing impairment (Wolff & Brown, 1987).

Meningitis is found to occur with significantly greater frequency among American Indians than among other ethnic groups (Hodge & Weinmann, 1987). The *1988–89 Annual Survey of Hearing Impaired Children and Youth* (Center for Assessment and Demographic Studies, 1989) lists meningitis as the most frequently reported known etiology for Indian respondents. Specific research with Deaf Indian children is needed to determine the relationship of otitis media and meningitis to cases of deafness.

EDUCATION OF THE AMERICAN INDIAN POPULATION

Any discussion of the educational characteristics of American Indian children is incomplete without reference to the historical role of formal education efforts. Between 1783 and 1871, several U.S. treaties with Indian tribes included specific provisions for schooling. Most of these early educational efforts with Indian children were administered by missionary groups (Szasz, 1974).

In the post-Civil War decades, the federal government pursued a policy of total assimilation of the American Indian into mainstream society. Off-reservation boarding schools were seen as the best means to this end. The Indian Bureau's practice of forcibly separating children from their families to attend schools sometimes hundreds of miles away from their homelands was widespread. The bureau's plan was to remold the Indian system of values. One Hualapai elder recalled, "When we went to school, the interpreter told us, 'Forget your Hualapai language. Forget your Indian food. Forget your stories. Forget the names of the mountains and the rivers. And above all, forget your language. Just speak English' " (quoted in Trimble, 1986, p. 133).

After the turn of the century, reservation boarding schools and day school programs increased. These options were generally more acceptable to parents who objected to the idea of having their children taken long distances from home. According to Szasz (1974), however, these types of facilities did not greatly improve the status of Indian education. The decade of the 1920s brought with it many calls for reform, among them the Meriam Report of 1928.

This report advised that Indian education be closely connected to the community, with introduction of course work in Indian culture. During the 1930s many Meriam Report recommendations were put into practice. Several bureau schools added native history, art, and language classes to the curriculum and no longer forbade the practice of native religions.

Total reform of past assimilation policies of the past was slow in coming, however. In fact, the period from 1940 to 1965 saw many of the earlier advances reversed, and in 1969 the Kennedy Report concluded that many of the recommendations of the Meriam Report were yet to be accomplished (Szasz, 1974).

Although there has been increasing tribal control of educational programs, sixty-eight Bureau of Indian Affairs (BIA) schools remained operational in 1979 (Snyder, 1982). The majority of these schools are concentrated in the Southwest United States. According to the Native American Research and Training Center report, in 1986–1987 only twenty hearing impaired children were reported by BIA (O'Connell, 1987). Indian Health Service (IHS) reports also showed small numbers of Deaf students in Indian schools. Among the Navajo tribe, for example, prevalence of severe to profound hearing loss in one IHS mass screening was artificially low (Hodge & Weinmann, 1987). This was attributed to the fact that children with this degree of hearing impairment were, for the most part, in special programs off the reservation and were not counted in the screening.

Sufficient data are not yet available to describe accurately the educational placement patterns of Deaf Indian students across the United States. The *Annual Survey of Hearing Impaired Children and Youth*, however, reported that, of 331 American Indian respondents, 61 percent attended local schools and 39 percent attended special schools for the Deaf (Center for Assessment and Demographic Studies, 1989). Perhaps the students in local schools represent those living in urban areas, whereas students in schools for the Deaf represent those from reservation communities. Without direct information regarding the placement patterns of this specific population, one can only speculate as to the meaning behind the annual survey statistics.

Academic achievement levels of American Indian students have been well researched. According to Croft (1977), there is general agreement that Indians do not differ from other groups in inherited intellectual ability, but they are seriously disadvantaged educationally, nevertheless. Croft cited Meyer's dismal commentary: "The first American, the Indian, is the last educationally, as he is economically, socially, and politically" (p. 15). Martin and Luebbe (1986) reported that among seventy Indian clients referred for vocational evaluation, the average reading level was five grades lower than the average grade level attained. Whether or not Indian students in programs for the hearing impaired are equally disadvantaged is less clear.

Several researchers have investigated the educational performance of Deaf children from other culturally diverse backgrounds. As Cohen, Fischgrund, & Redding (1990) pointed out, "It is likely that culturally biased curricula, inappropriate school placement and/or tracking, and lack of understanding of learning style differences, coupled with a lack of awareness about cultural differences, family practices and value systems, have contributed to educational practices that have ill-served minority Deaf Children and youth" (p. 9). Specific investigation of the educational performance of Deaf American Indian students is necessary in order to determine the extent to which achievement levels of other Deaf ethnic groups parallel this unique population.

Despite the lower-than-average academic achievement levels and graduation rates of American Indians in general, a stereotype that labels all Indians as poorly educated must be avoided. Fuchs and Havighurst (1972) described a 500 percent increase of Indian post-secondary students from 1958 to 1970—with 18 percent of Indian high school graduates entering college in 1970, compared with 22 percent of the total non-Indian population.

Increasing numbers of American Indians are obtaining advanced degrees and entering a wide variety of professions.

Although academic achievement levels and postsecondary enrollment rates for Deaf Indian students are not readily available, the following anecdotal reports illustrate the individual differences among these students. In 1987, the valedictorian of the Arizona State Schools for the Deaf and the Blind (ASDB) was a hearing impaired Navajo student. Other Indian students from ASDB have gone on to successful completion of course work at community colleges and the National Technical Institute of the Deaf. Clearly, the reported lower-than-average academic achievement level of Indian students should not lead to lowered teacher expectations regarding the abilities of Deaf Indian students.

Employment patterns shed light on the feasibility of providing vocational rehabilitation services to disabled American Indian youth. The Native American Research and Training Center report includes an investigation of unemployment rates for Indians both on and off the reservation. The 1986 Bureau of Indian Affairs statistics cited in this report indicated an unemployment rate of 38 percent for Indian people during that year, a rate over five times higher than that reported for the total civilian labor force (O'Connell, 1987).

American Indians with disabilities are much more likely than disabled individuals from the non-Indian population to reside in isolated rural areas with limited resources, transportation barriers, and great distances to existing resources. O'Connell and Minkler (1987) found that among Navajo vocational rehabilitation clients, the average distance to the vocational rehabilitation office was 33 miles, with a range of 0 to 150 miles. Such factors contribute to underutilization of vocational rehabilitation services by American Indians.

Vocational rehabilitation services for hearing impaired Indian clients were examined by Nickoloff (1975) and Holland, Lee, and Kee (1982). Nickoloff reported that a majority of vocational rehabilitation cases among hearing impaired Arizona Indians were unsuccessfully closed due to the reason of "unable to locate," in part because of the remote nature of reservation lands. Holland et al. (1982) described the need for interagency cooperation among federal, state, tribal, and private agencies in providing services to hearing impaired Navajo individuals.

American Indian people are distinguished from the dominant society in many significant ways. Linguistic, socioeconomic, medical, educational, and vocational characteristics must be taken into account when attempting to provide services to hearing impaired members of the Indian population. In addition, and perhaps most important, the unique cultural traditions of American Indians cannot be overlooked.

CULTURAL TRADITIONS

"You were born with that spirit but it's up to you to feel responsible to it and to develop it in a way that you would be proud to say, 'I'm a Navajo.' It's a tradition. It's a language. It's an identity" (Trimble, 1986, p. 82). When discussing the cultural characteristics of an ethnic group, generalizations are used. Care must be taken, however, not to misinterpret these generalizations into stereotypes. In their presentation on early intervention with Deaf Indian children, Kile and Meiners (1983) elaborated, "We do not wish to insinuate that all Native Americans are 'cast from a mold' " (p. 3). The many Indian tribes and Alaska Native villages contribute to a great deal of cultural diversity among the American Indian population. Differences in language, beliefs, and traditions can be found across individual tribes. Cultural characteristics of one particular tribe may not be applicable to members of other Indian groups.

Despite the unique cultural characteristics of individual tribes, several researchers have identified cultural values and beliefs common to American Indians (Forbes, 1973; Joe & Miller, 1987; Locust, 1985). A comparison of these cultural values with those of the dominant society illustrates significant differences that must be considered by non-Indians working with Indian people. The values of one culture should not be considered more "correct" than those of another (Joe & Miller, 1987).

The cultural values described in Table 9.3 have significant implications for professionals working with Deaf Indian children and youth. The importance of the group orientation of American Indians cannot be overemphasized. In the lives of many Indian children, the extended family plays a central role; service providers who overlook or discourage the involvement of family members other than parents may perform a great disservice to the Deaf Indian child. "If you must have a decision on an important matter, expect to wait a few days, weeks, or months. The family will want to discuss a decision with the clan (extended family) before giving a final response" (Holland et al., 1982, p. 121).

Kinship patterns differ among various Indian tribes. Among many southwestern tribes, ancestry is traced matrilineally (Witherspoon, 1975). The mother's clan is primary, and residency patterns generally revolve around the wife's and mother's property. Kinship terms in the Navajo language reflect the importance of maternal kin among this tribe; for example, *shima yazhi*, the term for maternal aunt, literally means "my mother little." Maternal cousins are often referred to as sisters and brothers, much to the confusion of unfamiliar non-Indian people. Although not all tribes trace ancestry matrilineally, a common tribal characteristic is the important role of elders (Joe & Miller, 1987). Grand-

TABLE 9.3   American Indian/Anglo-American Quasi-Universal Cultural Values

American Indian	Anglo-American
Group life is primary.	The individual is primary.
Respects elders, experts, and those with spiritual powers.	Respects youth, success, and high social status.
Time and place are viewed as permanent, settled.	Time and place are always negotiable; plans for change.
Introverted—avoids ridicule or criticism of others if possible.	Extroverted—seeks analysis and criticism of situations.
Pragmatic—accepts "what is."	Reformer—changes or "fixes" problems.
Emphasizes responsibility for family and personal sphere.	Emphasizes authority and responsibility over a wide range of social life.
Observes how others behave; emphasis is on how others "behave," not on what they say.	Eager to relate to others; emphasis is on how others "feel" or "think."
Incorporates supportive nonfamily or other helpers into family network.	Keeps network of family, friends, and acquaintances separate.
Seeks harmony.	Seeks progress.

SOURCE: Joe, J., & Miller, D. (1987). *American Indian cultural perspectives on disability* (p. 4). Tucson: University of Arizona, Native American Research and Training Center. Reprinted with permission.

parents generally are afforded a great deal of respect and often assist in raising grandchildren. Therefore, elderly family members should be encouraged to participate in planning services to hearing impaired Indian children and youth.

The typical role of Indian fathers differs from that of many non-Indian fathers, in that a clansperson or a maternal uncle may be more significant in a child's life than the father (Cunningham, Cunningham, & O'Connell, 1987). In some cultures, the visibility of fathers may be affected by taboos. Among the Navajo, for example, a man is forbidden to have face-to-face contact with his mother-in-law (Witherspoon, 1975). Although traditional taboos such as this may not be upheld by all members of a particular tribe, professionals working with families of Deaf Indian children are well advised to familiarize themselves with such cultural considerations.

Non-Indians working with Indian people are often struck by the obvious differences in time orientation between the two cultures. The dominant non-Indian society seems driven by the clock; in this culture, "times flies." Future orientation is readily evident in the fields of special education and rehabilitation counseling. Long-range goals with short-term objectives, the standards of program planning, emphasize the future rather than present.

American Indian people, on the other hand, operate primarily with an orientation to the here-and-now (Joe & Miller, 1987). This emphasis on the present can be frustrating to non-Indians who schedule appointments that may be broken by Indian families when events arise at the last minute. To many Indians, an activity occurring right now will always take precedence over something scheduled to take place sometime later. Cultural sensitivity is needed to understand that broken appointments do not necessarily mean that Indian people do not value the services of non-Indian professionals working with their Deaf children.

Unlike Anglo-Americans who seek to change or correct problems, most Indian people accept difficulties and attempt to live in harmony despite them. As Joe and Miller (1987) have pointed out, "When faced with a consensually-held 'problem,' Indians may seek solace, acceptance, or explanations in the familiar sociocultural framework rather than attempt to change the 'nature of life' " (p. 5). Evidence of this pragmatic nature may be seen in Indian families' reactions to the use of hearing aids with young children. Kile and Meiners (1983) found that many Indian parents do not force children to wear amplification. Perhaps a combination of permissive parenting and a pragmatic acceptance of impaired hearing results in this attitude regarding amplification.

The American Indian emphasis on how others behave rather than what they say has important implications for professionals working with Indian families. According to Anderson and Fenichel (1989), Indian parents tend to judge professionals slowly. In the words of a Navajo tribal chairperson, "We Navajos will look you over for a couple of years, and then decide if we are for you or against you" (quoted in Anderson & Fenichel, 1989, p. 13).

Differences in nonverbal communication between American Indian and Anglo-American groups are evident and worthy of attention. Many Indian people speak in soft voices and avoid eye contact with unfamiliar people (Holland et al., 1982). Although these characteristics are not found among all Indians, an awareness of the culturally acceptable rules behind such behaviors eliminates misunderstandings. These nonverbal communication factors have major implications for Deaf Indian children. Intervention efforts related to signed language, auditory training, and speech reading may need to be tailored in ways that are sensitive to the cultural behaviors of Indian families.

In addition to the cultural values described by Joe and Miller (1987), many American Indian tribes have common beliefs regarding health and wellness. In most Indian cultures, health and religious beliefs are closely intertwined (Anderson & Fenichel, 1989). Locust (1985) observed, "For the Navajo and Tohono O'odham, as well as other tribes, it would seem that there is little or no difference between religion and medicine, between a church and a hospital" (p. 1).

Locust went on to describe the following Indian beliefs: "Man is a three-fold being made up of a body, mind, and spirit. Illness affects the mind and spirit as well as the body. Wellness is harmony in body, mind, and spirit. Natural unwellness is caused by the violation of a sacred or tribal taboo. Unnatural unwellness is caused by witchcraft" (p. 2). The importance of native healing ceremonies among many Indian families must not be overlooked. Ceremonies often require the involvement of all family or clan members and may last for several days (Joe & Miller, 1987). Non-Indian staff need to be respectful of the role that native healing may play in the lives of Deaf Indian children and their families. Through the following quotations, Joe and Miller (1987) illustrated the misunderstandings that can arise from lack of awareness regarding native healing on the part of residential facility workers: "One time a child came back from home (after a week at home), and the parents didn't let us know that the child was not to be washed until the fourth day after her (Navajo) curing ceremonies." The child was given a bath as part of the facility's routine, and when the parents learned of the bath, they wanted to take their child out of the facility.

"Sometimes Navajo parents don't let us know when they were having medicine men treat the child, and that the child might be gone for a few weeks, during which time the child might not get his medicine or even miss an important medical appointment. Some parents, I guess, don't trust us or they probably think that we would disapprove of medicine men treatment so they don't let us know" (p. 11). The general concepts of Indian spiritual and health beliefs described should not be taken as absolutes for all tribes or Indian individuals. Acculturation levels vary, affecting the degree to which an individual identifies with traditional Indian spiritual and health practices. Hodge and Edmonds (1988) found that 78 percent of disabled American Indians surveyed felt that native healing ceremonies were helpful; in addition, 60 percent of respondents also saw physicians for their disabilities. Although the Navajo Vocational Rehabilitation Program offers native healing services to disabled clients, they report that Deaf clients request such services less frequently than do members of other disability groups (D. Clashin, personal communication, October 13, 1980). This difference is most likely the result of the communication difficulties between native-language-speaking healers and Deaf individuals.

The bicultural nature of many American Indians is evident in their perspectives on disability. According to Joe and Miller (1987), Indian families often hold both private and public explanations of disability. The private, traditional view describes the condition in terms of a cultural worldview; for example, congenital deafness has been attributed to a Navajo mother's having seen a snake during pregnancy. In contrast, parents may also publicly recognize a more "modern" etiology, such as maternal rubella. As with any group of individuals, attitudes regarding disability and deafness, specifically, will vary among Indian people.

American Indians generally view childhood in a different light than do non-Indians. An Indian child is not seen as a blank slate to be molded and fixed, but rather as a complete, whole person, even at a very young age (Cunningham et al., 1987). As an Apache medicine man stated, ''You water your children like you water the tree'' (quoted in Trimble, 1986, p. 64). Parenting tends to be somewhat permissive, affording Indian children ample opportunities to explore and learn through experience.

Another difference noted between American Indians and the dominant society is the Indian's nonmaterialistic nature (Forbes, 1973). Despite the negative connotations of their lower-than-average socioeconomic status, Indian people seem to view wealth in different terms. Status among many Indians is achieved not from owning, but from sharing. Whereas the mainstream culture perpetuates the Puritan ethic of living to work, American Indians generally work to live. Deaf Indian children may reflect similar attitudes regarding work and wealth; therefore, professionals involved with Indian children may need to tailor their expectations to match the individual cultural values of the children they are serving.

Much attention has been given to the visual learning styles of American Indians (Dillard, 1983; Philips, 1983; Sidles, MacAvoy, Bernston, & Kuhn, 1987). According to Dillard, learning among American Indians is best accomplished through observation. An Apache man's words emphasize this point: ''Watch, be a part, see. Through that you can come to an understanding'' (quoted in Trimble, 1986, p. 103). In her study of communication among Indians in the Warms Springs community of Oregon, Philips found that Indians make greater use of the visual channel than do non-Indians. In turn, less emphasis is placed on productive language competence, and audition is used in a qualitatively different way in the socialization of a child. Similarly, Kile and Meiners (1983) reported that among Indian families, oral communication is not emphasized with either hearing or hearing impaired children. As a result, a visual/spatial mode of communication is generally accepted for use with Deaf Indian children. Home signed language systems families are currently being researched. Initial data indicate that such systems are more complex and more widely used among Navajo families of Deaf children than they are among non-Indian families (S. Supalla, personal communication, July 11, 1990).

There is a great deal of individual diversity among the Indian population, and this extends to their level of acculturation. The traditional values outlined by Joe and Miller (1987), for example, may not be fully embraced by Indian people who have adopted many of the ways of the dominant society. The degree to which an individual Indian child reflects Indian values depends on the child's level of exposure to the ways of two distinct worlds. ''An American Indian's life is a half/half life—the traditional cultural values underlie the personality while the Anglo social structure presses down, creating constant tension and imbalance'' (Joe & Miller, 1987, p. 9).

Deaf Indian children who attend residential schools face even more complex cultural situations. Not only are they separated from their families with little exposure to their tribal language, foods, ceremonies, and beliefs, but these Deaf Indian children are also exposed to the unique culture of the Deaf community. Upon leaving school, many Deaf Indian youths must make difficult choices about where and with whom to establish themselves: on the reservation with hearing Indian families and friends, in urban areas within the Deaf community, or in border towns with limited access to each of these social groups.

The following description of the Ben family of the Navajo Nation illustrates the differing levels of acculturation that must be taken into account. Of eleven children, four are Deaf and two are hard of hearing. A paternal cousin is also Deaf. The two eldest Deaf sisters never attended school. They communicate in a unique, complex home signed language system, which other hearing family members also use with varying levels of proficiency.

The two live together in a traditional hogan near their immediate family members on the Navajo reservation. They raise sheep and weave rugs in addition to providing childcare to their nieces and nephews.

The hard-of-hearing brother also resides near his immediate family. He speaks only Navajo in addition to the family's home signed lauguage system. Like his elder sisters, this brother never attended school. Having sustained an injury while working for the railroad, he now tends the family's livestock.

The two younger Deaf sisters attended the state school for the Deaf and communicate in American Sign Language (ASL). They live in a metropolitan area, where one is employed in the health profession. They visit their family several times a year and also communicate in their sisters' home signed language system.

The hard-of-hearing sister attended both Bureau of Indian Affairs (BIA) boarding schools and schools for the Deaf. She is fluent in ASL, speaks both Navajo and English, and uses the family's home signed language system. She currently resides in the same metropolitan area as her Deaf sisters and, like them, interacts primarily with the Deaf community.

The Deaf cousin attended the state school for the Deaf and communicates in ASL but also uses the same home signed language system with his family members. He currently resides in a town near the Navajo reservation and is employed as a machinist and a signed language instructor. He returns home regularly on weekends and is also involved in the Deaf community.

Each of the hearing impaired members of the Ben family seems comfortable with his or her cultural identity. Each deals with the dominant non-Indian society, the Navajo tribe, and the Deaf community in varying degrees. The cultures of three distinct communities are uniquely reflected in the Deaf members of this family, as is the need for cultural sensitivity among non-Indian people working with such families.

The cultural traditions of American Indian families have major implications in the development of Deaf Indian children. These characteristics directly influence the child's identity and cannot be underestimated. Educators and other professionals working with Deaf Indian children must recognize and respect the diverse cultural backgrounds of the families they serve.

ASSESSMENT CONSIDERATIONS

"Those who assess culturally diverse children have an enormous responsibility, for assessment results are used to make decisions that directly affect the lives of culturally diverse children" (Olion & Gillis-Olion, 1984, p. 204). Assessment issues regarding American Indian children have been addressed by researchers for more than a quarter of a century. During that time there has been much debate as to which formal assessment tools, if any, provide accurate, culture-free measures of the intellectual potential, the present levels of performance, and the presence or absence of specific learning disabilities or developmental disability in the Indian child with normal hearing.

The existing research regarding assessment issues and the Indian child and young adult addresses only those with normal hearing. When hearing loss is addressed in this work, the impairment is generally caused by frequent and chronic otitis media. A review of the literature produced no information regarding assessment of Indians with significant sensorineural hearing loss. Obviously, the evaluation and assessment of Deaf American Indians requires further study, and it is safe to assume that an assessment process which includes the culture and the language of the family will be most effective.

Research regarding formal assessment of hearing Indians may be of special interest to psychologists, psychometrists, and educators working with Deaf Indian children. This is because hearing Indian children frequently indicate a significant variance between their verbal scores and performance scores on most intelligence tests (Hynd & Garcia, 1979; Zarske & Moore, 1982). Therefore, many researchers have recommended using evaluation tools that stress nonverbal skills when assessing the cognitive potential of an Indian child with normal hearing. This practice is in agreement with the test selection process for hearing impaired people (Zieziula, 1982).

The following assessment tools have been most frequently researched for use with hearing American Indian children and young adults. None of these tests, however, have been normed on significantly large samples of Indians from a variety of Indian tribes. There is also disagreement among researchers as to the amount of culture-free content in each of these tests. Therefore, anyone using these tests with Indian students should exercise caution when interpreting the results. The evaluation tools most frequently mentioned include: Harris–Goodenough Draw-A-Person, Knox Cube Test (KCT), Minnesota Multiphasic Personality Inventory (MMPI), Ravens Progressive Matrices, System of Multicultural Pluralistic Assessment (SOMPA), Weschler Intelligence Scale for Children–Revised (WISC–R), and Wide Range Achievement Test–Revised (WRAT–R).

Another area of interest to professionals in the field of deafness is the type of cultural behaviors that researchers have noted when testing hearing Indians. A knowledge of these behaviors may assist anyone who is formally or informally evaluating the skills of a hearing impaired Indian child. Many behaviors that may be exhibited by some American Indians have been mentioned previously in this chapter. The limited eye contact and minimal spontaneous verbal interactions may affect the assessment scores of an Indian child. It is not uncommon for an Indian child to become very passive or to withdraw completely when faced with a situation in which self-control is limited and disclosure of personal information is required (Dana, 1984).

Hearing Indian children will often respond more readily when the required response is a pointing response, a yes or no answer, or a one- or two-word answer. The children often respond orally by speaking very softly and looking away from the examiner. These behaviors can make testing a hearing impaired Indian child with oral skills difficult for an examiner who is also hearing impaired. A request by an examiner to "speak up" or "speak louder" may be met by the child with a lowered head and a refusal to make eye contact, a softer voice, or no response at all. That situation is usually best handled by changing to a task that requires a nonverbal response, such as pointing or writing. Some Indian tribes, however, teach their children that it is impolite to point at people or objects. For example, instead of pointing with a finger, Navajo children frequently purse their lips and nod their heads in the direction of the object to which they are referring.

Behavioral characteristics such as these must also be kept in mind when an examiner is questioning an Indian parent or guardian. Adults may exhibit the same behaviors in an assessment situation. For example, when administering a parental report evaluation such as the Vineland Social Maturity Scale, it is not uncommon for the examiner to encounter unfamiliar behaviors exhibited by the parent.

Some researchers have found timed evaluation tasks to be inadequate for evaluating hearing American Indians (Sidles et al., 1987). Another factor these researchers have attempted to consider is the influence of acculturation on an Indian child's performance. Research results are inconclusive as to what extent, if any, acculturation plays in the Indian child's test profile (Hoffman, Dana, & Bolton, 1985; McShane & Plas, 1984; Sidles et al., 1987). Also of note, some research indicates discrepancies in the area of test reliability between different Indian tribes (Gonzales, 1982; McShane & Plas, 1984). Obviously, assessment of American Indians, hearing and Deaf, requires further study.

What may be most important to service providers are the test behaviors previously discussed and the typical profile of a hearing Indian child on nonverbal/performance tests. Many researchers have found hearing Indian children to have strengths in the area of visual spatial skills (Kirk, 1972; Middleton, 1976).

A note of caution: When working with an Indian parent or an oral hearing impaired Indian child who speaks a language other than English, translations of test items can cause unforeseen difficulties. In a study by Rosenbluth (1976), it was found that an effort to translate the Boehm Test of Basic Concepts effectively resulted in a Navajo version of the test that was more difficult than the English version. The Navajo translation also resulted in different meanings for several of the items. When professionals interview Indian parents or guardians in English and the parent or guardian speaks English as a second language, many misunderstandings can occur unbeknown to either the professional or the parent.

For example, when asked in English, "Don't you have a pencil?" a hearing Navajo child would probably answer simply "yes." That answer could mean, "Yes, I *don't* have a pencil," or, "Yes, I *do* have a pencil." A Navajo parent who is asked, "Do you want your child to ride the bus, or do you want to pick up your child here at school?" may answer a simple "yes." This could mean yes to either part of the question, or it could mean that the parent did not understand the question. The non-Indian should be alert to ambiguities in the English language when talking with parents and students who do not speak English as their first language.

SUGGESTIONS FOR PROFESSIONALS

How can current and future educators of Deaf Indian children acknowledge their students' special cultural backgrounds and assist them in the learning process? A child is first and foremost a member of a family. With the passage of Public Law 94-142 and the more recent passage of Public Law 99-457, educational programs must involve parents and families in the educational process. Knowing that their family supports their educational placement and program may contribute to the motivation a child needs to succeed in school.

One of the more common laments of educators working with American Indian children is the sometimes limited parental involvement (J. Joe, personal communication, August 29, 1990). This is also true for many Deaf Indian children. The reasons why some Indian parents may not seem involved in their children's education are complex and varied. The history of the federal government's attempt to educate Indians by forcibly removing them from their families and cultures for years at a time continues to affect Indian parents today when they are faced with placement decisions regarding their own children.

Other factors may also enter into the school–family dynamics that could affect the

Indian family's ability and desire to be involved in the educational program of their hearing impaired child:

> Distance from school,
>
> lack of transportation to school,
>
> inability to speak English or discomfort in speaking English when talking with a professional who is using professional jargon,
>
> inability to find a caretaker to watch the younger children or an infirm elderly relative,
>
> lack of money to finance a long trip if the child attends school far from home,
>
> fear of traveling in a large city if the family lives in a rural or remote area (a "big" city could be anything larger than the city or town nearest the parent's home), and
>
> difficulty in including a grandparent in placement decisions.

These are just some of the many reasons why Indian parents may not be perceived as being involved or interested in their Deaf child's education. If at all possible, home visits by school staff are extremely valuable in coming to understand the American Indian Deaf child and his or her family. Home visits allow a staff member to evaluate the importance of the extended family, the daily living skills and daily chores and responsibilities of the child while at home, the level of acculturation present in the family, and other culturally relevant information. Indian parents may feel more confident visiting a school if they have already met the school staff.

Some traditional Indian families appear hesitant to allow non-Indian strangers into their homes on a first visit. This may be because of cultural taboos regarding visitors, or it may be as simple as an Indian family's fear that the non-Indian will judge them as inadequate parents due to the cultural differences or poverty of their lives. It is not unusual for southwestern Indian parents to prefer that home visits be held outside of the family's residence, whether this means sitting on the ground, a bench or chairs outside, a fence, or even on the bed of the family pickup truck just outside the house. If the weather is inclement, then a parent may wish to conduct the home visit in the professional's vehicle. Other common meeting locations include tribal buildings, health clinics, neighborhood schools or preschools, or a trading post within the family's community. According to Gilliland, Reyhner, and Schaeffer (1988), "To be effective teachers of culturally diverse students, we must be prepared to understand and accept as equally valid values and ways of life very different from our own" (p. 3). There are numerous techniques to provide training to non-Indian staff in the specific cultural beliefs and life styles of Indian tribes. Some of the following suggestions are specific to working with the families of Deaf students. By working cooperatively, non-Indian staff will better understand their students' native cultural beliefs, and Indian parents will learn and understand more about deafness and their own children.

Traditionally, Indians have taught their children proper behavior and moral values through oral storytelling (Gilliland, 1988). The same stories can be adapted for use in an educational setting. Many educational programs serving hearing Indian children have found success in teaching reading and language through the stories and legends of Indian tribes. This technique is easily adapted for use with Deaf Indian students. Traditional Indian stories can be found in a variety of resources, including programs listed later in this chapter.

Parents are another resource in locating Indian stories and legends. By using these stories in a classroom setting, non-Indian Deaf students may develop respect for Indian culture, and Indian students may develop more pride in their own traditions.

Three specific programs have been used successfully with Deaf Indians in Arizona. The first was called Navajo Parent Days. The parents and extended families of all Navajo students attending the Arizona State Schools for the Deaf and the Blind (ASDB) were invited to spend three consecutive days on campus. During their visit, the families had the opportunity to observe their children throughout the day and to meet individually with all school staff members involved with their children. Many of the families brought arts and crafts items with them to sell in Tucson in order to help finance their trip. The Indian students proudly displayed their parents' and grandparents' art to their teachers and classmates. Later, parents gave demonstrations to classes on beadworking, rug weaving, and cooking "fry bread," a staple in the traditional Navajo diet. In this setting the ASDB staff met parents and other family members—some of whom were very traditional in their interactions with non-Indians, others who were comfortably acculturated, and still others who functioned somewhere in between.

Another program sponsored at ASDB is the Indian Club. This club provides a variety of cultural activities designed to provide socioemotional support for the Indian students as well as education regarding Indian culture for the non-Indian students. The club has received support from Indian student groups of the University of Arizona and Pima Community College, the Tucson Indian Center, and Indian individuals in the community who present programs on dance, cooking, and arts and crafts.

A focus on Indian culture for Deaf American Indians can be seen in the efforts of the Community Outreach Program for the Deaf (COPD) in northern Arizona. In providing community-based services to hearing impaired Indian clients, COPD staff became aware of the limited access to in-depth knowledge of traditional culture that many Deaf Indians face. Similarly, Indian families and tribal workers in northern Arizona generally have little exposure to information regarding the culture of the Deaf community. Leaders from both communities, Deaf and Indian, were called upon to present cross-cultural information through a variety of experiential activities, organized and held with the assistance of the American Indian Rehabilitation Research and Training Center and the Native American Research and Training Center. This three-day workshop included presentations by Deaf individuals regarding the medical, audiological, educational, linguistic, vocational, and cultural aspects of deafness. Deaf people held mini-courses in ASL for Indian family members and tribal representatives. Emphasis was placed on cultural aspects of the Deaf community.

In addition, Indian leaders conducted lectures and presentations regarding tribal legends and ceremonialism. An open forum for Indian family members led to a lively discussion on traditional healing practices; a Deaf man who, with his father, works as a medicine man, contributed personal insight. A sweatlodge (prayer) ceremony was held, and a walk in the nearby mountains afforded the opportunity to learn more about the traditional uses of medicinal plants. All activities were made accessible to Deaf participants through signed language interpreting. Participants represented five tribes, and several people traveled great distances to attend. Responses to this workshop were extremely positive. Requests have been made for activities of this kind to be held on an annual basis. All participants—Deaf, hearing, hard-of-hearing, Indian, Anglo, African American, Hispanic, young, and old—benefited from exposure to the unique, positive aspects of both Indian and Deaf cultures.

The initial step that the non-Indian professional must take when working with Indian students is to acknowledge the differences between cultures and to value the understanding of those differences. This will assist the professional in recognizing when misunderstandings occur in the classroom. An example of this follows: A teacher at Arizona State Schools for the Deaf and the Blind had begun to perceive behavioral difficulties with a new Navajo student in her class. This ten-year-old boy with moderate to severe sensorineural hearing loss was interacting with the teacher with what appeared to her to be negative behaviors. He would answer "no" to most of her questions, and, when asked if he had his homework, his hearing aids, or a pencil, he would answer "no" or "I don't know," only to produce the requested object a short time later. The teacher requested a conference with an educator familiar with the Navajo culture to discuss the implications of her student's behavior. After an observation of the student and a discussion with the teacher, the consultant explained that the child's behavior was actually a common form of teasing in his culture.

Usually, the child did not smile when he demonstrated this behavior, so the teacher had not originally considered the behavior as positive. When she was told that children only use this teasing behavior with adults they respect and like, the teacher understood what she had perceived as a negative behavior was actually a form of respect from her student. This enabled her to respond to her student's teasing behavior in a positive manner and to reinforce his respect for her (K. Caputo, personal communication, May 29, 1990). What was a simple misunderstanding between teacher and student could have been much more serious had the teacher not requested culturally appropriate consultation.

Another area in which ASDB staff members developed cultural sensitivity is the cutting of students' hair. The school often made free hairstyling services available for students who resided in the residence halls. At the recommendation of an Indian staff member, ASDB developed a release form that indicated whether a parent or guardian gave the school permission to trim the student's hair. Some American Indian parents did not want their children's hair cut because of traditional beliefs, such as those involved in some ceremonies at puberty. But because the parents or guardians of all ASDB students signed this form—indicating their desires regarding hair length and style—it was determined that many non-Indian parents also did not want the school to cut their children's hair. Thus, a form developed for one cultural group has led, overall, to increased parental input to staff regarding all students.

The importance of the non-Indian professional's interest in and respect for the Indian student's culture cannot be overemphasized. Gilliland et al. (1988) elaborated on this issue: Educators sometimes speak of American Indian students as being "disadvantaged." In reality these native people have the double advantage of knowing and living in two cultures. The teacher, on the other hand, may know only one culture, and may have accepted that culture as being superior without any real thought or study. It is the teacher, then, who is disadvantaged. However, if the teacher does not know, understand, and respect the culture of the students, then the students are at a disadvantage in this teacher's class.

Fortunately for the non-Indian professional, there are numerous resources available throughout the United States and Canada to assist in developing an awareness and understanding of American Indian cultures. Several of the larger programs have been mentioned previously. The Bureau of Indian Affairs (BIA) and the Indian Health Service (IHS) provide programs on reservations and also in some urban areas. Most Indian tribes have programs that address cultural and educational issues pertaining to their specific cultures. In many areas, public schools with a concentration of Indian students have developed specific programs for their students and staff with federal funding from Title V or Title VII programs. Many urban areas have Indian centers, also known as Native Peoples Friendship Centers in Canada, that provide a variety of services to the Indians residing in these communities. Some state Councils on Developmental Disabilities also offer specific services for developmentally disabled Indians and their families. Twenty-seven states have State Commissions on Indian Affairs within the structure of the state governments.

The following list of resources includes programs that offer various resources to the non-Indian professional. As the awareness of multicultural issues grows among educators, so does the number of resources available to assist in programming for American Indian children and youth. These resource programs are primarily designed to provide services to American Indians. Many offer publications and research and have Indian members who are available to provide training and consultation to non-Indians.

These are only a few of the local, state, regional, national, and international resources available. Most of these programs are funded with federal monies; therefore, the level of services offered as well as their very existence may vary each year with fluctuations in federal funding levels. By utilizing available resources, professionals providing services to American Indian Deaf children and youth can obtain information leading to increased awareness and sensitivity regarding cultural considerations. Exposure to the values, beliefs, and traditions of Indian people will allow educators, counselors, and other service providers to be respectful and understanding when working with Deaf Indian students. Such cultural sensitivity will also assist professionals in providing appropriate assessment and placement services to the benefit of Deaf Indian children, youth, and their families.

BIBLIOGRAPHY

Anderson, P. P., & Fenichel, E. S. (1989). *Serving culturally diverse families of infants and toddlers with disabilities.* Washington, DC: National Center for Clinical Infant Programs.

Center for Assessment and Demographic Studies. (1989). *1988–89 Annual survey of hearing impaired children and youth.* Washington, DC: Gallaudet University, Gallaudet Research Institute.

Cohen, O. P., Fischgrund, J. E., & Redding, R. (1990). Deaf children from ethnic, linguistic, and racial minority backgrounds: An overview. *American Annals of the Deaf, 135,* 67–82.

Croft, C. (1977). The first Americans: Last in education. *Journal of American Indian Education, 16,* 15–19.

Cunningham, K., Cunningham, K., & O'Connell, J. C. (1987). Impact of differing cultural perceptions on special education service delivery. *Rural Special Education Quarterly, 8.*

Dana, R. H. (1984). Intelligence testing of American Indian Children: Sidesteps in quest of ethical practice. *White Cloud Journal, 3,* 35–43.

Delgado, G. (Ed.). (1984). *The Hispanic Deaf: Issues and challenges for bilingual special education.* Washington, DC: Gallaudet College.

Dillard, J. M. (1983). *Multicultural counseling.* Chicago: Nelson-Hall.

Dumbleton, D. D., & Rice, M. J. (1973). *Education for American Indians.* Athens, GA: University of Georgia, Anthropology Curriculum Project.

Forbes, J. D. (1973). Teaching Native American values and cultures. In J. A. Banks (Ed.), *Teaching ethnic studies: Concepts and strategies, 43rd yearbook.* Washington, DC: National Council for the Social Studies.

Forbes, J. D. (Ed.). (1979). *Multicultural education and the American Indian*. Los Angeles: University of California, American Indian Studies Center.

Fuchs, E., & Havighurst, R. J. (1972). *To live on this earth: American Indian education*. Garden City, NY: Doubleday.

Gilliland, H., Reyhner, J., & Schaffer, R. (Eds.) (1988). *Teaching the Native American*. Dubuque, IA: Kendall/Hunt.

Gonzales, E. (1982). A cross-cultural comparison of the developmental items of five ethnic groups in the Southwest. *Journal of Personality Assessment, 46,* 26–31.

Gregg, J. B., Roberts, K. M., & Colleran, M. J. (1983, October). Ear disease and hearing loss, Pierre, South Dakota, 1962–1982. *South Dakota,* pp. 9–17.

Hodge, F., & Edmonds, R. (1988). *Socio-cultural aspects of disability: A three-area survey of disabled American Indians*. Tucson: University of Arizona Native American Research and Training Center.

Hodge, F., & Weinmann, S. (1987). *Disabled American Indians: An overview of the etiology of disability in Alaska, Montana and Navajo areas*. Tucson: University of Arizona Native American Research and Training Center.

Hoffman, T., Dana, R. H., & Bolton, D. (1985). Measured acculturation and MMPI–168 performances of Native American adults. *Journal of Cross-Cultural Psychology, 16,* 243–256.

Holland, S. L., Lee, B., & Kee, J. (1982, March). *Networking services to deaf individuals on the Navajo reservation*. Paper presented at the meeting of the American Deafness and Rehabilitation Association, Seattle.

Hynd, G. W., & Garcia, W. I. (1979). Intellectual assessment of the Native American student. *School Psychology Digest, 8*(4), 446–454.

Joe, J., & Miller, D. (1987). *American Indian cultural perspectives on disability*. Tucson: University of Arizona, Native American Research and Training Center.

Kile, P., & Meiners, L. (1983, July). *The use of the Ski*Hi model with Native American families*. Paper presented at the Ski*Hi National Outreach Conference, Logan, UT.

Kirk, S. A. (1972). Ethnic differences in psycholinguistic abilities. *Exceptional Children, 39* (2), 112–118.

Lansford, L. M. (1978, June). *Performance of American Indian children compared with Koppitz normative population on the Bender*. Paper presented at the World Congress on Future Special Education, Stirling, Scotland.

Leviton, A. (1980). Otitis media and learning disorders. *Developmental and Behavioral Pediatrics, 1,* 58–63.

Locust, C. (1985). *American Indian beliefs concerning health and unwellness*. Tucson: University of Arizona, Native American Research and Training Center.

Martin, W. E., Jr., & Luebbe, D. T. (1986). *The effects of language difference on an accurate assessment of Native Americans who are disabled*. Unpublished manuscript, Northern Arizona University, Native American Research and Training Center, Flagstaff, AZ.

McShane, D., & Mitchell, J. (1979). Middle ear disease, hearing loss, and educational problems of American Indian children. *Journal of American Indian Education, 18,* 7–10.

McShane, D. A., & Plas, J. M. (1984). The cognitive functioning of American Indian children: Moving from the WISC to the WISC-k. *School Psychology Review, 13*(1), 61–73.

Middleton, A. H. (1976). Structure of intellect in American Indian children. *Dissertation Abstracts International, 37*(8), 4156B. (University Microfilms No. 77–2792)

Morton, E. (1988). *To touch the wind*. Dubuque, IA: Kendall/Hunt.

Nickoloff, E. G. (1975). *The hearing-impaired American Indian in the vocational rehabilitation process*. Doctoral dissertation, University of Arizona.

O'Connell, J. C. (Ed.). (1987). *A study of the special problems and needs of American Indians with handicaps both on and off the reservation* (Vols. 1–3). Flagstaff, AZ: Northern Arizona University, Native American Research and Training Center.

O'Connell, J. C., & Minkler, S. A. (1987). *Barriers to successful rehabilitation on the Navajo reservation.* Unpublished manuscript, Northern Arizona University, Native American Research and Training Center, Flagstaff, AZ.

Olion, L., & Gillis-Olion, M. (1984). Assessing culturally diverse exceptional children. *Early Child Development and Care, 15,* 203–231.

Pepper, F. C. (1985). *Effective practices in Indian education: A teacher's monograph.* Portland, OR: Northwest Regional Educational Laboratory.

Philips, S. U. (1983). *The invisible culture: Communication in classroom and community on the Warm Springs Indian Reservation.* New York: Longman.

Rosenbluth, A. R. (1976). The feasibility of test translation between unrelated languages—English to Navajo. *TESOL Quarterly, 10,* 33–43.

Shaw, J. R., Todd, N. W., Goodwin, M. H., Jr., & Feldman, C. M. (1981). Observations on the relation of environmental and behavioral factors to the occurrence of otitis media among Indian children. *Public Health Reports, 96*(4), 342–349.

Sidles, C., MacAvoy, J., Bernston, C., & Kuhn, A. (1987). Analysis of Navajo adolescent's performances on the Raven Progressive matrices. *Journal of American Indian Education, 27*(1), 1–8.

Skelly, M. (1979). *Amer-Ind gestural code based on universal American Indian hand talk.* New York: Elsevier.

Snyder, F. (1982). *Native American directory: Alaska, Canada, United States.* San Carlos, AZ: National Native American Cooperative.

Sorkin, A. L. (1978). *The urban American Indian.* Lexington, MA: Lexington Books.

Szasz, M. C. (1974). *Education and the American Indian: The road to self-determination since 1928.* Albuquerque, NM: University of New Mexico.

Trimble, S. (1986). *Our voices, our land.* Flagstaff, AZ: Northland Press.

U.S. Bureau of the Census. (1983). *1980 census of the population: Characteristics of the population (Vol. I, Series PC80-1-C1).* Washington, DC: U.S. Government Printing Office.

Witherspoon, G. (1975). *Navajo kinship and marriage.* Chicago: University of Chicago.

Wolff, A. B., & Brown, S. C. (1987). Demographics of meningitis-induced hearing impairment: Implications for immunization of children against hemophilus influenzae type B. *American Annals of the Deaf, 132*(1).

Zarske, J. A., & Moore, C. L. (1982). Recategorized WISC-R scores for non-handicapped learning disabled, educationally disadvantaged and regular classroom Navajo children. *School Psychology Review, 11,* 319–323.

Zieziula, F. (Ed.). (1982). *Assessment of hearing impaired people: A guide for selecting psychological, educational, and vocational tests.* Washington, DC: Gallaudet College.

RESOURCES

American Indian Professional Training
  Program in Speech–Language Pathology
  and Audiology
Marilyn Sipes, M.S.
University of Arizona
Speech and Hearing Department
Room 301, Speech Building
Tucson, AZ 85721
(602) 621-1644
This program, funded by the U.S. Department of Education, provides personal, academic, and financial support to American Indian college students pursuing degrees in speech and language pathology or audiology. Since its inception in 1979, the program has produced fifteen graduates, twelve of whom have master of science degrees in speech and language pathology and three who received degrees in audiology. Nine of the fifteen students have graduated since 1988.

American Indian Rehabilitation Research and
    Training Center (AIRRTC)
Marilyn J. Johnson, Ph.D., Director
Northern Arizona University, Institute for
    Human Development
P.O. Box 5630
Flagstaff, AZ 86011-5630
(602) 523-4791
Established in 1983 with the mission of
improving the quality of life for Native Americans with disabilities.

Native American Research and Training
    Center (NARTC)
Jennie Joe, Ph.D., Director
Department of Family and Community
    Medicine
University of Arizona
1642 East Helen Street
Tucson, AZ 85719
(602) 621-5075
Since its inception, NARTC has focused on
health-related research and training programs
to serve and benefit American Indians and
Alaska Natives.

Navajo Resource Center
Rough Rock Press
RRDS, P.O. Box 217
Chinle, AZ 86503
(602) 728-3311
Established to produce culturally sensitive educational materials for the Rough Rock Community School. Rough Rock Community School, established in 1966, was the first school in the United States established for American Indian children and operated and controlled by the surrounding Indian community. Resource center publications include educational materials developed for Navajo children as well as cultural information for children and adults.

Navajo Vocational Rehabilitation Program
    (NVRP)
P.O. Box 1420
Window Rock, AZ 86515
(602) 871-4941, Ext. 1338, 1409, 1412
TTY: (602) 871-5076

Established in 1978 as a result of the Rehabilitation Act Amendment of 1986 (Public Law 99-506), NVRP is administered by the Navajo tribe to serve the disabled population living on the Navajo reservation. All NVRP employees are Navajo. NVRP is one of fourteen American Indian vocational service programs in the United States funded under Public Law 99-506. NVRP serves Deaf clients living on the Navajo reservation, and some of its rehabilitation counselors have signed language skills. As well as providing the typical range of rehabilitation services, NVRP funds traditional Navajo healing ceremonies for clients who desire these services.

Other Available Programs

American Indian Cultural Workshop
Room 206
165 Broadway
New York, NY 10001

American Indian Culture Research Center
    (AICRC)
Blue Cloud Abbey
Marvin, SD 57251
(605) 432-5528

Arrow, Inc.
1000 Connecticut Avenue, N.W.
Suite 401
Washington, DC 20036
(202) 296-0685

Association on American Indian Affairs,
    Inc.
432 Park Avenue South
New York, NY 10016

Education Resources Information Center
Clearinghouse on Rural Education and Small
    Schools
P.O. Box 3AP
Las Cruces, NM 88001

Library of American Indian Affairs
Clearwater Publishing Company
792 Columbus Avenue
New York, NY 10025

National Center for American Indian
Alternative Education (NCAIAC)
941 East Seventeenth Avenue
Denver, CO 80218

National Indian Education Association
1115 Second Avenue, South
Minneapolis, MN 55403
(612) 333-5341

National Indian Youth Council
201 Hermosa, N.E.
Albuquerque, NM 87108
(505) 266-7966

National Urban Indian Council (NUIC)
18505 South Bellaire
Suite 525
Denver, CO 80222
(303) 756-1569

North American Indian Association (NAIA)
360 John R.
Detroit, MI 48226
(313) 963-1710

Northwest Regional Educational Laboratory
Research and Development Program for
Indian Education
101 S.W. Main Street
Suite 500
Portland, OR 97204
(503) 275-9500

Project Ta-kos Alta Mira Specialized Family
Services, Inc.
3201 Fourth Street, N.W.
Albuquerque, NM 87107
(505) 345-6889

Society for American Indian Studies and
Research
P.O. Box 443
Hurst, TX 76053
(817) 281-3784

SUGGESTED READINGS

Cultural

Andrews, L. V. (1981). *Medicine woman*. San Francisco: Harper & Row.
Bahti, T. (1968). *Southwestern Indian tribes*. Las Vegas, NV: KC Publications.
Baylor, B. (1977). *Yes is better than no*. New York: Scribner's.
Hillerman, T. (1990). *Coyote waits*. New York: Harper & Row.
McLuhan, T. C. (1971). *Touch the earth: A self-portrait of Indian existence*. New York: Promontory.
Niehardt, J. G. (Ed.). (1961). *Black Elk speaks*. Lincoln, NE: University of Nebraska.
Niethammer, C. (1977). *Daughters of the earth: The lives and legends of American Indian women*.
   New York: Collier Books.
Nomaday, N. S. (1966). *House made of dawn*. New York: Harper & Row.
Rock Point Community School. (1982). *Between sacred mountains: Stories and lessons from the
   land*. Chinle, AZ: Author.
Silko, L. M. (1977). *Ceremony*. New York: Viking.
Trimble, S. (1986). *Our voices, our land*. Flagstaff, AZ: Northland.
Waldman, C. (1985). *Atlas of the North American Indian*. New York: Facts on File.
Waters, F. (1971). *The man who killed the deer*. New York: Pocket Books.
Yorgason, B. M. (1979). *The windwalker*. Salt Lake City, UT: Bookcraft.

Professional

American Indian Studies Center. (1979). *Multicultural education and the American Indian*. Los
   Angeles: University of California.

Dillard, J. M. (1983). *Multicultural counseling*. Chicago: Nelson-Hall.

Fuchs, E., & Havighurst, R. J. (1972). *To live on this earth: American Indian education*. Garden City, NY: Doubleday.

Gilliland, H. (1988). *Teaching the Native American*. Dubuque, IA: Kendal/Hunt.

Kehoe, A. B. (1981). *North American Indians: A comprehensive account*. Englewood Cliffs, NJ: Prentice-Hall.

McCarty, T. L., Lynch, R., Bia, F., & Johnson, G. (1983). *A bibliography of Navajo and Native American teaching materials: Dine Kerli Naaltsoos Bee Nida nitinigii*. Rough Rock, AZ: Navajo Curriculum Center, Rough Rock Demonstration School.

Pepper, J. M. (1985). *Effective practices in Indian education: A teacher's monograph*. Portland, OR: Northwest Regional Educational Laboratory.

Sorkin, A. L. (1978). *The urban American Indian*. Lexington, MA: Lexington Books.

Wallace, S., Bia, F., Lynch, R., & Yellowhair, M. (1983). *Publications from the Navajo Curriculum Center Press*. Rough Rock, AZ: Navajo Curriculum Center, Rough Rock Demonstration School.

SECTION III

The Future

The concluding section of this text calls for a new view of education for children who are Deaf. Rather than applying a superficial approach to "fixing" assessment, curriculum, and instruction, professionals are challenged to *rethink* the basic assumptions on which educational practice is founded. As we approach the twenty-first century, Deaf and hearing professionals at all levels and representing all ethnic and racial backgrounds must consider ways to work together within a broad societal context for the benefit of *all* Deaf children.

CHAPTER 10

Rethinking the Education of Ethnic/Multicultural Deaf People: Stretching the Boundaries

Joseph E. Fischgrund and C. Tane Akamatsu

> *But times do change and move continually.*
> *Edmund Spenser,* The Faerie Queene

This chapter proposes that real change in educational practices with children who are Deaf can occur only when the assumptions regarding assimilation and pluralism are reexamined and the power relationships are clarified among all persons, Deaf and hearing, who are involved in decision making.

In recent years increasing numbers of educators of deaf children and youth have come to recognize the unique status of multicultural Deaf students. Both researchers and practitioners have focused on the inappropriateness of current educational or assessment practices, and how those practices might change in order to become more equitable for these students. Examples of this approach dominate the literature, meager as it is, on multicultural Deaf students (e.g., Chapters 4 and 5 in this text; Delgado, 1984; Stewart & Benson, 1988). Much of this work, while calling attention to, and suggesting changes to ameliorate, the long-standing practices of discrimination, unequal treatment, low expectations, and depressed achievement patterns of multicultural deaf children, rests on the fundamental assumption that changes in the current system can address these problems effectively. This basic proposition can be broken down into more specific belief statements:

1. Equity and quality in the education of multicultural Deaf students can be achieved within the current educational framework.

2. Resolving questions of nonbiased assessment and appropriate curriculum and instruction is well within the control of educators within the system.
3. Equity among school-age individuals is essentially a school issue, and the notion of cultural affiliations and feelings of membership outside of the school are of lesser importance.

In other words, the well-documented problems experienced by multicultural deaf students can be resolved in the context of a particular program or school and are independent of various phenomena in the larger society, such as racism, "melting pot" assimilationism, and the power relationships in American society. This chapter rejects such an hypothesis and argues instead that it is in exactly those larger contexts—power relationships and cultural boundaries—that issues relating to multicultural Deaf children must be approached.

Some of what precedes this chapter in this text does assume that if we did things differently in educational programs for Deaf children, then the educational prospects of multicultural Deaf children would improve. Questioning this hypothesis and instead placing the issues in a broader societal context should in no way be seen as criticism of these efforts. Ongoing work on the practical issues of how to improve and provide appropriate and effective instructional and related services to Deaf students must continue and should not be abandoned. As numerous studies have shown, the current situation for Deaf students is, simply speaking, unacceptable by any measure. By stretching the boundaries of how we think about the issues involved, we might indeed make the process of change in the education of Deaf children more sensitive and effective and lead to true equal educational opportunity for all students who are Deaf.

KINSHIPS, CENTERS, INSIDERS AND OUTSIDERS

In a challenging article in the *Harvard Educational Review*, Fordham (1988) utilized the concept of *fictive-kinship* to establish a context for discussing the tensions experienced by African Americans who attempt to assimilate successfully into white society. Fictive-kinship, she noted, "denotes a cultural symbol of collective identity" and, in the case of African Americans, "is based on more than just skin color." According to Fordham, the term

> also implies the particular mind set, or world view, of those persons who are considered to be [of that group] and is used to denote the moral judgement the group makes on its members. . . . One can be [of that group], but choose not to seek membership in the fictive-kinship group. One can also be denied membership by the group because one's behavior, attitudes, and activities are perceived as being at variance with those thought to be appropriate and group-specific, which are culturally patterned and serve to delineate "us" from "them." (p. 56).

This concept of a fictive-kinship is useful in analyzing the notion of "deaf culture" and the status of racial, linguistic, and ethnic minority individuals in the larger deaf community. Deaf people, like African Americans, certainly share a fictive-kinship relationship, one that is centered around deafness itself.

In their book *Deaf in America*, Padden and Humphries (1988) used the notion of "center," a point of reference for oneself, or for a community. Experiences are measured in terms of deviance from this center. The example they so eloquently presented was of the meaning of *hard of hearing*. To those who can hear, hard of hearing typically refers to someone who *cannot* hear well. Yet, to a Deaf person, hard of hearing usually means someone who *can* hear, even if only a little. This concept is further codified in the semantics of American Sign Language (ASL). In the following excerpt from Padden and Humphries (who are Deaf), English glosses for ASL signs are given in capital letters:

> HEARING means the opposite of what we are.
> The sign HEARING has an official English translation, "can hear," but in ASL HEARING is aligned in interesting ways with respect to DEAF and HARD-OF-HEARING. In ASL, as in English, HARD-OF-HEARING represents a deviation of some kind. Someone who is A-LITTLE HARD-OF-HEARING has a smaller deviation than someone who is VERY HARD-OF-HEARING. In this way, ASL and English are similar—and yet the terms have opposite meanings in the two languages. The reasons for this is clear: for Deaf people, the greatest deviation is HEARING.
> This is the crucial element in understanding these "backward" definitions: there is a different center, a different point from which one deviates. In this case, DEAF, not HEARING, is taken as the central point of reference. (p. 41)

This notion of different centers was also expressed in the play *Whiskey Chicken*, by Wayman Wong (1990). The play is set in San Francisco's Chinatown in the early 1950s and revolves around an immigrant Chinese family. All but the father dream of eventually earning enough money to leave Chinatown for the suburbs. In his opposition, the father declares, "White people come to Chinatown to see how *normal* people live."

The notion of center is important because it implies that one is at the center, or heart, of something. Today, it is well accepted that Deaf people comprise a distinct society in this country, with concomitant language and social institutions (Padden & Humphries, 1988; Woodward, 1972). It is evident that Deaf society has existed for a long time, but the recognition of this society was late in coming (Lane, 1988).

Perhaps one reason for this late recognition is that membership in the Deaf community is not as clear-cut as membership in an ethnic community is. Baker and Cokely (1980) pointed out that there is no single distinguishing characteristic shared by all members of the Deaf community, except the notion of *attitudinal deafness*. This term refers to the self-identification of an individual as a member of the Deaf community. Such an individual supports the values of the community and is accepted as a valid member by others already in the community.

According to Baker and Cokely (1980), there are four avenues to membership in the Deaf community. The *audiological* avenue, available only to hearing impaired people, is the fact of hearing loss. The *political* avenue is the ability to exert influence on local, state, or national issues that directly affect the Deaf community. The political avenue is somewhat closed to hearing people because they cannot have much influence within the Deaf community. However, hearing people may advocate alongside Deaf people and help to influence establishment powers-that-be. Proficiency in ASL is the *linguistic* avenue, open to deaf people and to hearing people. Children of Deaf parents, some teachers, interpreters, and friends of Deaf people, as well as Deaf people themselves, have access to this avenue.

Finally, there is the *social* avenue, which consists of participation in social functions of the Deaf community, feeling at ease while attending, and having Deaf friends.

It is important to note that not all individuals with hearing loss are members of the Deaf community and some hearing individuals can be members if they display appropriate attitudinal deafness. Identification with at least two of the four factors constitutes appropriate attitude (Baker & Cokely, 1980). Figure 10.1 diagrams these ideas. The center, where all four domains overlap, is known as the core of the community. Obviously, hearing people cannot be members of the core.

It is clear that Deaf society is not homogeneous but rather has relative degrees of membership. The core usually is comprised of Deaf people whose parents are Deaf, who attended special schools for Deaf children, who use ASL as a native language, and whose social and political beliefs and activities revolve around the Deaf community. However, the one incontestable criterion, necessary but not sufficient for membership in the Deaf community, is attitudinal deafness. There are also fringe members of the Deaf community—people who for various reasons come into regular contact with the Deaf community and who may participate in its social, linguistic, and political institutions to varying degrees. To this extent, then, some hearing children of Deaf parents raised within Deaf social institutions may be characterized as members of the Deaf community. The same is true for certain hearing people, such as teachers, interpreters, hearing children, and spouses

FIGURE 10.1   Avenues to membership in the deaf community

SOURCE: C. Baker & D. Cokely (1980). *American Sign Language: A teacher's resource text on grammar and culture*. Silver Spring, MD: T. J. Publishers. Reprinted with permission.

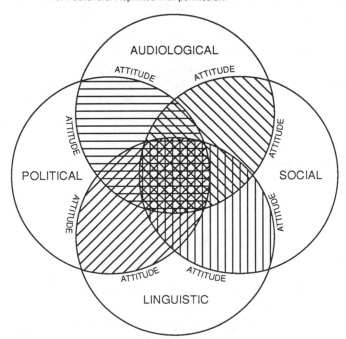

of Deaf people (and deaf people themselves who choose not to identify primarily with the Deaf community).

Multicultural deaf people may in fact share in more than one fictive-kinship, each with a different center. For many deaf students this poses the same kind of problem that African American fictive-kinship membership poses for African American students who are forced to reject their fictive-kinship in order to achieve academic or career success. African American and Hispanic deaf students often are encouraged by both hearing people and deaf people to be "Deaf first," to be part of the "Deaf culture." Ways of behaving that they share with their African American and Hispanic brothers and sisters are often rejected in schools for Deaf children. To succeed, African American, Asian/Pacific Islander, Native American, and Hispanic deaf students—the focus group of this text—have been encouraged by the system to develop, in Fordham's (1988) terms, a "strategy of racelessness."

Ironically, many Deaf people, in order to assimilate into the hearing society, have had to adopt a similar strategy. Once again using Fordham's (1988)words, but substituting *Deaf* for *black*, "Students who assimilate seek to maximize their success potential by minimizing their relationship to the [Deaf] community and to the stigma attached to [deafness]" (p. 57).

Fordham (1988) pointed out that many African American students do indeed reinforce and legitimize their indigenous culture and fictive-kinship, even though it may lead to failure in assimilation-oriented schools. The parallels here with Deaf individuals and especially multicultural Deaf individuals are not so clear. Within the white deaf community, reinforcement of one's fictive-kinship—establishing oneself in relation to the center— is very important. Graduation from a residential school has more status than completion of a mainstream program, even though the latter may have led to higher academic achievement and career success potential.

For many multicultural deaf individuals, the situation has been different. In the past, many were excluded from what the Deaf community considers a prestigious residential school experience and instead attended either a segregated residential program (Bowe, 1971) or a local day program in an inner city, where their racial or ethnic affiliation, in addition to their deafness, was devalued. Even those who did attend a residential school were seldom later included in alumni association planning, National Association of the Deaf (NAD) chapter activities, or leadership roles. (Anderson & Bowe, 1972). The formation of Black Deaf Advocates (BDA), a response to the de facto exclusion of African American Deaf people from meaningful involvement in NAD, is testimony to this. Clearly, for those who established BDA, African American fictive-kinship was a powerful force; yet their fictive-kinship as Deaf people was also much in evidence.

Thus, multicultural deaf people are tugged at by a variety of forces, forces that segregate them in subtle ways from both the mainstream deaf community and their ethnic or racial community. There are also forces that allow them to integrate into these communities. And, in some cases, the pull of these forces results in the establishment of a new fictive-kinship group, such as the unique sense of identity found among African American Deaf students (Grace, 1989). Some of these forces are described in the next section.

SEGREGATIVE AND INTEGRATIVE FORCES

It is important to realize that although there are very few explicitly stated rules for membership within a society, society nevertheless has boundaries that are difficult, if not impossible, to cross. In addition, each society has a certain inviolable core, which only few may occupy, often only through birth or political coup. The core is where power is concentrated, and power is usurped from the outside only when the core has become too weak to withstand pressure from the outside.

Segregative forces may be seen from two perspectives. On the negative side, these forces provide the fuel to keep those different from the core at bay. Proponents of the "English only" movement are an example of such forces. Their inflammatory rhetoric would suggest that those who speak another language natively choose not to speak English, and their wish to have information printed in other languages reflects their unwillingness to "Americanize," therefore making them a burden to society. The choice not to become raceless is perceived as antithetical to the American way. "English only" proponents choose to ignore both (a) the recognition by these speakers of other languages that English is an important tool in society, and (b) the overflowing adult English classes in areas with high proportions of recent immigrants and refugees, which supports that recognition.

A positive use of segregative force is to maintain a cultural identity to pass on the next generation. The establishment of ethnic social institutions can be seen as an example of the positive side of a segregative force.

Integrative forces recognize the intrinsic value of other cultures and promote their positive aspects. They seek the betterment of society as a whole by working to eradicate inequities in the system. They maximize the existing human resources that two cultures make available.

For example, Japanese Americans and Japanese Canadians united to achieve redress for their incarceration during World War II. Alone, these groups would have been unable to muster the power necessary to achieve their goals. With allies in the majority society, however, they were able to effect change. Likewise, the Gallaudet University Deaf President Now (1988) movement was led by Deaf people. It also received much media attention and support from outsiders in the mainstream and marked a significant change in the history of Deaf people.

People who are part of the integrative forces face much pressure from both inside and outside their communities. There is suspicion about their motives for integration and fear that communities (and identities) will become diluted. For ethnic groups, there is the fear of recolonization by the majority group.

AN ALTERNATIVE ASSIMILATION MODEL

Kitano and Daniels (1988) suggested a four-celled assimilation model, based on both ethnic identity and assimilation as defined by integration in work and schooling, identification with the majority, and marital assimilation. This model is presented in Chapter 7. As you review Figure 7.1 you will note that Cell A (high assimilation, low ethnic identity) refers to those who are highly assimilated into mainstream culture, who retain only vestiges of ethnic identity, and whose participation in any ethnic traditions is primarily symbolic. The one factor that prevents full assimilation is the physical difference between them and the majority community. Individuals in Cell A may be thought of as being on the very fringe of the ethnic community and well into the mainstream community.

Individuals in Cell B (high assimilation, high ethnic identity) perceive themselves as

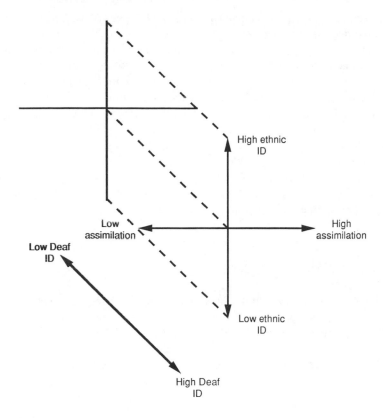

FIGURE 10.2   Eight-celled assimilation model

well assimilated but choose to retain identification with their ethnic group. Choices in career, friendships, political institutions, and the like reflect a strong bicultural perspective. Those in Cell B participate freely in both communities.

Cell C (low assimilation, low ethnic identity) represents those who are essentially alienated from both the mainstream and their ethnic identities. They avoid participation in mainstream institutions, but are also uncomfortable with their ethnic identities. Cell C individuals are on the fringe of both the ethnic community and the mainstream community.

Finally, Cell D (low assimilation, high ethnic identity) reflects those who have spent most of their lives within an ethnic community, or who are relative newcomers to this country. These people are well integrated in the ethnic community but are not in the mainstream much, if at all.

It would appear that *bicultural people* are those who can move back and forth between an exclusively ethnic (or mainstream) position into an integrative space. Until recently, members of ethnic groups, typically underrepresented in the power structure, have had to use this space to get ahead in school and work, whereas for majority people biculturalism was a matter of choice. Given the rapidly changing demographics of the United States (by the year 2000, 85 percent of the U.S. work force will be made up of women and people of color), it is likely that majority people will have little choice but to become multicultural. *In the case of education of Deaf children, hearing people must become multicultural if they are to participate in the needed changes.*

The assimilation model, as it stands, may be inadequate to explain the pressures on underrepresented ethnic Deaf people. Perhaps an eight-celled model, suggested in Figure 10.2, would be more suitable. Such a model would consist of two four-celled matrices. One would be the Kitano and Daniels (1988) ethnic identity assimilation matrix on which individuals can locate themselves in terms of strength of ethnic identity. The second, orthogonal to the first, might be termed the "deaf identity assimilation" matrix, in which *assimilation* refers to assimilation in the hearing community. Thus, a deaf member of the focus groups of this text could, for example, be highly ethnically identified, highly Deaf identified, and work successfully among white, hearing people without losing either identity. By *not* adopting a strategy of racelessness or avoidance of Deaf culture, this person can realize the full human potential that comes from the different components of his or her background.

POWER RELATIONSHIPS

A second broad context in which to rethink educational change with respect to deaf students in general, and the focus group of this text in particular, is the issue of power relationships. In another challenging article in *Harvard Educational Review*, "The Silenced Dialogue: Power and Pedagogy in Educating Other People's Children," Delpit (1988) argued that students must come to understand "the implicit and explicit rules of power as a first step toward a more just society" (p. 280). Delpit identified five aspects of what she called "the culture of power."

1. Issues of power are enacted in classrooms.
2. There are codes or rules for participating in power; that is, there is a "culture of power."
3. The rules of the culture of power are a reflection of the rules of the culture of those who have power.
4. If you are not already a participant in the culture of power, being told explicitly the rules of that culture makes acquiring power easier.
5. Those with power are frequently least aware of—or least willing to acknowledge—its existence. Those with less power are often most aware of its existence. (p. 282)

An example of how these rules come into play, especially number 1, is exemplified by Padden's (1990) discussion of the need for small class sizes of deaf children. The small class size, argued Padden, stems from "a pathological model of deafness [and] the need to control how much information we give to the deaf student" and leads to a "one-to-one teacher–student relationship in which the teacher carefully controls each child's input. . . . The teacher feels she is the only one in the class that can provide valid input" (p. 26). Padden proposed instead a model that alters the rules of power in the classroom, in which larger classes would lead to "much more interaction, more talking back and forth, and more sharing among students. The teacher would ultimately be in control, of course, but the students would also be learning from each other. And the reason that we need to *share* control is because it gives more opportunity to the students" (p. 27).

There are not only rules of power being played out between deaf and hearing people in and out of classrooms, but also rules of power that are played out *among deaf people.* As

Padden's discussion illustrates, it is clear that the education of deaf students is still dominated by hearing people and a hearing cultural outlook, since it is hearing people who have established the rules of power. Recent developments at Gallaudet University, beginning with the Deaf President Now movement, have begun to change that perspective, at least at that particular university. This awareness may lead to similar changes at other levels of the educational system.

But in a different sphere, where the influence of deaf individuals over their own lives has increased, it has done so primarily for white deaf individuals. What is commonly referred to as "Deaf culture" is in fact white Deaf culture, and what is commonly referred to as the "Deaf community" is often narrowly defined as the community of white Deaf people. In some instances there is an even more narrow definition and even more restrictive criteria for membership: the culture of white, ASL-signing Deaf people whose heritage derives from the residential school tradition. The question then is not so simple: If deaf people are to make decisions for deaf people, will it once again be a case of those deaf individuals who know the rules of power making decisions for "other people's children"? With respect to the position of educational reformers and the needs of both deaf children and their parents, Delpit's comments (1988) bear repeating:

> For many who consider themselves to be members of liberal or radical camps, acknowledging personal power and admitting participation in the culture of power is distinctly uncomfortable. . . . [White educators] either by virtue of their position, their numbers or their access to a particular code of power of calling upon research to validate one's position . . . had the authority to establish what was to be considered the "truth," regardless of the opinions of the people, and the latter were well aware of that fact. (p. 284)

Deaf people thus face complex challenges and questions. First, deaf people must come to understand the rules of power within the Deaf community. Then, they must decide whether learning and using these rules as an integrative force is desirable. For the white Deaf community, it is a question of both recognizing the existing culture of power and determining how well Deaf culture can reflect the pluralism that exists but is not often positively acknowledged. For African American, Asian/Pacific Islander, Native American, and Hispanic deaf people, the issues are far more complex.

CONCLUSION

This discussion suggests that developing a truly responsive system for educating all deaf children is not simply a matter of making reforms in specific areas, adjusting practices, or conducting more appropriate staff development activities. Real change can happen only when underlying assumptions concerning assimilation and pluralism are examined and power relationships are understood by Deaf and hearing persons involved in all aspects of the educational process. It is a question not only of what we do, but also of what we think about what we are doing. It may require, in the end, what Cummins (1986) called for in his landmark article:

> In order to reverse the pattern of widespread minority group educational failure, educators and policy makers are faced with a personal and a political challenge. Personally, they must redefine their roles within the classroom, the community, and the broader society so

that these role definitions result in interactions that empower rather than disable students. Politically, they must persuade colleagues and decisionmakers . . . of the importance of redefining institutional goals so that the schools transform society by empowering minority students rather than reflect society by disabling them. (pp. 33–34)

This text calls for a redefinition of education for Deaf students from diverse cultural backgrounds, and, in fact, all Deaf students.

BIBLIOGRAPHY

Anderson, G., & Bowe, F. (1972). Racism within the deaf community. *American Annals of the Deaf, 117,* 617–619.

Bowe, F. (1971). Non-white deaf persons: Educational, psychological, and occupational considerations. *American Annals of the Deaf, 116,* 357–361.

Baker, C., & Cokeley, D. (1980). *American Sign Language: A teacher's resource text on grammar and culture.* Silver Spring, MD: T.J. Publishers.

Cummins, J. (1986). Empowering minority students: A framework for intervention. *Harvard Educational Review, 56,* 18–36.

Delgado, G. (Ed.). (1984). *The Hispanic deaf: Issues and challenges in special education.* Washington, DC: Gallaudet University.

Delpit, L. (1988). The silenced dialogue: Power and pedagogy in teaching other people's children. *Harvard Educational Review, 58,* 280–298.

Fordham, S. (1988). Racelessness as a factor in black students' school success: Pragmatic strategy or pyrrhic victory. *Harvard Educational Review, 58,* 54–83.

Grace, C. (1989). Increasing staff awareness and sensitivity toward the needs of black deaf children: A training manual. Jackson Heights, NY: Lexington School for the Deaf/New York State Education Department.

Kitano, H., & Daniels, R. (1988). *Asian Americans: Emerging minorities.* Englewood Cliffs, NJ: Prentice-Hall.

Lane, H. (1988). Is there a "psychology of the deaf"? *Exceptional Children, 55,* 7–19.

Padden, C. (1990). Panel response. In R. C. Johnson (Ed.), *Unlocking the curriculum: Principles for achieving access language in deaf education.* Washington, DC: Gallaudet Research Institute, Occasional Paper 90-1.

Padden, C., & Humphries, T. (1988) *Deaf in America: Voices from a culture.* Cambridge, MA: Harvard University.

Stewart, D., & Benson, G. (1988). Dual cultural negligence: The education of black deaf children. *Journal of Multicultural Counseling and Development, 16,* 98–109.

Wong, W. (1990). *Whiskey chicken.* Play produced by the Asian American Theatre Company, San Francisco, CA.

Woodward, J. (1972). Implications for sociolinguistics research among the deaf. *Sign Language Studies, 1,* 1–7.

Looking Forward to a Multicultural Commitment

Kathee M. Christensen

Crows scoured the wet evening clean
above our heads.
Two languages interchanged.
We came to a halt
with our half-certainties . . .
that love is
to clasp simply,
question fiercely;
and the artistic act . . .
long library bodies, their pens
distinct against the sinking sun.
      Thomas Kinsella, Out of Ireland

Chapter 11 challenges professional educators of children who are Deaf to commit themselves to a multicultural perspective on teaching and learning. Educators who embrace a multiple intelligence view of cognitive development and a multicultural view of language acquisition will find themselves better prepared to meet the educational needs of children in the twenty-first century.

Interest in multicultural issues is not a twentieth-century phenomenon. From the time of the ancient Greeks, authors have considered cross-cultural themes. For example, Aristophanes thought about women's liberation in *Lysistrata* and Plato presented a discussion of the innate intelligence of uneducated servants in *The Meno*. Although notions of equality and access are not new, some contemporary educators appear baffled by the challenges of a multicultural/cross-cultural philosophy of instruction.

BENEFITS OF A MULTICULTURAL PERSPECTIVE

Chapter 2 suggested that cognitive development, particularly in the transition from concrete to abstract thought, can be enhanced by the introduction of multiple perspectives shared through a variety of cultural viewpoints. If this approach begins early and continues throughout the educational journey of each child, then cultural clashes may be replaced with multicultural respect and understanding. It would not be an easy process, but the rewards of a successful implementation of a multicultural curriculum could be positive for children, their families, their teachers, and their communities.

Consider the classroom as a mini-community and a vital component of the larger world community. It is in the classroom that children learn important early lessons of cooperation, responsibility, and respect for themselves and others. These values, introduced at home, grow and flourish in the classroom. Children learn either to ridicule or to respect based on the treatment they encounter from teachers and others in their daily environment. Children can learn to use their natural, cultural voices with pride, or to stifle what is natural and replace it with what is required by another person's priorities.

Deaf children from diverse cultural backgrounds may encounter a fundamental barrier to entrance into what Vygotsky (1978) has called the *zone of proximal development*. This barrier is formed when previous cultural experience is not used as the foundation for new knowledge and experiences in school. A flexible environment in which the child is able to link past learning with new experiences is required if optimal learning is to occur (Trueba, 1989). The research of Trueba (1983), Rueda (1987), and others suggested that children may perceive cultural conflict in school as a type of mental assault. The extent to which Deaf children share this perception when confronted by teachers and others whom they cannot understand and who make no attempt to communicate in an accessible manner has not been documented. At this time, we can only speculate as to the degree of mental assault perceived by Deaf children at school.

We can, however, take active steps toward ensuring that all Deaf children with whom we come in contact will be treated with respect and given the opportunity to achieve the highest levels of inherent intellectual and emotional potential. We can accomplish this basic goal through ongoing cross-cultural dialogue with children, along with the application of "best practices" in the classroom and beyond. In a multicultural model, the teacher becomes an ethnographer who perceives each student individually and objectively and attempts to understand all students in terms of who they actually are. Teachers ensure that all children receive equal amounts of positive attention. All children in the class are called on frequently to share their original ideas, are given leadership opportunities, and are complimented openly for a unique approach to problem solving.

When learners perceive that learning is an active process in which they are expected to think creatively and where difference is valued rather than stifled, they begin to take pride in themselves for coming up with new ideas and to respect the opinions of others, no matter how they might differ. When mutual respect is achieved, both learners and teacher can progress toward academic and psychosocial milestones of development. Without mutual respect, school attendance becomes an unrewarding chore and lessons are given low priority. Cultural clashes ensue, and children are labeled "unmotivated" or as having one or more behavior problems. The true "problem" might be that of an insensitive educator.

The work of Gardner (1983) and others in multiple intelligence theory is highly applicable to a multicultural curriculum. In multiple intelligence theory, some basic assumptions of teaching and learning are called into question. Gardner suggested that there may not be a single faculty called *intelligence* and that, perhaps, the concept of intelligence (whether singular or pluralistic) may not be well founded (1989, p. 95). At any rate, what we call intelligence includes, but is not limited to, linguistic and logical mathematical performance. At least five other aspects of human behavior combine in a variety of ways to form the particular intellectual profile of a human being. Trained observers can discern a child's strengths in areas such as musical, spatial, bodily/kinesthetic, interpersonal, and intrapersonal intelligences. In the twenty-first century, it may be that educational curricula will take a left turn toward cultural and intellectual pluralism.

We continue to live in a multicultural society. The three Rs are significant only as they relate to the three Cs: communication, cognition, and culture. In a multicultural society, intellectual development is nurtured by positive interaction with individuals from a variety of cultural perspectives. Since all acts of communication are subject to interpretation, it makes sense to have multiple sources from which to draw information when creating interpretations. If a multicultural philosophy is put into practice, then the classroom can become a place where human potential flourishes and reflects multiple versions of academic and social success.

TEACHER PREPARATION

It is time for us, as educators, to become self-critical rather than just critical. What do we need to do to prepare for the challenges of the twenty-first century? What are our goals for the year 2000? Will we be ready for the children who trust us with their educational futures?

The Council on Education of the Deaf (CED) is a board that represents the four largest educationally oriented, national organizations in the field of deafness: The Convention of American Instructors of the Deaf (CAID), the Conference of Educational Administrators Serving the Deaf (CEASD), the A. G. Bell Association for the Deaf, and the Association of College Educators of the Deaf (ACE–D). This board meets twice a year to review and determine the standards for the certification of teachers of deaf students. College and university teacher preparation programs are evaluated according to CED standards. At the CED board meeting in December 1990, a new standard was adopted, which requires that "teacher training programs will ensure that courses and curriculum on both the undergraduate and graduate levels reflect ethnic and multicultural issues related to deafness, education, and general development" (CED, 1990 revision, p. 10). In order to meet the certification requirements, therefore, every teacher preparation program in the United States will need to demonstrate how it includes multicultural information in course work and practicum settings. Prospective teachers will be required to understand multicultural issues in research, assessment, and instruction of Deaf students. With this impetus, it is possible that issues regarding Deaf culture and the cultural environments of African American, Hispanic, Asian/Pacific Islander, and American Indian Deaf learners will direct educational reform in the next century.

SOCIAL UNITS

Some of the authors in this text have suggested that an ethnocentric attitude exists among hearing people who view Deaf individuals as "disabled" rather than as members of a different cultural group. They have alluded to ethnocentricity within the white Deaf culture, which can exclude members from diverse ethnic and racial backgrounds from assuming leadership roles. Recent hiring practices contradict this view. The current assistant secretary in the U.S. Department of Education, Office of Special Education and Rehabilitation Services is Dr. Robert R. Davila, an Hispanic Deaf man. African American Deaf men hold leadership positions in state residential schools for the deaf and in government offices. Organized special interest groups have formed within NAD (National Association of the Deaf), CEASD, and CAID to encourage involvement at all levels by people from diverse ethnic backgrounds. This represents a start in the right direction. Clearly, there is a need for greater representation of ethnically diverse men and women in leadership roles throughout the educational structure, and it will take a unified effort among Deaf and hearing people of all races and ethnic backgrounds to make that happen. In the meantime, it is up to all of us to support one another in a mutual effort to make our community truly multicultural in all of its dimensions.

Most of us combine more than one culture in our social identities. It may in fact be a form of ethnocentrism to ask us to identify with one primary culture or to rank order the social units with which we identify. An Afro Latino, for example, who was raised in the Dominican Republic or Panama, would be hard-pressed to identify solely with either his or her racial or linguistic identity. To deny one or the other would be to deny a vital part of the individual. By the same token, it seems unfair to expect a Deaf African American to chose a "Deaf-first" identity or vice versa. To ask for such a rank ordering of social units is to oversimplify an extremely complex social issue. Cultures, like languages, can be additive. Perhaps we might come to the point of considering *humanity* as the broadest cultural concept within which exist a variety of diverse social units. That notion is possible if we follow the suggestion made in Chapter 10 and stretch the boundaries of education to include a multicultural perspective toward teaching and learning.

Many books that address multicultural issues are concerned with the assimilation of people from one cultural and linguistic community into a larger, multifaceted community. Metaphors of the mosaic or the patchwork quilt are often cited. Diverse communities, although uniquely individual, are considered to have similar needs and to deserve equity. A theme emphasized in several chapters of this text, however, suggests that Deaf individuals represent a culture that is fundamentally different in nature from the larger, dominant hearing community. In Deaf culture, *vision* is the basis for acquiring communication, developing cognition, and establishing cultural norms. The assumptions of a hearing culture do not necessarily translate with equal significance to a Deaf community. Furthermore, within the Deaf community are diverse ethnic and racial groups whose cultural foundations are based on experiences as members of dual identity groups, such as Hispanic Deaf or American Indian Deaf communities. Imposition of values from an Hispanic hearing culture on an Hispanic Deaf individual, without consideration of a dual identity, may demonstrate a lack of understanding and acceptance of the basic rights of a valid cultural group, regardless of the positive intentions of those who are considered the decision makers or power brokers of the larger cultural group.

This text describes ways in which Deaf people are members of a cultural community based on the use of vision as the primary sense. Within the larger Deaf community are diverse ethnic and racial groups with uniquely different experiences, which lead to the formation of cultural values and behaviors. All groups, regardless of size and location, are equally valid. They have the potential for bicultural or multicultural involvement in larger, diverse communities when given equitable opportunities for interaction, education, and leadership. The patchwork quilt metaphor does not make sense when considering the assimilation of the Deaf community into the larger dominant society of hearing persons from diverse ethnic and racial backgrounds. Perhaps a "separate but equal" philosophy better describes the relationship of parallel Deaf and hearing communities. If this philosophy were to be accepted, the Deaf community would not be considered disabled, but rather differently able. In the important challenge of acquiring English as a second language, Deaf children would not be subjected to the impossible task of learning to read English through a phonetic approach or of speaking English sounds, as a prerequisite for other linguistic tasks, without the benefit of auditory reinforcement. Educators would, instead, seek methods to achieve linguistic and other educational goals through visually salient and accessible means, for example, captioned media and a wide variety of visual supplements. Diverse ethnic and racial groups of Deaf people would become expert informants to the field of multicultural education as they describe their own unique encounters with people who have similar and different life experiences.

This book was not intended to provide answers to complex intercultural questions. In fact, if readers of this text are left with new and penetrating questions regarding their own roles as members of cultural groups charged with facilitating equitable multicultural educational and social opportunities for Deaf children, then an important objective will have been met. As we enter the twenty-first century, the vision for education of children who are Deaf includes new and informative multicultural research efforts and accomplishments.

BIBLIOGRAPHY

Council on Education of the Deaf (CED). (1984). Standards for the certification of professionals involved in the education of hearing impaired children and youth. Washington, DC: Author.

Gardner, H. (1983). *Frames of mind: The theory of multiple intelligences.* New York: Basic Books.

Gardner, H. (1989). *To open minds: Chinese clues to the dilemma of contemporary education.* New York: Basic Books.

Rueda, R. (1987). Social and communicative aspects of language proficiency in low-achieving language minority students. In H. Trueba (Ed.), *Success or failure? Learning and the language minority student* (pp. 185–197). New York: Newbury House.

Trueba, H. (1983). Adjustment problems of Mexican American children: An anthropological study. *Learning Disabilities Quarterly, 6,* 395–415.

Trueba, H. (1989). *Raising silent voices: Educating the linguistic minorities for the 21st century.* New York: Newbury House.

Vygotsky, L. (1978). *Mind in society: The development of higher psychological processes.* In M. Cole, V. John-Teiner, S. Scribner, & E. Souberman (Eds.), Cambridge, MA: Harvard University.

Index